CORFU, NOT A SC

RICK JOHANSEN

April 2016

# Introduction

In the beginning, there was a lone parent called Neeltje Verburg. She was born in Rotterdam, the Netherlands, and emigrated to Bristol, England, in the 1950s. She met and briefly married Anthony Johansen, a merchant seaman. They had a son whom they named, not christened, Richard Marinus Johansen. Richard hated being called Richard but when you are called Richard, that is what people tend to call you. Richard wanted to be Rick and, secretly, was Rick in his dreams and in his writings. But to everyone else he was Richard. It was so unfair.

Anyway, that's enough of referring to myself in the third party, which is a classic symptom of a number of conditions of which I do not suffer: Narcissism, self-importance and delusion. I love myself so much that I don't like photographs of myself, never mind selfies. I do not look in the mirror and like what I see.

Neeltje, or Elly as she became known for reasons unknown, frequently took me abroad with her. From a very young age we went every year to Rotterdam for the entire summer and school holidays. We did not fly; we travelled by train, train, boat, train and tram to reach our destination of Leopoldstraat. The long summer days were much like they were in Bristol, which is to say they were "changeable" which itself is another way of saying wet. In fact summers were just like they were at home. All that changed was the language, an effective public transport system, the food and the drink. I was so impressed with the Netherlands. You could buy this drink called 7 Up which was not available at home. And ice cream with fresh whipped cream on top. It was my summer holiday but it was a home from home too.

I do not know how many times I went to the Netherlands, but it must have been in double figures. I got to believe that this was what summer holidays were like. Later we went on holiday to West Bay in Dorset, every year for many years. I discovered Hamburgers in West Bay, I also realised that the weather in Dorset was just the same as it was at home. Why were all the advertisements for British seaside holidays emblazoned with sunshine and blue skies when all we got were the same slate grey skies we got back in Bristol, with added drizzle? Weather-wise, a summer holiday had little to do with the weather. You just stayed somewhere else and enjoyed – or is it endured? – the same weather you got at home. It never occurred to me that there might be a holiday where you could virtually guarantee warm, sunny weather.

Anyway, we were poor. My Dutch grandmother paid for our travel and food costs when we stayed with her, my English grandparents shared the costs when we went to West Bay. I later learned that in fact my mother gave up luxuries like food in order to pay for our holiday to Dorset. That made me feel horribly, and justifiably, guilty having constantly moaned about the weather and indeed anything else pubescent boys felt like moaning about, which was pretty well everything.

To sum up, summer holidays were holidays somewhere else, but with much the same weather. If you got a suntan, it was more down to luck than judgement.

My first serious expedition away from England came in 1975 when I visited my dad who, by now, had settled in Canada, remarried and got divorced again. I didn't see this as a holiday, more of a bonding session with a man I barely knew. Even though I was still very young, I had associated holidays as being opportunities for doing as little as possible. Travelling around Canada, seeing all the sights and all the rest of it was an amazing experience but not a holiday. But it was warm and sunny almost all the time. At least that's how it looks in my photo album. And I rather liked going somewhere warmer. I could get used to this. Years later I got very used to it.

I reverted to type in the years that followed, venturing only as far as Holland. In fact we even had a "lads holiday" in the sleepy seaside resort of Katwijk in the early 80s and, for the first time ever, I experienced a hot summer abroad. The beaches were lovely, the girls were topless, and the beer flowed. This going abroad malarkey was a lot of fun. I must do it again sometime.

Apart from the Netherlands, Canada, Belgium (one day when I was small) and, also in the early 1980s, Cap d'Agde, the naturist capital of Europe (this, I swear, was an accident and anyway, we didn't actually mingle with the naturists. Shame), I was not exactly well travelled. The truth be known I'm probably still not.

I knew the names of countries around the world and, if pushed, could even find some of them on a map of the world. But the names were all I really knew. I had heard of Greece and had heard of Cyprus mentioned on BBC Radio's Worldwide family favourites, by way of its RAF base from which dedications would be made, normally by armed forces personnel. I think I had heard of Athens and knew it was the capital of Greece, but that was as far as it went. For Greece, and Spain, add just about anywhere else. It may surprise some of you that the world really was a very small place, even going back to the 1970s. You learned about the rest of the world through books and maybe on the odd telly programme, but foreigners were largely all the same and it probably didn't occur to us that there might be places with different cultures. We were, by nature, Little Englanders, imprisoned by our ignorance. Now you can switch on a computer and look at almost anywhere in the world. Then, a computer was something they had on rockets to the moon.

I do not remember people going abroad for their holidays. People went away to various parts of Britain, but no one, to the best of my knowledge, went on package holidays. At least people like me didn't. Aeroplanes were the province of the upper classes, not for ordinary working people like us. If you wanted to go anywhere it would be by car or by rail. But by the early 1980s I became aware that some people were going abroad on holiday. I remember in the early 1980s my neighbours proudly announcing that they were going to Majorca for a holiday. I would have nodded and smiled approvingly, but the truth was I had no idea where or what Majorca was and I was far too embarrassed to ask. When they returned, they could hardly stop gushing about it: "The food was a bit greasy (well, it was foreign food, after all, and it gave me a bad guts), the locals didn't speak very good English but we always managed to find a nice bar or café that sold a top quality full English or Sunday roast. The beer was all lager, but you can't have everything. And hot? We were burned to a cinder on the first day." They went back to the same resort, same hotel for as long as I lived next door to them. They never went anywhere remotely different. Good for them, I say. Until I was well into my twenties neither did I.

If I knew next to nothing about Greece, then I knew even less about her islands. Corfu, Rhodes, Zakynthos – these were names that never got near my psyche. But then, as I now know, the kind of people who went to the Greek islands in those days, the 1970s and 1980s, were not like me. Mass tourism was a long way away, the working and middle classes were beginning to discover Majorca and the Costas, but there was a whole unexplored world out there. By the 1980s, the levee broke and package holidays all across Europe and later beyond were everywhere. That was when I discovered travel agents. For me, it is a thing of the dim and distant past, but that trip to the travel agent, eh? Wait your chance to be served, all sit down round the agent's desk and he or she would gaze at a screen and type in various bits of information. I don't recall ever being allowed to see the screen; it was a great big mystery. "If you don't mind leaving on a Thursday from Gatwick instead of Birmingham on a Wednesday, it will save you £50 each in flight supplements. And two of you will be sharing accommodation for three so there will be the low occupancy supplement. So the overall cost will be" and the answer was approximately twice the amount you had worked out, travelling from a different airport on a different day. "Can you book it, please?" After a couple of hours getting more stressed, I'd have willingly signed anything.

So, to my mum, I owe a degree of thanks for planting the seed of travel, which would slowly grow. She also encouraged me to draw (I couldn't draw) and write (you can be the judge of that). I dedicate this book to the late Neeltje Drury who departed this earth in 1999 and will obviously not have a clue about the dedication on account of her death. Anyway, this one's to you, mum, amongst others.

If I learned anything at school, you can probably tell it wasn't geography. I don't think I actually learned what the subject actually was until I had long left education, but that is the same for just about every subject I studied, except for English.

For some reason I could always spell, even if I couldn't always accurately describe what each word actually meant. When I was at Wick Road Junior School in Brislington, Bristol, there was a teacher called Mr. Steed. He was forever holding spelling tests that, even then, I thought were pointless since you could either spell or you couldn't. I remember the tests had 20 words, always 20 words. I was no "keener" but when it came to spelling, if in nothing else, I was fiercely competitive. If only I had been more competitive in subjects like maths, the sciences and even practical subjects like woodwork, I might have taken different and better life choices. In the words of the Gibb Brothers, "It's only words and words are all I have."

I wanted to write, but I had no idea what I wanted to write about. In senior school, the only subject I was interested in, again, was English Language. Other subjects were an educational car crash. It was six years wasted in so many ways. I liked English Language so much that I effectively took the same O level exam twice just for fun. I knew I liked English, but it took a teacher to make me love the language. And she wasn't even English: she was Portuguese.

Mrs. Defonseca was a short, slightly plump lady, with her hair tied back. She had a loud, raspy voice, which made you sit up and listen, all with a powerful Portuguese inflection. Some people "took the Mickey" out of her, behind her back of course. How on earth could you have an English teacher who wasn't English? I learned that you certainly could and moreover that teacher became the most important teacher of my entire life. She taught me the value of words, she taught me the power of my imagination, she taught me to always stretch my mind, to test the boundaries of the language as far as I could, to always seek out the subjects that got me to imagine and then put that imagination onto paper. She gave me all the time I needed and so much more. When my O level exam came along, there were a variety of subjects, which one could choose and then write an essay about them. Rather than get into a complex self-argument about the merits or otherwise about the effects on people of violence on TV, I chose the subject that was headed, "Describe an orange." An orange? What is there to write about? But when I set my imagination free, I went on for pages of free-flowing prose, to the extent that I had to wrap up quickly before time ran out on the exam. My scores were sensational as I scored top marks in English Language and bottom marks in almost everything else. Mrs. Defonseca sought me out the following year. "Well done for choosing the orange to write about," she said, smiling. "Just having a go probably added a few points to your total." "Was it any good, though?" I asked. "Brilliant!"

The world was my lobster, it seemed. When we had the careers evening at school, I met with various journalists from the Bristol Evening Post. That was it. I was going to be a journalist. I would write for a living. For reasons I shall return to later, my dream – you could not call it a plan or grand design – never came to fruition. Instead I drifted into 39 unfulfilling years in the civil service. Denied the opportunity of further education because of a) the need to put bread on the table (my mum worked in women's fashion and was paid poverty wages), b) mental health problems and c) my natural academic shortcomings, I went to work.

The desire, the need, to write came back with a vengeance when I finished full time work. I had been writing for more than a decade for the Bristol Rovers programme "The Pirate" as Eclectic Blue. I then set up a website www.eclecticblue.org.uk. Whenever I had a spare moment, I wrote, and when I was tired of writing, I wrote some more.

Mrs. Defonseca was a pivotal person in my life. Although she has not taught me since the early 1970s, I owe her everything for teaching me to love words. The words in this book are all mine, but the inspiration is all hers. This book's for you, Mrs. D.

My best friend in all the world is Cath Johansen, nee Jones. I never asked her to take my name in marriage, although I was happy enough to get married. I never liked the terms husband and wife, preferring the term partner. To call her "my wife" or, worse still, "the wife" makes her appear some sort of appendage to which I am, not necessarily happily, attached. After one short-lived and utterly disastrous marriage to someone else (obviously), we got together in

1989 and I've never looked back since. I am not the easiest person in the world to be with, let alone live with, and we agree on so little when it comes to culture it is amazing that we are able to talk at all. But we do talk, constantly. And she has been my biggest supporter.

When I first had the idiotic idea (I felt) to write about a holiday island out of season, which would entail a period of solo travel to Corfu, I thought she would say I was mad. Well, she did say that, actually, but she was also fully supportive. She knew I had this dream of writing a book and that I didn't just want to write it, I needed to.

My two sons, Arie and Stefan, have been incredibly supportive too. They're pretty well grown up now (as I write, 21 and 17 respectively) and I suspect I am every bit as hard work for them as they have been to me, which is not quite the normal order of things. This book is for Cath, Arie and Stefan, too.

It was not until later in life when my father, Anthony Johansen, and I got close, as fathers and sons should be. Miles alone should not truly separate families, but they separated ours for far too long. Anthony and Neeltje separated when I was far too young to know, but then again I don't remember a time when my dad lived at home with us. That's probably because he didn't live at home with us because he was in the Merchant Navy fulfilling his highly successful first career.

In the Second World War, Anthony Johansen, at age 15, sailed with the North Atlantic convoys bringing much needed food and goods to hungry and desperate Brits. The ships dodged the German U Boats and he knew that, at any time, his ship could be attacked and his life would, almost certainly, be over. It was only later in life that I found out what a war hero he was. His father Alfred, who married Nellie Ladd, came to England from Norway in the early 1900s. (I calculate that I am quarter English, quarter Norwegian and half Dutch.)

Anthony moved to Canada, married and divorced again, as we have previously mentioned, but along the way he had two more sons, Noel and Vaughan, who both live in Vancouver. After going to McGill University in his late 30s, early 40s, he worked in the National Harbour Board of Canada and worked in the private office of the Canadian prime minister Pierre Trudeau. Not bad for a working class boy from the west country, eh? In Ottawa he met the true love of his life, Joy Phillips-Johansen, and he had a long, fulfilling retirement until his passing in 2011 at the age of 81.

By the time of his passing, he and I were as a father and son should be, albeit 6000 miles apart. I went to his 75th birthday in 2005, his 80th in 2009 and, saddest of all, his funeral in 2011. He was an astonishing man and if you want to know more about him, Joy's book "Fair wind and a following sea" tells quite a story.

He was always encouraging regarding my writing, but never suffered fools gladly. Whilst I do not consider myself to be a fool, I know I can be very hard work at times. For a long time he may have feared that I might not be reaching the same standards he set himself and he may well have been right about that. No, he was right. I did not have his drive, his vision, his determination or his ambition. I suspect this bugged him for many years but by the time we last parted in 2009, he finally got me and I got him.

This book is for you, dad, and it's for you, Joy. It's also to my beautiful brothers Noel and Vaughan whom I desperately miss. Imagine having two brothers you pretty well never see and, barring a lottery win, you fear you might see only occasionally for the rest of your life, if at all?

This book would never have happened but for Corfu. Well, obviously. If Corfu had not been there, I would have had nothing to write about, but it was, so I did.

Corfu itself is much more than a holiday island to me. There are, without doubt, more attractive and less (over) developed Greek islands, but I can only write about what I know and what I know is Corfu.

For over a decade, we have stayed at Anna's Studios in Arillas. There are 18 apartments in pristine condition, a bar, a lovely pool and above all the Krasakis family, Anna, Kostas and their sons Tasos and Theo. Technically, we have a commercial arrangement with the family, but in reality it is like visiting our holiday home. Yes, yes, I know they have a business to run but I am proud that they are our friends too. There is no feeling on earth that compares to arriving at Corfu Airport and then arriving at Arillas. Other resorts are available, many of them are quite wonderful but we all have our preferences and Arillas is mine.

This book is for you, Anna, and your lovely family. They gave me huge assistance and advice when I visited Corfu in January 2015 and I am very grateful indeed.

Dimitris Kourkoulos is the owner of the Brouklis taverna in Arillas. He is also chair of the local business community in which they seek to improve, not develop, Arillas. Charismatic, good-looking, multilingual, running one of the finest tavernas in Corfu, I should hate him really, but I don't. He's the man behind the www.arillas.com website which is always well worth a look. Dimitris was very generous with time (and oranges) when he kindly allowed me to spend a morning at his beautiful house up the hill from the taverna. If there is anything worth knowing about Arillas, Dimitris will know it. If there is anything worth eating, he will cook it. This book is dedicated to Dimitris, his family and his staff.

Nikos Goudelis owns the Akrotiri Café on the hill between Arillas and San Stefanos. He is one of the nicest people in the world and he owns a café with some of the finest views in the world too. When in Corfu, a holiday is incomplete without as many visits as you can manage to the Akrotiri. Nikos has given me some great assistance with this book too and this book is for you.

Theo Gasteratos runs the best boat trips in all of Corfu. If you have not been with Theo's Boats, you have probably not lived. Theo was also generous with his time whilst I was in Corfu, once speaking to me whilst in his bath (may I point out that I was not actually in the bath with him!). He is a lovely bloke, I thank him so much for giving me his time and this book is dedicated to you, Theo.

And then there is Perikles Katsaros. As you will learn in this book, I met Perikles on four separate occasions, including at Athens Airport when I was changing flights. He owns the legendary Taverna Nikolas in the tiny village of Agni in the rocky north west of Corfu. Along with Brouklis, there is nowhere I would rather spend a lunchtime, afternoon or evening than at this taverna. The service and hospitality is always wonderful, the food is always fresh and perfectly cooked and prepared. Perikles, who is no longer a spring chicken on the age front, still works mammoth 18 hour days, usually late into the night. He knows that many of his guests love to see him in the restaurant; such is the price of running such a fantastic taverna.

Perikles could write a book about his life in Corfu and I hope that one day he does. He even suggested to me, not jokingly I felt, that he and I might one day drive across the Greek mainland together and that I write about that too. He owns a hotel on the mainland so maybe we could stay there at some point?

I love the bloke to bits and this book is for you, Perikles, my dear friend.

And then the other people I met when I was there, some by accident, some by design, some happy for me to use their full names, others who weren't.

Helen Souref, the receptionist at the Ariti Grand Hotel at which I stayed in the winter of 2015. Thanks to her flawless English (you will see why if you read on), she was my guide, my confidante and my friend during my stay. She is an enormous asset to the hotel, always calm, always friendly and endlessly patient, especially with British guests who find difficulty reading a basic map. Thanks, Helen, and this one's for you.

In Roda I was privileged to meet Mike and Jackie Connors and Rick and Debbie Mansell. As you will discover, these wonderful people now live in Corfu and, better still, live like Greeks. Yes, they have their ex pat friends but they also work so hard to integrate with the community in fascinating ways. Indeed, Mike and Jackie were having lessons in Greek when I was there. They were generous too with their time, taking me to their local kafeneon and to Mike and Jackie's delicious home. They could not have been more kind during the time I spent with them and their advice and guidance was invaluable. Oh, and they were very good company too. An evening with the Connors' and Mansells might not be one to forget, or should that read remember? Anyway, this one is for you, guys.

And then there are my friends, without whose support this book would certainly never have happened.

Nick Day, Bristol Rovers match day announcer, radio presenter, businessman and all round top bloke, has been a staunch, loyal friend and supporter for many years. When things were getting me down – I'll come to that in a minute – Nick has been there for me, urging, imploring and encouraging me to complete this project. This book is for you.

Kevin Spencer, formerly of Filton, Bristol, now of Newton Abbot in Devon, lucky chap, who reminded me of the importance of always putting family and friends above everything. This book is for you, too.

Chris Brown, Bristol Rovers fan and the author of Bovver and Guilty Tiger, has been a friendly and honest critic. I dedicate this book to you, Chris.

Jules Scanlon, my sister of another mother (and father!), who remains the closest friend and the wisest of counsel.

The list really could go on forever but I am aware that you, my loyal reader, might actually wish to read something of substance so I'll just say thank you to everyone who has been there for me. This one's for you.

You will have heard the old saying, "Everyone's got a book in them" and I'm not so sure about that. You might as well say that everyone's got a painting in them too and if you have ever seen any of my efforts, you would be setting the bar of artistry very low indeed. Actually, I always convinced myself that there was a book there; it was just the subject matter than might be the issue. And then came Corfu.

It was Rodgers and Hammerstein who gave us the most profound advice:

"Happy talk, keep talking happy talk,
Talk about things you'd like to do,
You gotta have a dream, if you don't have a dream,
How you gonna have a dream come true?"

And how right they were.

I have had all manner of dreams over the years, many of which have fallen by the wayside as time has gone by. The impending arrival of old age, plus a natural lack of football ability, has meant the chances of playing for Liverpool, always remote to say the least, have receded to nothing. I am unlikely to drive a train, apart from by way of a computer simulation game and the likelihood of dating Natalie Imbruglia is not looking good either. So what's left?

There remain things I want to do and places, other than Corfu, I want to see but having this idea of writing about Corfu in winter and then making a book of it has actually come true. I did it. There are lots of things you quite fancy doing, others you are desperate to do, but things get in the way. One day, if you want something bad enough, you have to take the plunge. Book that flight, reserve that hotel room – whatever it is you want, you need, to do – and make that commitment. Once I had booked my flights and hotel, I had that "Oh my god!" moment quite a few times. "I can't do it, I need to find a way out, I am not good enough to write about it, this is all a big mistake." I had the best part of five months to think about it before I actually got on that Aegean Airlines A321 at Heathrow. This was the moment I knew it was all for real. I was "gonna have a dream come true."

Aren't the worst words in the world, 'what if'? What if I had gone to Corfu to see what it was like in winter and what if I had then written about it? That wouldn't have been one dream unfulfilled, it would have been two. And I would have visions of myself in old age, filled with regret, gazing at the past and how I had wasted it.

It would have been worse for me too because I've been a mental health basket case since I don't know when. Part of the depression, my own

Black Dog, is the lack of belief in my own ability to do anything, that constant feeling of failure and disappointment, the absence of meaningful achievement. I was very aware of that too and how failure to take this chance, maybe a once in a lifetime opportunity, would be very damaging to me as a person. I determined not to let it drift past me.

But now it's done and it is an achievement. I have confounded the pessimist, the unbeliever, in myself. No, I might not be Paul Theroux or Michael Palin – and I certainly do not expect to see me conducting a tour around Corfu in winter for broadcasting on the BBC, more's the pity I say, although Michael Portillo would be my own choice for film of the book! – but there's still time to climb the greasy pole.

So to all my counsellors and therapists, this book would certainly not have happened but for your help and interventions and this one is for you, too.

I am the least suited person on the planet to be able to offer coherent advice on how to conduct your life and how to make it better, when I struggle enough with my own, but I have learned that if you do not take the opportunities that come along in life, if you don't take a punt on something very different, if you choose not to stretch yourself and do something way out of kilter with anything you have ever done before, you sell yourself short.

So ride that motorbike, surf that big wave, fly that plane; all the things you ever dreamed of doing all your life.

What follows is the story of me fulfilling a dream and putting to bed forever the "what if I went to Corfu one winter".

Now this dream is over and I am going to find another one.  I have an idea of what the next one is going to be and it's fermenting as I write.
Do not expect a neat, well-ordered, well organised trip across Corfu; this is me you are talking to, but I hope I have been able to convey what a lot of fun it was for me.

# 1. The Big Idea

"One day, I'm going to go to Corfu in the winter. I want to see what it's like when the tourists aren't there. Then, I'm going to write a book about."

That was the gist of what I had been telling family and friends for many years. It was always "one day". I didn't know whether that "one day" would ever come along. I didn't really do much to make it happen. The idea just sat there whilst life went on around me. We went to Corfu most years for a summer holiday because it was just about affordable for a family of four on a modest income. And because we loved it.

I always believed, as many of us do, that I had a book in me. I had made many false starts, usually running out of enthusiasm or ideas, or both, but there in the middle distance was the subject matter. I had the idea of writing about Corfu in summer, but anyone could do that and anyway my experiences would probably be exactly the same as everyone else who went in summer. Got up, had breakfast, went to the beach, had a few beers, ate some nice food. I couldn't see much of an audience for that. People would rather do it themselves rather than read about someone else doing it.

Could I really justify the expense? It wouldn't be cheap, what with buying a scheduled flight, staying in an hotel, hiring a car and generally living in the island for a certain period. As the years went by, the scratch had reached such a stage that it needed itching. Whilst I was in good health and I was some years from my bus pass, time was running out. I was well aware that if I was going to commit to the project, I would have to do it sooner rather than later, or abandon the idea altogether. There are no two words worse than "What if?" What if I had done this, that and the other? Assuming I reached old age, I did not want to find myself filled with regret. I knew the book would probably not be Paul Theroux or Bill Bryson, but there was surely a story to tell and I wanted to be the person to tell it.

Then something happened in my life that changed everything. In 2014 I accepted a voluntary exit package from my Civil Service employer. I had given 39 years of public service and if I am being honest I was treading water. During that time I had lost both my parents and all my senior relatives, as well as countless friends and acquaintances. I had become well aware of my mortality. I knew this would involve a financial hit and that I would need some part-time employment, but I had nothing left to give to the government. It wasn't quite that I saw each day as a day nearer death, which was of course it was, but that each passing day saw a lost or wasted opportunity. I could have been doing something I wanted to do when I was at work doing something I didn't. Leaving my job was the easiest decision of my life and walking out of my government building on 15 May 2014 was a joyous day I will remember forever.

In the summer of 2014, "Corfu...not a scorcher!" became more than a dream and I thought about it constantly.   In Arillas, our bolt hole in the northwest of the island, I found myself telling people, the Corfiots we knew and our friends from the UK, that I was going to write a book on Corfu in winter.  It was a way of committing myself to the project.  If I told people this was definitely what I was going to do, I could not wriggle out of it.  I remember sitting one evening on the bench at the end of the jetty, watching the sun go down to the west, slipping slowly beyond the horizon.  My mind was buzzing with ideas. Looking back to the land, the bars and tavernas were packed, there were even some locals drying off after a post work swim in the warm sea.   The beach was long and smooth with all the pebbles piled neatly at the rear by the road. It was obvious they had not got there on their own and I imagined how the beach would look in winter.  I imagined how the sea front would look too.  I had never seen the place virtually unpopulated but the urge in me to see it was growing.

Every night I drifted off to sleep playing out in my mind what it would be like to come here out of season.   I imagined catching the bus to Heathrow Airport, flying to Athens (there are no direct winter flights from the UK to Corfu), staying in a hotel alone and driving round the island meeting people, on my own.   It was a frightening thought in some ways because my very clever partner usually made all the holiday arrangements and I was largely spoon-fed.   It was a bit of a shock to have the prospect of making all the arrangements and decisions myself!

Turning the dream into a reality was another thing. By September a return to autumnal England finally made up my mind: I was definitely going to do it. Once I had made up my mind, it was a matter of putting everything in place. I had asked Corfiot friends for advice on where to stay. It had to be in or around Corfu Town because geographically it made the most sense, as it was roughly equidistant to everywhere I wanted to go and Corfu Town was likely to have the most facilities for a winter visitor. With their advice and that of my old friend Trip Advisor (other sites featuring the whinges of holidaymakers are available), I selected the Ariti Grand Hotel in Kanoni, which was a short bus ride from Corfu Town and had the added advantage for a plane spotter of having rooms, which overlooked the airport runway.

Flights were easy too. Realistically it was Aegean Airlines from London Heathrow via Athens or nothing. Theoretically I could have flown from Bristol Airport, but it would have involved connections along the way – via Amsterdam and Athens, for example – and would have taken as long as a day to complete the journey.

I knew from the outset that my itinerary would need to be flexible. There were places I would have to visit but the timings would be determined by people's availability. Once I decided that I would travel in January 2015 I began to contact people I knew in Corfu. Not everyone wanted to be named publicly in this book for various reasons, but most of them were happy about it. I saw it very much as work, even though this was the holiday isle. Not everyone saw it quite that way! But I would ask: why would I spend a relative arm and a leg going on holiday to Corfu in the middle of winter? It would seem to be as absurd as going to a Swiss ski resort in August. Corfu was where you went for your summer holidays to get your tan. Winter, there was nothing to go there for, was there?

At first I certainly didn't think that Corfu would have anything to offer the winter visitor, and how could it? So much of the place was geared to the summer. The beaches, the trips, the water parks and the unheated accommodation. If you wanted a winter break you would go to the Canary Islands. It did not even vaguely occur to me that a Greek island might have more to offer than the prospect of summer sunshine, nor that I would later become almost evangelical about it.

By October I had booked everything and thought of little else, but somehow it didn't feel real. It was such a departure from the humdrum world of work and a life of routine that it almost seemed it was happening to someone else! If I had drifted off to sleep in Corfu during the previous August, thinking about my winter trip, by Christmas I was utterly obsessed. It actually helped my sleep because if I woke up in the night, I went back to sleep with positive thoughts.

Going alone didn't faze me. It wasn't as if I was going somewhere with which I was not familiar. As the narrative will reveal, it did not help that it had not occurred to me to brush up on my very basic Greek, or to take an Anglo-Greek phrasebook. I know that this is not exactly unusual for us Brits because wherever we go in the world, we expect the locals to speak fluent English and if they don't we tend to speak English to them, albeit much slower and louder. I cringe when I think about it now. I was going to a foreign country, one that I knew well, but without making even the most basic provision for speaking to the people in their native language. I never made the slightest effort when I was there and my rare efforts at speaking Greek ended in the Greek person speaking fluent English. That you rarely need to bother to speak Greek in Corfu doesn't, I know, make it right to not bother and I am genuinely sorry for that.

Would there be enough to do given how long I spent gently grilling under the Ionian sun in summer? I anticipated that most visitor attractions would be closed, as would the resorts themselves, some of which existed only for tourists. I doubted that I would be able to find the history of the resorts in the short time I would be in Corfu. Some had started as small resorts and had grown bigger, others were tacked on to existing villages. Others, I sensed, had come from nothing.

Would I be disappointed by Corfu in winter? I had no idea, but I doubted it. I knew it would be colder and probably wetter – and possibly snowy too – but it was still going to be the same place, wasn't it? This, I suppose, was the point of it all. I didn't know what it would be like other than it would look broadly as it did in summer, there just probably wouldn't be anyone else there.

I knew that if I was not the only British tourist on Corfu in January, then I would be one of the very few. There are ex-pats aplenty on the island, some living the Greek life, others living the British life in Greece, but not tourists, not many that I could see anyway. I quite liked the idea of bumping into a Brit tourist abroad, but I doubted it would happen.

It might not seem like it to you, dear reader, but this was quite an adventure for me. I wasn't Phileas Fogg and I didn't have my Passepartout. I was a pound shop Michael Palin.

I knew the content of the book could well be somewhat haphazard and chaotic. I am not going to apologise for that because that's exactly how I expected my visit to be. I wanted to be able to make things up as I went along, within the need to visit all the places and see the faces. It was never going to be a forensic, deeply descriptive guide to the island in winter, although my utter fascination with Corfu Town took me close to doing just that at one stage. It would be, for me at least, a voyage of discovery, several ambitions fulfilled and God knows what, if anything, would happen as a result.

The aim was to indulge my curiosity of how my little summer paradise would be in winter, but also to try and convey how it felt to the casual or even committed Corfu lover and perhaps to enthuse those who have never been. A broad ambition for such a small subject, I know, but I had to do it.

People always told me I could write which was particularly handy since writing, after my family and friends, has always been my greatest passion. As an aviation nut, a Corfu fanatic and frustrated author, here was the potential for a joyous combination of my passions in life. It wasn't quite now or never but I treated it as such.

I had not always followed my dreams because, too often, I didn't have dreams to follow. But now I had one and I wasn't going to let it go. I really enjoyed writing it and I so hope you enjoy reading it. Do not expect to be greatly educated by what follows because I have aimed to give you more the feel rather than the bricks and mortar of Corfu in winter.

## 2. In the beginning

It was in the early 1980s when I began to hear about Corfu.  At the time I was not particularly well travelled.  In my early twenties I had never been anywhere in Europe other than the Netherlands and, briefly, for one day, Belgium.  People were going to Corfu on holiday but I had little idea of what or where it was.  I'm afraid I didn't even know it was part of Greece.

A girl called Jenny, with whom I worked, was going to Messonghi Beach on her holidays.  I feigned knowledge, nodding sagely, as she described her forthcoming stay at the Messonghi Beach Hotel.  I figured it must be somewhere exotic, the West Indies perhaps, or the Indian Ocean.  One thing was for sure: it would be hot and sunny and she would return with a dark, deep suntan.

Two weeks later, Jenny returned from Messonghi Beach, tanned as described, having had the holiday of her life.  Messonghi Beach was not where I had imagined it might be: it was on the Greek island of Corfu, wherever that was.  Beautiful blue waters with matching blue skies, unencumbered by the slate grey skies of the British summer.   There were cocktail bars, tavernas (what were tavernas?), lazy days passed into giddy late nights, dancing the night away.  Some nights Jenny and her friend would hop in a taxi to head for the "party" resort of Benitses, just up the coast.  A former fishing village, Benitses had morphed into a place where nightclubs, countless bars and cheap and cheerful accommodation sprouted up on every corner and all parts in between. I was far too embarrassed to admit that I had never heard of Benitses, or anywhere else in Corfu for that matter, but it sure sounded like fun.

My lack of knowledge about Corfu, and just about everywhere else, was not particularly exceptional for the time. There was no Internet and knowledge was gained either through holiday brochures or the anecdotes of others who went there. Actually, there was another way of getting information about holiday destinations: television.

The BBC ran a show, imaginatively called "Holiday", which sent presenters to destinations all over the world. Nice work if you could get it! Presenters like Cliff Michelmore (ask your parents, kids) became household names and they played a pivotal role in bringing the world of foreign holidays closer to ordinary people who before then had not even considered a foreign holiday. Later ITV produced their rival show, "Wish You Were Here?" featuring Judith Chalmers and it provided a very similar service to the BBC. What was once a distant dream gradually became an every day reality. I remember seeing one show which featured Corfu. That was where Jenny went.

In all honesty, I don't remember where the presenters went, other than it was on this Greek island. It wasn't Messonghi Beach and it wasn't

Benitses. It was somewhere else in Corfu. The beaches looked so inviting. The beaches didn't look anything like the beaches of my childhood, no one was hiding behind a windbreak, there were no tourists trudging around in heavy raincoats. This was what summer was supposed to be like, I surmised, except that it was never like this in England. One day, perhaps. One day.

A couple of years went by and I ran into an old school friend called Nigel Moody. Blonde, with a neat side parting, strongly built, average height (most of were of average height in those days), I had known Nigel, or Moggy as we called him in the playground since Infant School. Having drifted apart for a few years we started going out for a beer and a game of darts again, usually in the Kings Arms pub in Brislington, Bristol, which became not my second home but almost my first.

I was doing 'lads' holidays by now. They were not exactly daring lads' holidays. We weren't partying through the night, not in the quiet Dutch resort of Katwijk in 1984, or the naturist capital of Europe, Cap d'Agde, the year before. (We really did not know it was the naturist capital of Europe until we arrived, honest!). I was never one for nightclubs. A day on the beach and a few beers, and usually more than a few beers, was sufficient for me. Nigel was going to Corfu every year.

In fact, Nigel had been travelling to Corfu for some years. He had the bug. He would buy a flight – I didn't even know you could buy a flight on its own: I thought you had to have accommodation included – and stayed in a house in Corfu Town (Corfu was a town as well?) whose owner rented out rooms. The house was basic, there were few facilities beyond a small bedroom and a shared bathroom, but he didn't need anything more. During the day, he would mount his hired motorcycle and head off around the island (Corfu was an island?) to a different place, a different beach, every day. I wasn't quite so sure about the motorcycle bit, I couldn't drive at the time, but there were bound to be buses. I might have to think about this.

It was time to look at my atlas to find out a bit more about Corfu. It took some finding, but there it was. It was really small and – heaven forbid – it was even further away than Italy. But the seed was now well and truly planted. It was now 1985 and it would be the year of Corfu.

But first, who to go with? My friends Paul and Gary had already booked a fortnight's holiday at a resort called Kavos. Benitses was regarded as the hot spot for young people but Kavos was the new kid on the block. It also had more of a Greek sounding name. This turned out to be the only thing that was remotely Greek about it. I had imagined it would be a picturesque fishing village with quaint tavernas (I had since learned what tavernas were) and little old ladies, clad in black, riding round on donkeys. In subsequent visits, I saw lots of places like that, but never in Kavos. I settled upon my old friend Pete Nicholls, another work colleague.

He was slightly shorter than me, had dark hair and, crucially, drove and owned a car. I was in my Ian Botham-in-the-1980s phase, with a mass of blonde highlights and a big moustache to boot. I liked Pete a lot, he'd be good company and we wouldn't be beating each other up.

Nigel was my Corfu guru. When he went to Corfu, he'd write a letter to a man called Agoris who ran a café just across the road from where he stayed and Agoris would translate the booking to the proprietor who rented the rooms out and whose English was as threadbare as my Greek. When that was all sorted, he'd book a flight and off he'd go. Now I asked him to book the room for us and spoon-feed us on how to book the flight which, in 1985, still involved visiting a travel agent.

It was surprisingly easy to book the flights. We were to fly on an early morning flight from Gatwick Airport, south of London, on a flight operated by the charter airline Dan-Air. Now Dan-Air had something of a reputation. They had earned the cruel moniker "Dan Dare", an airline that flew by the seat of it pants. Formed in 1953, the Dan Air name was a byword for a mixture of danger, cronky old planes and sour-faced cabin staff. The fleet of aircraft certainly wasn't state of the art, with elderly Boeings and geriatric BAC one-elevens. (I didn't know for years what 'Dan Air' stood for, assuming some Danish connection or perhaps that the founder was called Dan. In fact, it stood for Davies and Newman which was the name of a London shipbroking business.) If you were flying to Europe on a charter flight, the chances were that you would be flying Dan Air. I had very limited experience of flying so it did not really occupy my mind until the date of departure got nearer.

I spoke regularly with Nigel who told me that we really should hire motorcycles in order to take in as much of the island as we could. There were buses from Corfu Town which went to most resorts and small towns and villages, they were generally reliable, if packed, they were inexpensive and they left at odd times. He explained that the last bus back to Corfu Town from a relatively distant resort might be lunchtime. As it turned out we did not hire motorcycles for two reasons. One, I had no experience of riding one and two I had heard all kinds of stories of people in the Greek islands hiring and then falling off their motorbikes, getting seriously injured in the process. The yellow streak down the middle of my back held me in good stead and indeed relative safety.

It certainly felt like an adventure. This was somewhere I had never before been to. I had no idea what it would be like, what the food would be like, how hot it would be. I was going to be a stranger in a strange land. As our departure drew ever nearer my excitement levels grew, as did my levels of apprehension. The what ifs were all over the place. What if we couldn't find the room where we were staying? What if we got lost? What if we didn't like it? What if is not a very positive state of mind.

Paul and Gary travelled ahead of us flying directly from Bristol, the day after the Manchester air disaster where an Airtours plane tragically caught fire on take off, killing 55 passengers, en route to Corfu. At the time I was a nervous flyer and this awful, tragic incident didn't exactly settle my nerves. At least our flight was a couple of days later.

Before we went, I had to consider what to take with me. How warm would it be? Well, as it turned out, very, but I still ended up taking the kind of clothes I would normally take for an autumn break in Cornwall, including a couple of pairs of jeans, jumpers and a rain coat. A raincoat indeed. Why on earth would I need that? Two weeks later, I found out!

In the meantime, we had to get to the airport and unlike our friends, we were travelling from London Gatwick. This meant the overnight bus to Gatwick Airport for the stupid-O'clock departure. A few hours of fitful sleep later, and a very stiff neck, we were at the airport. Only three hours to kill until departure. It was still pitch dark and, being England, cold and wet. Good move wearing jeans and a raincoat.

We dragged our cases around the airport, eventually navigating through security which in those days usually involved a cursory glance at our passports, a cheery smile and, hey presto, it would almost be time for boarding.

We boarded our plane, a Boeing 727, not, I hoped, the one Dan-Air had purchased from a Mexican airline following a collapse of its undercarriage that had seen the aircraft written off, only for it to be repaired and sold. The 727 had three engines, all at the back of the plane. As we squeezed down the aisle it was clear that, at least on the inside, this plane had seen better days. The carpets were old, worn and slightly ripped. The seats moved seemingly at their own free will. I had flown Dan Air a few years before en route to Beziers in France. On that occasion as the 737 rotated for take off, the door to the flight deck shot open with a huge bang as it hit the toilet door. There was a surprised captain looking back down the plane rather than ahead of him. Somehow, I had imagined he would be desperately wrestling with the controls. It stayed open well into the flight too. I managed to visit the flight deck – you could, prior to 9/11 – and the captain was a former RAF jet pilot and he chain-smoked Marlboro cigarettes as he cheerfully pointed out the vineyards over which we were flying. This flight was rather less eventful.

This flight was completely event-free and three hours or so later we were well into the descent for Corfu. It was a cloudless sky, everything was blue. I vividly remember flying over the island, directly over the airfield, which was pointed out by the captain. Even then it was impossible not to observe the rich greenness of the island, mile upon mile of trees. How could this happen on a boiling hot Greek island where it never rained?

Later, I was to learn that it rains in winter. And it rains and it rains and it rains.

Over the channel between the Greek mainland and the island, we made a massive and seemingly tight right hand turn with Corfu to the left. Having done so little preparation about the island I was about to visit, I cannot pretend I observed the landmarks near Corfu Town. Mouse Island, the causeway separating the area of Kanoni and Perama or the runway itself which was built on a lake.

The runway, I had been warned, was desperately short, one of the most dangerous in Europe. You either approached the runway by coming in from the south, descending so low it appeared you actually land in the sea, or you landed from the north, almost level with the chimney pots and TV aerials (this was long before the arrival of satellite dishes). In fact I made the mistake of reading a book of lists before I left, which informed me that Corfu was not just one of the most dangerous airports in the world, it was the most dangerous airport in the world. Nowhere else came close, so the thought was deeply etched in my mind that I was risking life and limb by just going to Corfu. The truth, I later discovered, was rather less dramatic. Whilst the runway certainly does have the sea at one end and the town at the other, plus a lake on both sides, it is relatively long. It was very bumpy, and still is, but dangerous? No. It was just another runway and all the doom and gloom stories were no more than that.

We seemed to be about to land in the sea when 'THUMP!' The rear wheels didn't so much touch down as crash down and then there was an enormous roar of reverse thrust. Welcome to Corfu. And everyone started to clap, more in relief than any kind of praise for the pilot who had managed to land the plane.

Everyone stood up, collected their bags from the overhead lockers and then waited, with their bodies contorted at crazy angles. Why we didn't all stay seated I didn't understand. We were keen to disembark this elderly plane as quickly as possible but we probably all knew nothing would happen any quicker by us standing up.

The tradition of getting up as soon as the plane has stopped on the apron has carried on to this day, especially on package flights. Gather up all your hand luggage, stand up and bend your back at a 90-degree angle and wait for the doors to open, which can take a good while in Corfu where, even at the airport, no one is in a hurry. There is a strange silence at times like this because, I suspect, everyone knows really that standing up straight away is pointless. You still have to disembark from the aircraft, stand in an endless queue to have your passport not checked by a disinterested official and when that's all over, stand round the baggage carousels, along with the hot and sweaty passengers from any number of flights that have arrived at the same time as yours.

The steps finally arrived and people gradually squeezed through the doors. There were two things that struck me immediately. The heat was like nothing I had felt before. I was completely overdressed and by the time I reached the terminal building I was, frankly, a sweaty mess. Don't wear jeans when you are having a summer holiday in the Greek islands. The second was the smell, or rather the smells. Ours was not the only aircraft and there was a strong smell of kerosene, a smell I rather like, although I appreciate it probably does not offer a great deal in terms of health benefits. It blended with a strange, almost floral smell, which I have noted too on subsequent visits. The smell of Corfu, a kind of familiar welcome home smell.

And there was the noise. There was no such thing as quieter aircraft back in the 1980s and even when idling, the engines created a hell of a din. I got to know that noise very well in the two weeks that followed.

If the apron was hot, inside the building it felt more like a sauna. The disinterested official was in place, far ahead of a long, somewhat disorganised queue, smoking a cigarette, not really looking at our passports, certainly not looking at the hordes of weary holidaymakers who just wanted this to be all over and board their buses to the resorts. Many people were probably more stressed now than before they even left home. Of the two carousels, only one was working and I estimated at least four flights had landed around the time that we did. To make matters worse, even this one was not yet working because none of the luggage had yet arrived at the terminal building.

It is hard to explain just how crowded it was. Imagine being outside a major store in the January sales, but in 30c heat, with your children in tow and it was ten times worse. "Oh come on: start working!"

After what felt like an age, there was a clank, followed by a rattle, then finally a "did-a-dig-a-dig" noise which indicated the carousel had reluctantly spluttered into action. There was no baggage coming through, of course. That would be too much to expect, but at least the contraption was working. A collective "Ahhhh" went round the terminal building, a frisson of excitement that we might soon be on our way, but that was soon replaced by a muffled groan as the carousel stopped turning altogether. "For goodness sake!"

Other than a toilet there was not much in the way of facilities to help bide the time, something that has not changed in 30 years. But, hey, this is Greece. Nothing happens very quickly over here, which is part of the attraction, a rather large part of the attraction if the truth be known.

When the carousel eventually shuddered back into action, bags started appearing, first in dribs and drabs, then all at once. Splendidly the indication board wasn't working so no one from, I remind you, four flights – at a guess, some 500 people – had the first idea from which flight(s) the luggage belonged. Bemused, confused, we got as close as we could to the carousel and to our utter amazement, two of the first cases to arrive were ours. In future years, arrival at Corfu Airport's baggage reclaim would be something to dread, knowing how shambolic and chaotic it was and remains.

Suitcases in hand, we made our way through the small customs area, in which during the 30 years I have been visiting the island I have never, once, seen a customs officer. It is entirely possible that the officers might have taken cigarette breaks when planes were arriving – these are a permanent feature of Greek life – but a more likely explanation is that there is no point in having them for what are mainly charter flights. You are hardly like to smuggle in cheap cigarettes or booze to a place where these items are already far cheaper.

Into the arrivals area, then as now, which was full of people holding up cards with the names of passengers, holiday companies and even resorts stand in line. Slightly beyond were the package tour representatives, preparing to assign passengers to the various buses to take holidaymakers to their resorts. Mercifully, we were able to avoid this because we had arrived on a flight only basis and would be making our own way to our accommodation. In later years, I would soon find how boring and time-consuming aspects of package holidays could be. Buses are laid on to take people to their resorts, but most of them stop at other resorts and accommodation along the way. If your accommodation is last on the route, this can be a very long process. Many years later, we had an airport transfer to the north of the island which took three and a half hours, longer than the entire flight from the UK and this didn't take into account the time spent waiting on the bus at the airport for passengers who had arrived from other UK airports.

We made our way through the throng and joined the road from the airport to where we were staying, or rather to where we thought we were staying. "Upon exiting the airport, turn left, walk to the main road and turn right by the football ground and keep going," was the general thrust. "It isn't very far."

So far, so good. The football ground, though seemingly half-built (it still appears to be half-built, if I am being honest), was unmissable. Turning right, passing a mix of houses and shops another smell hit us. Sadly, it was not aeroplane fuel or flora: it was the unmistakable smell of drains, of sewage. Where on earth was that coming from?

A quarter of a mile onwards and there it was, our humble abode for the next two weeks. Our road took a gentle right turn, to the left was a road which, we later discovered, took one all the way into the centre of Corfu Town. On the right was a sign, "Rooms", which was a bit of a clue. Across the road was a café run by a man called Agoris. I didn't know his surname but he was Nigel's man on the ground to book the room with the owner whose grasp of English was similar to my grasp of Greek, which was virtually non-existent. In our two weeks there, I never got to learn his name and when we needed to communicate, we did so by way of hand signals and "Gringlish", which was basically speaking Greek and a half-cocked Greek accent.

Agoris took us across the road, leaving us in the hands of the owner, who took us down a narrow, dark corridor, left into a dark room in which there was a small window at the back, two single beds and a sink. Just a long from our room was a bathroom, which contained a toilet and a shower with no curtain. Next to the toilet was a pedal-bin. Our host grabbed a piece of toilet paper and demonstrated that, following its use, the paper should be placed in this bin. Nigel had warned me about this. Throughout Corfu, toilet paper should be put in a separate bin, not the toilet. The drains couldn't take it. Being told about it was one thing, seeing it for real was quite another.

Agoris's café became our regular haunt for breakfast, the occasional lunch and the occasional supper. He sold a range of hot pies and donuts, as well as a delightful range of snacks which tasted nice enough even though I had little idea of what I was eating.

Every afternoon Agoris went off with his towel to go to a private beach about 10 minutes away. This explained his deep swarthy tan, which was a complete contrast to his wispy silver hair. I don't know how old he was at the time we visited although I would guess he was in his late fifties or early sixties. I liked him an awful lot and it was sad to learn that he died some years ago. In a short period he had become our friend, our main cook, our guide and our translator, all for the price of a coffee and a sausage roll.

Leaving our house, turning right, was the Bay of Garitsa, maybe five minutes walk away. The view was impressive, except the water, which was – how shall I phrase this? – not the bluest of blue. To put not to fine a point on it, the water was a dreary dark colour. I would not go so far to say it was brown, but I think you know what I am saying. To all intents, it was an open sewer. Immediately ahead, as the bay twisted round to the right was the magnificent Old Fortress. Further beyond was the Greek mainland, to the left Corfu Town. The Old Fortress is a highlight of the island, built in 6 AD, it stands over the Esplanade or Spianada Square and is linked to the town by a fixed iron bridge 60 meters in length. For all its history, many of us associate it with the James Bond movie "For Your Eyes Only", many of us, that is, with dubious cultural leanings.

No one was swimming in the water at any time when we were there but at certain times games of water polo took place. There were plenty of small boats moored around the bay, but the water quality and its attendant odours did Corfu Town few favours.

Before too long, you arrive in the very heart of Corfu. Countess Flamburiari, whoever she was when she was at home (as I have said elsewhere; you will need to look elsewhere for proper history), said, 'Corfu Town is Venice and Naples, a touch of France and more than a dash of England, apart of course from being Greek'. That's as good a description as you could possibly imagine. Influences from different countries and cultures are everywhere and there was certainly a dash of English, with cricket being played in front of the famous Liston. The pitch, such as it is, is in the middle of a very rough, bumpy grassy area. The wicket is artificial but the cricket certainly isn't. We would settle down beneath the cooling trees and then develop the international theme by having a couple of large Heinekens. Now and then, a ball would fly from the bat and land in the trees above the bars on the boundary, crashing through the branches, sometimes landing on tables. Other times, a large 'CLANG!' would be heard as the ball clattered into a car parked in the official car park, which went round half of the outfield. Sitting in Greece, watching a very English game played by Greeks and drinking Dutch beer. It didn't get much better than that.

Corfu Town is largely pedestrianised, not least because many of the streets are so narrow. The little lanes and alleyways reveal a wealth of history amid the stunning Venetian architecture. Shop after shop of jewellery, fancy items, fur coats (cruel, but a must in Corfu, I would imagine), cheap tat – you name it, it was probably there, even if the brand names of the products do suggest they might just be hooky. To this day I always walk round the shops of Corfu Town and when I have finished, I always wonder why I did! I detest shopping at home but if I could stop from time to time to imbibe some refreshments, I could probably live with it. Above all walking round Corfu Town, preferably during the evening, is a pleasure in itself. In 1985 it was certainly more "Greek" than it is today because now the town has embraced the international café culture and even imported a McDonalds housed within an elderly Venetian three-storey house.

Evenings we would always head into Corfu Town to dine at the tavernas and takeaways where you could purchase a lovely Giros or Souvlaki, or sit down for a traditional slap up meal. Greek cuisine is not renowned for being world class, but I would disagree with that. It is often meat heavy and not always suitable for the vegetarian (things have greatly improved on that front since the 1980s), but I have always enjoyed what has been on offer. Resorts in Corfu tend to offer the type of food that is appropriate for the type of tourist that visits. Corfu Town caters mainly for the people who live and work there and, as a rule, is as good a place to eat as anywhere else in Corfu.

Even the takeaways were excellent. One evening we came across a takeaway that displayed chickens being cooked on a large rotisserie. We came to realise this particular establishment, situated off the beaten track near to where we were staying, was well-frequented by locals, it being nowhere near the tourist trail. We took this as a major positive and went inside, more than once in our holiday as it turned out, and to my surprise and delight, all they sold was chicken and chips. The only choice one had to make was the amount of chicken you wanted. I soon discovered that whatever size portion you bought, it was always too much. But it was delicious. Sadly this place is long gone, as I discovered to my disappointment 30 years later.

One thing I noticed was how cheap everything was. The Greek currency at the time was the drachma and you would get many hundreds to the pound. A fiver would buy you a decent two course meal and perhaps a drink too. You always had a wallet stuffed with a vast array of notes which actually weren't worth very much, but you certainly got good value from them. The mistaken introduction of the Euro (a bit of politics there) has changed all that and whilst Corfu is still good value, it is no longer cheap.

Getting about in Corfu Town was relatively easy, even at night. We had walked to the centre of town along the bay, we would walk back that way. It had not occurred to us to buy a map (why would you need a map for staying in a town in which you had never previously set foot?) so some of it was guesswork. To reach the bay you merely and literally had to follow your nose. Within a few days we discovered how easy it was to walk back to the digs more as the crow flies, through the darkened streets, passing the small bars where old men would sit outside smoking – everyone smoked back in the 1980s, including me – and one small taverna after another.

I well remember our first night in our room. I bumped into various strangers in the dark (and it was dark even when the lights were on), people I assumed were also staying there, before flopping on a bed which couldn't have been much harder if it had been made of concrete. I was so tired I went out with the light. And then I woke up with a start. There was a plane taking off. Then a plane landed, another one took off and so on. And when there wasn't a plane landing or taking off, there was the relentless scream of engine noise that simply never stopped. There were no night flying restrictions in Corfu, given the importance of tourism, and the airlines exploited the lack of regulation to the nth degree. We would shut the window, but that made the room unbearably hot and you couldn't sleep in that either. Some days were much worse than others and I soon worked out that Mondays and Fridays were the main flight days in Corfu, the big turnover days, where the noise was constant and relentless. On other nights, the noise was sporadic but never confined to any particular time. No wonder I always fell asleep on the bus.

There were no tea making facilities in our accommodation so every day we went to see Agoris for breakfast. Traffic rumbled by just a few feet from the café, the locals conducted their conversations at a volume that suggested they were having a blazing row. At first I thought they were, so ferocious were the discussions, but Agoris assured me that it was friendly banter. No one got punched anyway, at least not when I was watching.

The next morning we crossed the road to see the cheery Agoris and drank coffee, planning the day ahead. Well, to say we were planning the day ahead suggests we had the first idea of where we were going. Of course we hadn't. I fancied a day on the beach, as I always do when I am on holiday. But was there a beach anywhere near? It turned out there was, a municipal pay as you enter beach, through a gate and there was a tatty bit of sand, some changing rooms and the uninviting brown coloured sea. We paid our drachma and found a couple of sunbeds. Wearing our speedos – yes, people really did wear them in those days – we neatly placed our towels, lay down on them and fell asleep. Pete shoved me at one point because I was snoring loudly, probably frightening the children, but God I needed the kip after last night. We didn't swim, that was just too risky.

A few days of this and my spirits were raised and it was time to branch out. We walked to the bay and got a bus to Kanoni, past the birthplace of Prince Philip at Mon Repos. Leaving the bus, we were greeted with THE view of Corfu. Looking south to all the resorts, the sea to the left, and the green-covered hills to the right. And in the foreground, Mouse Island and the church of

Panagia Vlacherna. To the right, a causeway linking Kanoni and Perama and the road south. 30 years on and this view still does it for me. There are hotels and bars from which you can take in the view. I can sit there for hours and of course do. To the right is the airport runway, all of it to be viewed from high, sitting literally in the middle of a lake, sea at one end, Corfu Town at the other. Many people go there just for the view but a good few, myself included, go there to see the planes. So Pete and I would sit at a table under the Ionian sun, eating a burger of undefined content, drinking overpriced beer and watching yet another jet roaring in.

A couple sat at a table with the best view of the runway. What particularly interested me was that the man had a VHF radio and he was listening to the pilots and the control tower. He was balding, around 55, wearing a short-sleeved shirt, khaki knee length shorts and – in traditional British style – sandals and socks (I ask you!). His wife was immaculately dressed in a floral frock and a big floppy hat. I didn't catch her name – never a strong point with me, remembering names – but I will always remember his: Basil, the only Basil I have ever met. Not only did he listen to the chatter from his radio, he noted all the plane types and numbers, putting them in a small book.

We got chatting, as you do when you have the same interests as a complete stranger, and I asked where they were staying.

"At the hotel overlooking the runway," replied Mrs Basil.

"Oh right. Have you stayed here before?"

"Yes. We come here every year."

"So what do you do during the day? Lie by the pool? Travel around the island? Go into town?"

"We come here."

"What: every day?"

"Pretty much yes. Basil loves listening to his radio, watching the planes. I sit here with my book, or perhaps I'll take a dip in the hotel pool. We even have lunch up here," she continued, pointing at a restaurant overlooking Mouse Island, perfectly positioned to catch the landing planes on final approach.

We, or rather I, sat with Basil and Mrs Basil for a few minutes, or "ages" as Pete later described it. I was interested, slightly though not obsessively fascinated, in what we were watching and I decided that one day I would get a radio like Basil's In the years that followed Kanoni became a visiting essential. Friends we would travel with would look up at the hotels looking down on the runway and lake and say, "Who on earth would want to stay in a hotel like that?" You will know, dear reader, the answer to that. The man who specifically requested a runway view when booking my visit in January 2015.

The view of the lagoon from the hotels at Kanoni is quite beautiful, even allowing for the fact that a busy airport runway cuts straight through it. The hotels appeared to be full, too, notwithstanding the 24-hour air operation that took place below their bedroom windows. It was hard to believe that some people booked these hotels specifically to acquire views of planes taking off. Back then, in 1985, aircraft engines were much louder than they are today, which I have to say was part of their attraction. I might not have been quite so keen being woken up at 3.00 am by yet another Dan Air Boeing 727.

We had pre-arranged with Paul and Gary, before leaving England, that we would meet up on a specific day in Corfu Town, head out on one of the buses to some resorts, later returning to Corfu Town and then, all of us, to Kavos where they were staying. I'm afraid I have no recollection of the first part of the day at all. I think we went to Kassiopi, because the following year that's where Paul, Gary and myself went, and the year after. But the story picks up on the trip to Kavos.

We boarded the bus and it was jam-packed. It was the last bus of the evening and there were a wide variety of passengers, from locals to dolled-up British tourists, girls in gownless evening straps rather than strapless evening gowns. The driver was not hanging about and soon we were tearing through Corfu Town before turning left onto the coast road to the south. We stopped occasionally – well, it was a bus after all! – then we approached a resort that was rocking. Young people everywhere, huge open air clubs, drunken young men in vests staggering across the road and boomingly loud music cutting through the warm evening air. The bus slowed down and then stopped alongside a row of bars and it virtually emptied within a few seconds. Benitses! It left just us four and a couple of Corfiots to complete much of the rest of the journey until Lefkimmi, a non-touristy authentic town. I seem to remember the road on to Kavos was barely more than a dirt track.

Leaving the bus, Paul explained that he and Gary had decided to visit every single bar in the resort for no reason other than that they could. A week later, they had been forced to give up, probably in order to save their livers, because they had discovered they had only seen around a quarter of the resort.

Now Kavos was different from anything I had ever seen before. I was not one for the nightclubs at home, more a heads down no nonsense mindless boogie for me, and I usually retired to bed around midnight. In Kavos, people were just going out at that time. We ate in a local restaurant and, being British tourists, we embraced the local culture by ordering the local staple: steak and chips. It was pretty grim, too, as I recall, the meat having all the taste and texture of old rope and the chips being on the cold side of cool. I probably deserved it for being such a food heretic. And then to the bars, outside of which were young people probably paying for their stays by handing out leaflets for cheap drinks and even cheaper nightclubs. I am not going to pretend we didn't enjoy it – I am usually up for a drink wherever I am – but this was almost, well it was, compulsory drunkenness. No one else was sober, I concluded, so why should I be? At some ungodly hour, we returned to their apartment following the dirt track under the light of the moon, with the smell of urine coming from the beach as legions of boys (and not a few girls) relieved themselves. I made a note of where not to put my sunbed the following morning.

The apartment, if you could call it that, was basic. Basically, there was a room with two short single beds, a tiny living room and what we call a bathroom, except that this was the size of a shoebox. And it stank. In Corfu, you do not put your toilet paper down the toilet after use, you place it in a bin next to the toilet and the maid empties it when she does her daily clean. Except that she had not done her daily clean that day. Our sleeping arrangements were also basic: we put two blankets on the floor, lay on them and engaged in fitful, low quality sleep for a few hours before waking with the stiffest of stiff necks (and just about everything else). The little beds in our room in Corfu Town were of orthopedic standard compared to the floor here. Frankly, I felt awful.

Mid morning and we had a full breakfast in the nearest café. Not, I hasten to add, a full Greek breakfast, but a version of a full English, swimming in olive oil. It slithered down easily enough but the unexplained crunchy bits in my sausages left me a little queasy. I don't know if it set me up for the day – my recollection is that, for a while, I became virtually incontinent – but it certainly got me moving.

Despite industrial-sized quantities of generic lager and cocktails the night before, I had not forgotten the sight nor smell of holidaymakers relieving themselves on the golden sands.  If anything, in the warm light of day, it stunk to high heaven, although it didn't seem to bother any of the sunbathers, not that there were many of them.  They didn't usually arrive until early to mid afternoon, if they made it at all.  They were hard at work on their bar tans.

In all honesty I didn't like what I had seen of Kavos.  True, it had a beautiful, if somewhat pungent, beach but for me the negatives, and there were many, vastly outweighing the positives, whatever they were.  It was a mass (or was it a mess?) of apartments, complexes, bars and clubs constructed next to a dirt track and it was in the middle of nowhere.  It was called "The Strip". How do they think of these things?

Before returning on the evening bus to Corfu Town, we booked a boat trip to the nearby island of Paxos to the south.  It was more of an 18-30 type trip rather than a sightseeing occasion and we saw little of the place beyond the capital Gaios where we met a large group of lads from Blackpool.  We sat outside a taverna which had no written menu.  When you required service, the waiter would simply read from memory what they served, at breakneck speed.  When he finished, we looked blankly at each other and someone said, "Oh, just get us squid and chips, please." And so we were served squid and chips, the former of which tasted to my dull palate as fish flavoured elastic bands.

Having seen next to nothing of Paxos, the boat next headed off to the much smaller Anti Paxos. As we reached the island, it was as if we had entered a Bounty advert: gorgeous azure blue waters, packed with multi-coloured fish and a beach inhabited only by fellow 18-30 revellers. A few low quality dives, feet first in my case, and it was time to go. I never really fancied this type of holiday and I fancied it less afterwards. Nothing wrong with it, but two weeks of getting bladdered and trying to pull was really not what I wanted from my holiday, I spent all year doing that anyway.

In the evening, we made our escape and got back to the relatively sedate Corfu Town, even if the Bay of Garitsa's odours (the odours are becoming quite a theme) were none too pleasant if the wind was blowing in the wrong direction. I had by now got used to it.

I liked Corfu Town. Where we stayed was cheap and cheerful, the people always friendly and helpful. We did Kanoni a few more times, we spent most evenings in Corfu Town, drinking and eating beneath the trees on the Liston, occasionally watching games of cricket. Miracle upon miracle, we even managed to navigate a route back to our room from the centre of town, even when it was dark. We bought corn cobs, grilled and covered in salt, not butter, and warm nuts from street vendors, and there was that chicken shop where you could purchase as much hot chicken as you wanted with as many chips as you could consume.

And then it was all over. Two weeks later we packed our bags and prepared to make our way to Ioannis Kapodistrias airport. It was mid morning and no one else seemed to be around at the house. We had intended to cross the road to say goodbye to the lovely Agoris and thank him for his excellent hospitality but it was raining so heavily, you could barely see across to the other side of the road. But we couldn't wait. We had a flight to catch. We put on our coats and off we went and within 10 yards I looked as if I had been standing fully clothed in a shower. We soldiered on through the monsoon, with massive forks of lightning and biblical claps of thunder quickly following suit. As we were walking under trees for much of the way I did wonder if this was slightly more dangerous than the journey were about to make home!

We reached the terminal building and it was complete and utter chaos. There were hundreds upon hundreds of people crammed in the hall where the check-in desks were and only a couple were open. One look at the departures board showed why: the storm that had drenched us to the skin had persuaded most captains to divert their inbound aircraft to Athens. But not all of them. There were three flights from Britain which had flown in through the storm and guess which airline they belonged to?  Dan Air, and our plane was one of them.

We dripped our way through the departure lounge and our flight to London Gatwick was immediately called.  We showed our boarding passes, walked down onto the apron where the rain was still chucking it down and climbed aboard this dear old Boeing 727.  So pleased to see you.

The captain came on the tannoy.  30 years on and I cannot recall his exact words but they went something like this, in a very well spoken almost upper class voice:  "Good morning ladies and gentlemen and welcome to this flight from Corfu to Gatwick.  We've had a very bumpy journey down here this morning and we were given the option of diverting to Athens but we decided to give it a go landing here first.  We'll be taking off towards the sea today because we're a bit too heavy to take off towards the town and we'd probably clip a few TV aerials. Sit back and enjoy the flight!"  Oh bloody hell.  I paid more attention that usual to the safety instructions as the plane rumbled to the end of the runway, the lights from the plane flashing almost as frequently as the lightning which still filled the air.  "Cabin staff to their seats please."

An enormous roar from the back of the plane and we were off.  It's an oft-stated myth that Corfu's runway is incredibly short.  It's not short but there is a town at one end, the sea at the other and a lake on either side.  And it's as bumpy as hell. Off we tore down the runway without any real indication that we would eventually leave the ground. Then, just as the sea and the causeway came into view we rumbled into the air in the slowest ascent of an aircraft I have ever known. We seemed to clear Mouse Island, which is a little way out to sea, by what seemed to be a few feet but was probably hundreds of feet and slowly, ever so slowly, we climbed into the fireworks display all around us. I know now that turbulence doesn't normally bring an aircraft down, but then, as the plane slipped up and down and from side to side in what appeared to be the centre of the storm, I wasn't quite so sure.

Within 20 minutes the skies below, still not that far below it seemed to me, were clearer and there was the west coast of Corfu. And it looked beautiful. There were great big chunks of yellow beach dotted all down the coast. We didn't see any of them during our stay, having done zero preparation before we went, but there would have to be another time. I had finally done Corfu, albeit as an innocent and incompetent tourist. I had to do it again and next year I did.

You will be relieved to read that the 'lads' holidays of 1986 and 1987 will not be described in intimate detail. Not because they were especially outrageous. How could they be? Kassiopi, where we stayed, remained at that time – just about – a working fishing village. Not for us the bar tans and sore livers of Kavos and Benitses, even if my 30th birthday was some time away. The three of us were not party animals in the conventional sense.   Late night, early morning beers was as lively as it got for us but it was still lively enough for me to have forgotten where in the resort we stayed.  The first time was an apartment at the top end on the road out of town to the south, which meant we were far enough from any real noise but near enough to the action, such as it was.

During the day we would walk down the narrow road to the beautiful harbour with its bobbing boats and an amazing view of what I remember as being the bleak lands of Albania.  It certainly looked sinister from a distance and there was lots of talk about Albanians sneaking into Corfu after nightfall.  Sadly, the only Albania we got to see was a dead body which gently floated in as we sat outside the Wave Bar, which was situated on the left hand side of the harbour as you looked out.  After dinner, we would inevitably head to the Wave Bar to drink and talk rubbish for hours on end.  The owner was a slight, balding, bearded, genial man called Kostas and he would occasionally be accompanied by a man called Jimmy – I have no idea if this was his real name – who, I seem to remember, was Greek/American, or it may have been the other way round.  He talked like Groucho Marx and looked like a less goofy Bernie Winters. Most evenings, a handsome, smart man would come in and perform vigorous Greek dancing, often with a table between his teeth.  Ladies of a certain age loved him and came back night after night.

The bars and restaurants would gradually begin to close after 1.00pm although Kostas would do his best to accommodate us until the matchsticks propping open his eyes began to fail. Sometime, at around 3.00am, he would ask us how many more beers we wanted, sell them to us, lock up and go home. He had to get up in the morning; we didn't. On several mornings, we stayed up to see the dawn, having drunk ourselves sober. The locals would be cleaning stuff – there was water everywhere on the streets – and the overwhelming, heavenly smell of freshly baking bread wafted through the town. By the time we'd got up, usually after lunch, the bread would long be gone.

We were fond of another bar situated by the harbour, a long thin bar with bar stools. We became friendly with a couple of Scots lads who said they spent most of their holidays there. One day one of them was doing The Sun crossword. "I'm stuck on one. Three letters, drinks counter." We all collapsed, assuming it was a well-timed joke but his mate insisted he meant it. "You're sat at it!" we said. "Oh aye."

Kassiopi is a very popular resort despite rather than because of its beaches. On one side lies a narrow shingle beach; at the far side of the harbour lies a very small shingle beach by some flat rocks. We always went to the beach, such as it was, but an awful lot of people never ventured beyond their swimming pools. As I grew older, I did the same.

We had promised our families we would not hire motorcycles. We had heard all the grim stories of Brits, wearing neither helmets nor leathers, just shorts and T-shirts, suffering awful injuries on the roads and we had seen the victims too. Broken legs, girls and boys with awful cuts and scratches that would leave permanent scars. Some people even died. So in the second week of our holiday, the three of us hired mopeds but not helmets nor any kind of protective clothing. Wearing shorts and T-shirts, and not even the latter for most of the journeys, the little machines took us from Kassiopi in the far north east of the island to Agios Georgios in the far southwest.

None of us had ever ridden mopeds before and what a place to start. Riding on the wrong side of the road, on a hilly switchback road with nothing between the road and the sea and the rocks below. What a good idea that was. We stopped once or twice for drinks but did the trip south pretty well in one go. Agios Georgios is part of a 12km stretch of a beautiful sandy beach, a resort basically tacked onto it. The nearest town is Argyrades, which is apparently (I hadn't been there yet), famed for its Venetian architecture and its cafes. I expect people who went there before the bars, tavernas and apartments appeared would now describe it as spoilt but if it was simply new to you, as it was to us, it looked pretty unspoiled.

We left the mopeds at the end of the road and went for a swim. Whilst splashing about, we happened to take a glance to where the mopeds were and we observed a large van with its back door open. A man jumped from the driver's seat and moved towards them. We realised immediately what was going on and dashed from the water at full tilt before our transport for the day disappeared to who knows where. I am not sure we looked all that terrifying in our speedos, which were common at the time, but the man suddenly turned away from the mopeds and hurried towards the van, got in and sped off, the back doors wide open and banging away on the side! That would have been fun to explain to the blokes who hired the bikes to us!

Having travelled south on the east coast road, we decided to return to Kassiopi through the middle of the island. Instead of turning right at Gouvia to follow the coast road, we went straight on up the legendary Trompeta Pass. What we thought was going to be a short cut turned out to be an exhausting slog, mile upon mile of a road which varied only in its gradients and bends. Exhausting and we were young men on mopeds. There was a taverna at the top of the hill but the light was dying and we decided to make for Kassiopi. Good move as it was nearly pitch black when we trundled back into town having taken numerous unintentional detours. That first beer did not touch the sides and neither did the half a dozen or so that followed.

Shamefully, I had not really taken much notice of the beautiful Ropa Valley in the middle of Corfu as we rode through it. In fact, I had barely noticed anything. But slowly and surely I was beginning to get the hang of this beautiful island.

We hired a boat too; a small motorboat, and one day chugged our way out of the harbour into the open sea between Corfu and Albania. "Don't go too far out to sea and make sure you are back within the harbour area after lunch!" we were firmly advised. Well, what could possibly go wrong? We made it down the coast, passing lovely uninhabited pebbly beaches, and there was a small harbour with luxury apartments up in the hills. This was Agios Stefanos and we decided to stop for lunch. Stomachs full and a few large beers consumed, we decided as it was now the middle of the afternoon to return to Kassiopi. The harbour was like a millpond but once we turned north into the open sea the wind had got up and there were waves, four or five feet high, buffeting us up and down and side to side. It was very exciting, sitting at the front of the boat as we crawled back along the coast especially as we had no life jackets and I was not the greatest swimmer. It really did not occur to me that if we, three completely inexperienced seafarers, tipped the boat over at least one of us might drown. We did eventually make it back to port, handed the keys of the boat back and went to the Wave Bar to celebrate making it back in one piece. In all seriousness, both the boat and moped hiring were among the most stupid things I had ever done.

I knew Corfu Town reasonably well after staying there in 1985 and after two years I was very familiar with Kassiopi. Well, the bars and tavernas anyway. Corfu Town was obviously a 'live' town, where many of the people we met in different resorts actually lived out of the summer season. And so, to a lesser extent perhaps, was Kassiopi. What on earth would Corfu look like in winter? The island was not like, say, the Canary Islands where it stays warm and largely dry all year round. Corfu was very warm in June, blisteringly hot in July and August and very warm in September. In winter, it rains. Sometimes, it even snows. Other times you can go on the beach. But often it rains. And then it rains some more. 30 years on, I would find out what Corfu was like in winter.

1989, I made an entirely forgettable week long visit to the island with my then partner. We went to Kassiopi and didn't leave the place all week. We spent many days in a bar called Edelweiss, which was usually empty bar us, and the owner had one music video he had on repeat all day and all night long. Whenever I hear Nenah Cherry's 'Buffalo Stance' and Jane Wiedlin's 'Rush Hour', I am returned to that bar. I wonder if it still there now? I rather think it isn't, unless trade picked following our visit.

But there are two outstanding memories.

On 26 May 1989 (and I had to look up the date which happily wasn't ingrained in my mind), I went to the Illusions bar in Kassiopi, situated just on the left as you go down into the harbour because there was a football match I wanted to see.    Bristol Rovers was my team but the unconscious glory hunter within me loved Liverpool too.  Liverpool faced Arsenal in a vital league game that had been rearranged following the disaster at Hillsborough that claimed the lives of 96 Liverpool fans.   Liverpool were playing Nottingham Forest in the FA Cup final. Well, we know what happened next.  As I write, in 2015, it is incredible to believe that this was 26 years ago when I was still quite young.  Now I am my sixth decade on this earth, yet still the victims of their families have not found justice.  I add this partly due to my anger and sympathy with the victims and their families and also to illustrate the rapid passage of time.

Anyway, Liverpool had only to not lose by a score greater than 1-0 to win the League which would, in a season marred by awful tragedy, have given the club the double.  I sat down in a crowded bar, without my ex partner to be, who hated the football almost as much as she was beginning to hate me, expecting the best. Instead, Alan Smith scored for the Arsenal.  That was okay.  That score would still see Liverpool crowned champions.   Then Michael Thomas broke through the middle and...oh, I'd rather not talk about it anymore.

The other memorable moment was the flight home.  We had flown to the island with an airline called Paramount.   They had achieved much publicity by being the first, or at least one of the first, non smoking airlines, hard to believe that not that long ago you could set fire in a flying petrol tank. There were rumours that the airline was in some financial trouble and that flights were being delayed or cancelled altogether. Our flight out, on a gleaming new MD83, was on time and trouble-free. So much for Paramount being in trouble! But the following week, we discovered there might be something in it.

Corfu Ioannis Kapodistrias airport is, as we have already discovered, not the place to be hanging around for too long. As the number of flights in and out has dramatically increased, the airport has virtually stood still. Even today, it looks much the same as when I first went there three decades ago. In 1989, it was crowded and very hot. And our plane wasn't there. And it wasn't there for ages. The travel company had deposited us some three hours before the flight was due to take off but a further five hours passed by before it arrived. And boy did it arrive. I had been looking through the windows for ages, watching plane after plane land and then take off again. Where was our little Paramount? Then, there was an enormous noise on the runway. Had something blown up? No, it was a very elderly Boeing 707 with no markings on. Phew: that's a relief. I am bloody glad we are not flying on that wreck. Then over the tannoy, "Paramount Airways announce the arrival of their flight from Bristol and apologise for the delay which was due to technical problems." Ah, technical problems! We boarded the shabbiest, tattiest plane I have ever been on. It made Dan Air look like Club Class. The seats were literally falling to pieces and the carpet looked like someone had taken a lawnmower down the middle of the plane. The sour-faced cabin crew who did not appear to be wearing any particular uniform rushed through their safety announcements and the plane roared into action. We were right at the back of the aircraft which is usually a good idea because planes rarely reverse into mountains.

The chief steward welcomed us to "this Paramount airways flight, today being operated by (and I am not making this up) Icelandic airways", adding that he hoped we would enjoy the flight. We reached the end of the runway, turned and whoosh, we were off in a deafening, rattling maelstrom and as the plane rotated, my seat collapsed backwards and I was lying down looking up at the ceiling or whatever the ceiling is called on an aeroplane. I don't know how long I was lying there but it felt like ages.

Eventually, I was able to free myself from the seatbelt and moved to another seat. No one from the cabin crew had even noticed. They didn't appear at all during the three hour flight to Bristol, there was not a murmur from the captain; nothing, but given the noise from the four geriatric engines it's possible I simply didn't hear it.

Having done Corfu four times in four years, it was time for a break, perhaps a permanent one, go somewhere else, see something different. I like the island, but I wasn't smitten. Not yet, anyway.

That was my introduction to Corfu. It started with just holidays with four different individuals and groups. In 1989, I met my future life partner, Cath Jones, as she was, and life began to change for the better. I was in the process of divorce at the time so we didn't holiday abroad for a few years after that. But when the Ts were crossed and the Is dotted, it was time to have a holiday, somewhere hot and sunny. As the years had gone by, I had become a bit more knowledgeable about Greece and her islands. After a lot of thinking we found our answer: in June 1992 we would go on a Thomson Square Deal holiday! This was the holiday company's way of getting rid of a few unsold holidays at short notice by not deciding where the guests were going to stay until they landed at the airport. In our case, that meant flying to Skiathos and being told about our accommodation there and then. We had heard great things about the island from people who had been there. Hopefully, it would be Skiathos.

After landing, we left the tiny airport (the runway is tiny too) and were met by the Thomas representative who looked through her papers and said we would be staying in...Skopelos! I had literally no idea what Skopelos would be like and as we boarded the hydrofoil called the Flying Dolphin, I admit I was slightly disappointed. But not for long. One look at Skopelos Town from the sea, a lovely little place built on a hill (we were right at the top) absolutely rammed with small churches. It really was a wonderful stay. It wasn't in any way a 'British' type of resort. In fact, there were few Brits staying there. I remember sitting in a bar one night watching the England football team playing in the European Championships with some German lads. We had a lot of great banter about football but one of them was very concerned about one of our players. "Zis Carlton Palmer. Iss he ze best midfield player zat England has?" I quickly changed the subject.

Most days, we would travel by bus to beaches near and far and usually deserted or very nearly so. The long, hot sunny days stretched out into long warm evenings drinking cold beers, cocktails and my new favourite nightcap: Metaxa, the Greek brandy. We read books, I listened to my Sony Walkman and the eight or so tapes I was able to fit into my hand luggage. Did I ever know the Billy Joel song book by the time we got home. It was lovely to be in Greece and this lovely island. We loved Skopelos and we loved Skiathos whilst making a day trip and vowed to go there on holiday one year. Then Corfu got in the way.

We were moving into our new house, or rather our old new house, in the north of Bristol, in the autumn. We decided that in September, prior to moving in, we would have another holiday. I really fancied going back to Corfu but this time to a different place. And so it came to pass that we booked a two week stay in Agios Georgios (South).

All we knew about the place was that it had a long, sandy beach with beautiful unspoiled dunes heading north to the man made Lake Korission. Well, what else does a resort need? We stayed in some small apartments slightly off the beaten track but only a short walk from the beach. I seem to remember the accommodation was called the Eleana apartments. The owner was wonderfully friendly and the rooms were neat and tidy. There was a smallish pool that was handy for staying cool during the late summer days or we could go to the beach amid all the flotsam and jetsam which seemed to be everywhere. The main road into town, such as it was a town, led to the beach road that ran parallel to the sea. You turned right for the bars, restaurants, tavernas and shops and eventually you ran out of road and it was just the beach. I remember a bar called Mad Mike's where the owner certainly lived up to his name. It was a wonderful place, madly eccentric, but the providers of, we were assured, the finest full English in all the world. I simply don't 'do' the full English when in Greece these days. It's partly my suspicions as to what is actually in the sausages (because British ones contain nothing but the finest ingredients, right? No lips and arseholes there, then) and my early experiences in Kassiopi found the olive oil fried breakfast didn't really agree with me, if you know what I mean. Let's not have too much information here.

When we returned almost a decade later the resort had been developed a whole lot more, but that's for later.

The beach was indeed beautiful. Even in September there were days when the sand was just too hot to walk on barefooted. People played beach volleyball, others, like us, lazed about in the sun. We did, once, try to get as far as the lake but failed dismally. It probably wasn't as far as we feared, but why take a chance? We got as far as the unofficial nudist beach and turned back. Skopelos and Skiathos were my first Greek experiences of naturist beaches and it seemed that usually they were populated not, as I secretly hoped (I'm afraid to confess), glamorous young ladies but middle aged couples and sometimes, disappointingly, middle-aged podgy men.

We did explore this time, a bus trip to Corfu Town which I had long fallen in love with. Cath was immediately smitten by the tree-lined Liston and the spider web of lanes with their little shops, bars and restaurants. And lots and lots of people. Everywhere else we went seemed to be largely British or German but Corfu Town was mainly Greek with a few holidaymakers like us. Normally, I would find a few hours shopping a nightmare to comprehend but in Corfu Town it was and remains a pleasure. In darkness, the town comes alive and there is nothing better than sitting beneath the trees with a traditional Ginger Beer.

We weren't there long enough to visit the two forts – it would be many years until we made the effort to actually embrace some history – but it was hard not to love the place.

We took the boat trip to Paxos. Unlike 1985, this was a quieter affair, a gentle chug to the island, very basic, no refreshments but more relaxing that the booze-fuelled Kavos version. Even at snail's pace, we made a mid morning stop at Lakka, a little harbour that had been recommended to me by my dentist, bless her. We disembarked with instructions to return to the boat for the next leg an hour later. This didn't sound long but it turned out to be long enough. There was little history to see, so far as I can tell, and not much to do, but that was the point of Paxos. Very quiet, largely unspoiled, very few inhabitants apart from millions of wasps who attacked us all day, especially in the café where we tried to enjoy a coffee and baklava, a kind of walnut and pistachio pastry confection. If you like the near nothingness of a picturesque harbour village with nothing to do bar sit and watch the boats in the harbour, the occasional bit of people-watching and, well, that's it, then this place is for you. It certainly was for me and I vowed that one day we'd go back here for a holiday. We're still vowing.

We also went out for a day in a hire car with some people we had met. I can't remember their names now but let's call them Jack and Jill. Hire cars were to become an integral part of our future holidays but this year we were in someone else's. Jack loved the north west of the island. We went to Paleokastrista with its legendary views, especially from the epic Bella Vista café, which we didn't visit. Eventually we pulled into a lovely little resort called Arillas.

There was a lovely beach on the front that extended to the right underneath some impressive cliffs and to the left alongside the road. As you reached the front, there was a lovely little jetty from which people were fishing or just chatting. There were plenty of tavernas and bars, all within easy walking distance of each other and all the necessary shops you would need. The pace of life seemed very laidback too. No one was rushing around, which was generally the case in Corfu and everywhere else I had visited in Greece. "No problem!" said everyone and usually nothing was a problem. As with Paxos, we vowed to come back one day. By 2004 we were staying in Arillas every year.

Evenings, which were much cooler than I expected but then it was September, were spent eating at the tavernas, drinking in the various cocktail bars and ending up sitting outside our apartment with a Metaxa in hand, gazing at the millions of stars above, the silence only punctuated by the occasional car or moped roaring down the road or an aircraft flying over before commencing the approach to Corfu. One night, were sitting there and just for a brief moment the INXS song 'Baby Don't Cry' could be heard playing from a distant bar, brought in by a breath of wind, maybe. Years later, I heard the song again and was immediately taken back by the TARDIS of my mind to our little place in Agios Georgios. I went straight to iTunes and downloaded it. In 1992, I was still with my Sony Walkman.

I was paying far more attention to this beautiful island now. Corfu Town didn't seem to smell anymore, at least not in a bad way, and I was seeing more and more places, always from the bus, where I would like to visit. The return bus journey from the resort to the airport took us past Messongi Bay, the West Indian luxury resort I had imagined it to be! Not! Through Moraitika and eventually through Benitses. Ah Benitses, the party capital of the island. We went by in the daytime but it seemed somehow different. There were some groups of lads and girls but it looked like a village that was reinventing itself. Years later, we found this was true. Benitses had dumped the clubs and the British binge-artists. They were transported to Kavos, out of the way of the tourists, it seemed to me, that Corfu really wanted to attract.

The airport was still a shambles though and the increase in tourism was not matched by an improvement in facilities. On this day, as with so many others, there were so many people waiting to fly that there were mammoth queues all down the road. We could miss our flights! We didn't and mercifully once we got into the departure lounge – some lounge – we barely stopped as boarding was already underway.

1993 and Cath was pregnant. So we went to Corfu again, to Agios Georgios, but this time the other one, in the North West. We stayed in a small apartment just off the main road. Basic, functional, clean. It was around 15 minutes walk to the beach and around the same distance but uphill was Theo's Hotel, from Thomson's Small and Friendly Brochure. Just off the main road with a lovely pool and some great views across the bay. Nice. And yes, we made one of our vows to stay there too, which is currently in the failed category.

As well as the usual Corfu Town shopping trips, we had a night out at the Korakiana complex where holidaymakers are bussed in from all over the island to see and join in with Greek dancing whilst eating – why do I remember this? – jacket potatoes and chicken, all washed down with 'village' wine from what appeared to be standpipes. After the first couple of large glasses I remember saying, "Mmm. This stuff really isn't too bad!" which went down like a lead balloon with a pregnant partner who was restricted to soft drinks. I was no expert on Greek dancing but the professionals seemed quite adept. Mercifully, I was not summoned to the dance floor, despite our near proximity and whenever the dancers got near I avoided eye contact. Some of the British 'dancers' were not exactly of a professional standard and a few of them, with serious amounts of alcohol on board, gave us all plenty to laugh about.

The beach at Agios Georgios North was one of the best on the island. A large bay surrounded by high cliffs, quickly shelving water, still lovely and warm. There was some lovely accommodation too, with beautiful views. And enough places, on the front and just off it, to enjoy a nice meal. One on the front did a very pleasant gammon steak and chips with HP Sauce, I am almost (but not quite) embarrassed to write, which was so good, I must have had it around four times in our two weeks. "Can't take you anywhere!" And she was right. I continue to be an absolute nightmare with eating in Corfu and if anything I've got worse!

Son number one, Arie, came along in 1994 and Corfu was off the agenda for a while, preferring as we did a half-board holiday in Menorca, Spain. It was lovely, for sure. A much shorter flight, everything you wanted was in the resort, there was no need to do anything except chase our son around. 1996 and we were back again, this time in Sidari in the far north west of the island.

Sidari was Corfu, but not as we knew it! Where Kassiopi was a quiet, almost traditional Corfiot fishing village, with added bars, tavernas and shops, Sidari had virtually every facility you could wish for. Watersports galore, a big waterslide, go-karts and numerous bars, tavernas and clubs. It was bustling all day and all evening. We were in a small complex on the road towards the north east Coast leading to San Stefanos and Arillas. Unfortunately, we were a long way up that road, right off the beaten track and, with a two year old in tow, it was a real effort to get into town, which you had to do every day if you wanted to eat. The beaches were even further away.

The walk to the town could be quite hairy. There were, obviously, no pavements and the road was barely wide enough for vehicles to pass each other. There was a ditch running by the road and our toddler and I almost ended up in it on numerous occasions. Sidari was very built up and became even more built up over the years. You might think I am about to put it down but you could not be more wrong. Yes, it is lively. Yes, it is more *British* than some resorts on the island and you can get your John Smith's beer and Sunday Roast if you want it, or an Indian meal or Egg and Chips. Yes, there is karaoke and yes there are bars showing the football. But if that is what you like on holiday, who is to argue? There was nothing threatening about the place, people were just as friendly as they were everywhere else; it was just different. And as people we are all different too. The beach was not sandy like on the wonderful west coast but it wasn't full of shingle like much of the east coast. It was more of a muddy sand but perfectly clean and respectable.

The building work was expanding everywhere around the resort, even as far as the legendary Canal d'Amour where if you swim, you meet the girl of your dreams, which could be bad news if you were there with your wife! For us, it was a mistake. Nothing bad about the place, very popular with the Brits, just not our cup of Retsina.

We were still not really discovering the island. We were staying somewhere, doing the odd tourist trip but we weren't exploring, seeing something new. We were, and probably still are, the archetypal British tourists.  Whilst the accommodation where we stayed wasn't the best we had ever stayed in, having since driven past we have noticed that it has all been modernised. Some years ago, it appeared on one of those TV 'holidays from hell' shows.  I don't think it was quite that bad.

Then came a four-year gap.  Son number two, Stefan, arrived in 1998 and it was Cornwall on a shoestring with a raincoat.  It is only when you stay at home to holiday that you realise just how expensive it is.  In part, that's because the weather is so unpredictable.  In Corfu, during the summer, the odds were that when you tumbled out of bed, there would be a welcoming sun bed with accompanying sun above. At home, you could not guarantee anything and when it rained, as it often did, and you had two children to entertain, it cost money.  Rubbishy, overpriced 'theme parks' were all the rage, usually provided by farmers who were diversifying.  Or the 'family pub', where all the prices were arranged to ensure everything cost as much as possible and, more often than not (in my own personal experience) mediocrity, especially with the food, was the winner.  I often came back from holiday wanting a proper holiday which involved getting on a plane from somewhere wet and cold and landing somewhere else that was warm and sunny.  Going away for the same weather and spending even more money to do and eat much the same things as we did at home: that wouldn't work, certainly not for long.  And holidays with young children can be more stressful than relaxing. When our boys were aged six and two, we thought it was time to go back again, back to Agios Georgios South.

The reason for Agios Georgios was a brand new complex called the Corfu Plaza, set back a few hundred yards from the beach. You could get snacks and cold drinks, you could get a beer anytime you wanted and it was half board. It's a large low level complex reached by a narrow road from the main road. Everything was designed with the family in mind. Child minding, kids clubs, play room, the lot. There was an amazing animation team led by a wonderful entertainer who went by the name of Marky Mark, who worked with two female reps, the gorgeous Julie and Helen. I don't think Marky Mark was his real name, for some reason, but that was all that was not real about him. These people work all hours, all day and every day, for relative buttons in return. And there was a song for the summer – Gloria Estefan's 'Party Time' for which the entertainers have devised a dance that my partner Cath remembers to this day. They have left us with memories that will last forever. I wonder where they are now?

The beach is still to die for even if the concrete was stretching further to the north, away from the large village of Argyrades. I am not being harsh when I say that the actual resort has little or no character and certainly no real history. It's functional, it's practical and it has been developed with the tourist in mind. I am notoriously disinterested in history – I'm sorry:

it's just me – so that didn't bother me one iota. Plenty of lovely tavernas and restaurants, Mad Mike's bar was still there. What more could a family want?

And what a word family is in Greece. At home, you were treated like a leper if you went anywhere with children. Unless you were prepared to visit some ghastly plastic pub with a 'Wacky Warehouse' type soft play area, pubs were a no no. By contrast, in Corfu the family came first and it was refreshing to find ourselves welcomed into every bar in the resort. Unlike at home when you would venture into a pub with the same fear as if you were dismantling a bomb, you just walked in here and you'd be welcome.

We really liked Agios Georgios, enough to return in 2002, but it wasn't the same. Never go back, they always say, and perhaps they were right. It wasn't a bad holiday but we had pretty well done it all and with our children now eight and four, we needed to try something new.

Either side of Agios Georgios, we did the all-inclusive experience in Ibiza. Time loves a hero and I certainly liked the island but if I think long and hard enough, I remember that the compulsory entertainment and terrible beer, along with the early morning scramble for sun beds (and we are talking from 5.00 am here); it was barely a holiday at all.
In 2004, we reverted to type and booked a holiday in Corfu yet again. And this time we went to the small northwest resort of Arillas for

a self-catering holiday. 18 rooms, a lovely swimming pool, a bar and bar meal service, the resort centre and beach a short walk away. And did we follow the 'never go back' rule? Of course not: we went back every single year thereafter.

The love affair with Arillas began about half an hour after getting off the bus at Anna's Studios. The bar area overlooked the bay, as did many of the apartments. There was a spotlessly clean swimming pool and did I mention the bar area? Ice cold beer sold in frosted glasses, the full variety of spirits and cocktails and a lunchtime menu to take care of all eventualities.

Anna's was, and remains, a family business that these days earns bookings not through travel agents but by reputation and recommendation.

Set in the north west of the island, 43 km from Corfu Town, Arillas has the lot. Well, not the lot if you are not me in which case you go somewhere else, but for me, it's as near to heaven as I will probably ever get. As the arrival in setting foot in Corfu is like coming home, so is arriving in Arillas. There is nowhere I don't know, there don't seem to be that many residents I don't know. They are, of course, primarily businessmen and women, but the friendliness and courtesy of the Corfiot is no act. It is far easier to attract custom and return visitors if a first class service is available – who wants to go back to somewhere that's a dump? – and they get that. But perhaps it's through familiarity and getting to know each other that many of the traders I now regard as friends. It makes me want to keep going back.

And I never get bored with Arillas. It is true that there is nothing much to do, but that's a positive advantage for me. I like nothing to do apart from, that is, from somewhere nice to eat, drink, sleep, swim and lie in the sun. I can do all these things in Arillas, as I can do anywhere else in Corfu. It's not a bad old place, is it?

I could write and repeat myself about Corfu for hours. In fact, I probably have already. I'd go to any of the resorts again, with the possible exception of Sidari, which is not my cup of Earl Grey (which I take with me).

The resorts are, in general, far better than they were 30 years in virtually every way. The powers-that-be got perilously close on occasions to allowing reckless over-development in places like Agios Georgios (South) and in some places in the northeast, they've done exactly that, but somehow their original beauty and character pulled them through. I suspect the locals had a bit to do with it. Any resort is an over-development waiting to happen. In some places, it may work as they morph into another type of resort, but in others they run the risk of destroying what attracted visitors in the first place.

As I began to prepare this book, I spoke with Nigel Moody, who was the one who provided the spark for me to visit Corfu in the first place. I explained what had happened, how he had given me a lifelong passion for this most amazing of islands and I thanked him for it. He has not been to the island for a few years now, but he well remembers the places that entranced and captivated him half a lifetime ago. Many of the people he knew in Corfu Town have since long passed on, but he recalls the names and faces as if it was yesterday. Corfu can do that to you. It's an incredible place.

I had seen Corfu in the height of summer, I had been there in the spring and I had been there in the autumn. Rather obviously, the weather was at its hottest and sunniest in July and August and not quite so hot and more likely to be unsettled in May and September. The weather differed from month to month, but not by much. In Britain, you know that the summer is usually over as soon as August starts, not officially, but you know what I mean. In Corfu, a version of summer can usually be available into November. For all that, Corfu did have a winter. How else could you explain the striking green colours around the island? It rarely seemed to rain when I was there, but I knew it rained a lot in the winter. So the seed was planted. What would Corfu look like when everyone went home, when the final flight left the airport, when whole resorts effectively and almost literally went into hibernation until the next summer?

I wondered if I might be disappointed. Perhaps it was not as beautiful as I imagined, maybe my views were distorted by the endless summer of

Corfu? I had experienced bad weather in Corfu, perhaps every few years, but the attraction of the island, as with so many holiday islands, is always the weather, specifically the hot weather. I know some people say "I'd still rather be in Corfu (for example) when it's raining than at home when it's sunny" but I don't. I know this doesn't apply to everyone, but I'll wager a good number of us wouldn't go abroad if Britain had a Mediterranean climate.

In the summer, many parts of Corfu are very busy, even the so-called quieter parts of the island, like Kensington on Sea, the Rothschild estate in the North East by Agios Stefanos. How would they look in the depths of winter? I suspected that a good number of resorts would be entirely closed down, the shops, bars and tavernas locked and shuttered up. I knew that some places were real 'live' villages and others existed solely for the summer season, after which everyone went home. The thought stayed in my mind for years, working from the dark recesses of the back of mind, steadily to the front. I couldn't work out how I would do it, or afford to do it, or what the point of it would be. I could drive up and down the island, visit all manner of places, take it all in, and then what?

The idea of writing about it, a kind of Pound Shop Paul Theroux or, as I said earlier, Bill Bryson (both great travel writers and trust me, I am not comparing myself to them in any way whatsoever), but with far less time to research and explore and even less idea of what I might do and then find. It might be nothing, in which case, what a dreary read that might be.

And who would be interested? A writer should know his or her audience: who were they? Perhaps it would be the people who knew and loved Corfu, particularly those who always wondered what the place would be like in winter? And maybe those who have never been there, but quite fancied a gentle ramble round a Greek island out of season?

I knew it would be preferable to have a narrative running throughout, which was the most difficult part of the project, otherwise it would, and initially was, a series of unrelated anecdotes. And yet it would be the anecdotes that would drive me forward.

I am deeply in love with Corfu. You may already have noticed this. It is as familiar as an old sweater, many of its people have become friends, probably for life. Those friends include those who visit the island to holiday there, those ex-pats who live there and the Corfiots themselves. There are countless other Greek islands I have yet to explore, most of which I will never explore, due to the constraints of life. It is an island of great contrasts in terms of geography, in terms of those who visit, in terms of the people who live there. In short, it has something for everyone. But only in summer. What it would have for anyone in winter, I was about to find out.

## 3. Not a holiday

"So, when are you off on your holidays?"

This question was asked many times in the lead up to my trip to Corfu during January 2015. At first I responded by saying, "It's not a holiday. Nobody goes on holiday to Corfu in the middle of winter. This is work. I'm writing a book." But, in the face of knowing winks and stifled guffaws I soon gave up trying to justify myself. It was all a bit of fan and banter anyway.

I could see what people meant. On the face of it I could see that it did look like a bit of a jolly. However bad the weather was at home in the UK, it would be far nicer in the Greek islands, or less bad. During the week before I left, there had been snow in Santorini and Crete and I did worry that if there was also snow across the Ionian Islands, I might not be able to travel up and down the island at all. I had no intention of driving up the switchback, barrier-free, utterly terrifying Mount Pantokrator, especially if there was the slightest chance of it being icy. It was bad enough driving on the correct side of the road in England, never mind on the "wrong side" in Corfu. A slight error of judgment and I might not be found until the following spring. For once, I would have to be sensible, sort of.

And in the months that preceded my expedition, there was always the fear in the back of my mind that Greece might enjoy, or should I say endure, a freak winter. "Corfu, not a scorcher! As Britain enjoys the warmest winter in living memory, the Greeks are investing in thermal underwear and thick coats to help them cope with snowdrifts across the islands. With its airport and harbour snowed in, Corfu has been isolated from the rest of Greece for two weeks, supplies are running out and there is no end to the big Ionian freeze in sight!"

This, I know, was an unlikely scenario – and unheard of scenario, one might think, rightly – but I had to be prepared for the worst, even though I knew in my heart of hearts that the main weather hazard was likely to be the rain.

My previous visits to Corfu were either of the package holiday variety, or by booking direct with a property owner and then booking our own flights. This was nearer the latter, really. I had to find out how to get there in mid winter and then find somewhere to stay that was actually open. Inevitably, such accommodation would be in Corfu Town, the capital, or somewhere near it, like Kanoni. That was no bad thing, either, because I wanted to be somewhere that was equidistant to both ends of the island.

After taking early retirement following a nondescript 39-year career, Corfu in winter was now a real possibility, if I wanted it bad enough. The day to day drudgery of a full time job got in the way, not just making it difficult to travel in winter, but then to have the time and space to write about it. Now I had both and it felt like now or never. The worst two words in the world are

90

"what if" and I did not want to leave this idea festering until I was too old. "What if I had gone to Corfu in winter? What would it have been like?" By the autumn of 2014, I had decided for sure. I would take the plunge and look to achieve a long-held ambition.

It's much easier these days to book flights. No traipsing to a travel agent, waiting to be seen and then watching as the assistant flipped through countless screens, none of which you could see. All I had to do was find out which airlines flew to Corfu in midwinter, or more to the point whether any flew there at all.

There was nothing from the UK that would take me directly to Corfu and nothing from anywhere else, for that matter, but it was possible to get there via Athens. There were three flights a day from London Heathrow to Athens from where you could get a connecting flight at the other end. As for hotels, I asked my Corfiot friends as to the best options. I settled for the Ariti Grand Hotel in Kanoni. I emailed the hotel to reserve a room and specifically requested a room overlooking the airport runway below. I wonder how many requests they get for that? Not that many, I would think.

I would need a car, too, so I contacted the Krasakis family in Arillas with whom we have been staying for over a decade. Apart from running the Anna's Studios complex, they also run a car hire business. As you will find, my knowledge of cars is less than non-existent so I merely ordered a small car and left the model to them.

I had booked my flights, via Athens, and my hotel, as well as my hire car, back in September 2014. So it was always going to happen but somehow it got stuck in the back of my mind. Even the preparatory work and the compilation of my 'history' with Corfu still didn't quite bring it home that this was actually going to happen to me and not someone else. Christmas came and went and I barely gave it a thought. It wasn't until the New Year that the reality finally dawned on me. Soon, I would need to pack. Now where was my holiday list? The summer list would be of little use.

I am by nature a worrier. Not only did I regularly scan the weather forecasts for Greece, in anticipation of the worst winter since records began, I scanned them at home too. Just my luck if the M4 was snowbound on the day of my flight to Athens! Or perhaps there would be an air traffic control strike across Europe? I would certainly need to leave home early; just to be sure I made the flight on time, or better still with plenty of time to spare. You could never be too early, even though I usually am, and getting to an airport early allowed plenty of time to carry out one of my favourite pastimes: plane spotting.

And so it came to pass, on Sunday 18 January 2015, that I prepared to leave for Corfu. Almost in the immortal words of John Denver, my bags were packed and I was ready to go. I was leaving on a jet plane but at least I did know when I'd be back again. My long-suffering wife, partner and best friend Cath drove me to Bristol Bus Station so I could catch the 7.30 National Express service to London Heathrow. By my standards, I was cutting things fine because this would allow me a mere three hours before my first flight left, Aegean A3601. We drove down a near empty M32 from our home in South Gloucestershire, just before dawn's early light. On a good day, you could see the hills to the south of Bristol from the M32, but this was a grim winter's morning, thick unbroken cloud and a steady cold drizzle and you couldn't see anything much, apart from the Tesco behemoth and IKEA by the Eastville exit and then the Cabot Circus shopping centre towards the centre of town.

Cath dropped me off and I dragged my small case and hand luggage into the bus station. There were maybe 10 fellow passengers for the Heathrow bus and none of any other destinations. I doubted that many of them were flying to Corfu via Athens! There were a few cleaners buffing the floors and there were echoey conversations between drivers as they arrived for work. Then, my bus arrived and before long we were boarded and jerking and bumping our way towards London.

I sat on the right hand side of the coach, which is something I always do on the M4 in order to get a decent view of aircraft landing and taking off at Heathrow. I had bought a newspaper to read but I couldn't bring myself to read it. Any idea why couldn't I read it?  Because I was almost literally sick with nerves.  Now the day had actually arrived, the enormity (to me) of what I was about to do finally registered.  Unlike holidays, when I am heavily reliant on others, usually Cath, to direct me from A to B (and all points in between, and indeed after), this time it was really all about me.  Every single aspect of my time in Corfu, not to mention getting there in one piece and then getting home again, was down to yours truly.  Occasionally, I thought about bottling out, but not for long.  I knew that I would probably not get another chance to do this.  It was what I had wanted to do for so long, I couldn't get out of it.  Truth be told, I didn't really want to get out of it, but I was nervous to the point of sickness and tears.

The nearer we got to London airport, the more it rained.  Steven the driver helpfully switched the TV on, which was situated high to the front of the vehicle, and for the remainder of the journey we were offered the unforgettable opportunity to watch the road ahead of us which, as luck would have it, was what I could also see by looking through the front of the bus!  As R Dean Taylor put it in his classic tune 'Gotta See Jane', the 'windshield wipers (were) splishing, splashing' as we headed through the gloom of the early morning and, as it turned out, the late morning English countryside.  All in all, the journey was bearable with the exception of the woman behind me who defied the recorded message that Steven played as our trip began which urged passengers to be considerate with their mobile phones. From Bristol to Heathrow bus station, her phone was constantly making that irritating whistle noise every time a text came in. At least the anger it generated took the edge of my pre flight nerves.

Upon arrival at Heathrow, I then embarked on the mini marathon, as Eddie Waring used to call it on 'It's a knockout' (ask your parents, kids, but not about the main host Stuart Hall: that's another story), to Terminal 2. Down one lift, down a long corridor, walking on a moving walkway and finally in the terminal. I soon found the Aegean check in desk and was confronted by all manner of self-check equipment which I had never seen before. Well, you wouldn't if you were travelling on a charter flight from little old Bristol Airport, would you? I fumbled with the machine for a few long seconds but luckily I was rescued by a young dark-haired man in a smart suit, who appeared to be about 12 years of age. I could sense he had met people like me before – that is to say middle aged technophobes who want everything done for them – and expertly he printed out a luggage label and attached it to my case.

There was a very helpful notice that advised me of the kind of things I could not take on board the aircraft:

Oxidisers such as bleaching powders.
Organic peroxides.
Tear gas devices or any gas cylinders.
Infectious substances such as live virus

materials.

Wet-cell car batteries.

Magnetrons. Instruments containing mercury.

Instruments containing magnets.

Fireworks and pyrotechnics.

Non-safety matches.

Fire lighters, lighter fuel, paints, thinners.

Poisons, arsenic, cyanide, weedkiller.

Radioactive materials, acids, corrosives, alkalis, caustic soda.

Creosote, quicklime, oiled paper.

Vehicle fuel system components which have contained fuel.

Explosives, ammunition, detonators and related equipment.

Smoke canisters and smoke cartridges.

Luckily, on this occasion I had brought with me none of these items (apart from a wet-cell car battery, obviously, some cyanide and a few Roman Candles), but once I had negotiated my way through the check-in procedures I decided to go straight through security. Having removed my trainers and belt, and then switched my laptop on and off, I went through the scanner, setting off the bleeper (I think that is the technical word for it). What could that be, I wondered? My keys and money were going through the X Ray machine. I didn't have anything else vaguely metallic on me. But I did. I received a body search from a man who appeared to be John Candy, but appeared now to have a London accent, and to my great surprise he found a golf pitch repairer in the pocket of my hoody! God alone knows how that had got there but it wouldn't be accompanying me into the departure lounge.

Terminal 2 is on two vast airy levels and I emerged from security into the upper area. Bristol Airport it isn't. The first thing to do was to get some breakfast, so I spent an interminable amount of time in the queue at a takeaway store before handing over £4 for a small roll with an even smaller rasher of bacon inside. My appetite barely satisfied, I launched on a tour round the departure lounge, working out where the various gates were so that when my flight was called I would at least have a vague idea of where my flight was going from. Walking in and out of various shops I then came across a celebrity: the one and only Zack Dust. No, I had never heard of him either, but there he was. I knew this because he was carrying a guitar case with the name Zack Dust on it. He was about 5 foot nothing, with a moustache and beard, wearing a long dark coat and a Stetson. My guess was that he was a musician! Thanks to the Internet being available on my mobile telephone, I was able to 'Google' Zack Dust and so establish that he was a country/blues/folk singer-songwriter from Croatia (I had already concluded that the language he was speaking in was German). I considered, briefly, approaching Zack and having a chat about his musical career and maybe taking part in a selfie but before I knew it, Zack was off, guitar case in hand, probably to make a million-selling record or to head off on a worldwide tour.

Anyway, when he becomes famous, just remember where you read first about Zack Dust. Having left my rock star behind, I headed downstairs and found that my flight had been allocated to Gate 34. It just so happened that this gate was adjacent to the take off runway and for a good while I just sat there and watched an endless succession of planes taking off. I still wonder to this day how on earth these huge lumps of metal get off the ground at all – I was never any good at science, or anything else for that matter! – But sadly the anorak in me feels compelled to stop and watch for as long as I can get away with it!

With around 40 minutes before the flight was due, boarding commenced. First the business class passengers, then those from row 17 and beyond and finally those of us at the front of cattle class. For once in my life, I had done something terribly right. Aegean Airways allows you to check in on line from 48 hours up to departure and I made the point of logging in precisely 48 hours before departure. The website helpfully directed me to a section where I could actually choose my own seat and it had automatically allocated me seat 10A on this Airbus A321. Since the seat was located behind the emergency wing exit it meant I had no seat in front of me and about six feet of foot space, with no one next to me either. Happy days.

As the doors were closed and preparations were made for take off, I started to relax for the first time. I used to be a very nervous flyer, fretting about every change in engine tone, every 'bong', every bit of minor turbulence, taking off and landing, but now I was relaxed, even chilled, about it. What could possibly go wrong? The captain made a lengthy announcement in Greek, followed by a short one in English and soon we were lining up on the runway. The engines were spooled up and we were hurtling along and then airborne before anyone could say, 'Are we in the air yet?' A steep climb out of Heathrow, through and then above the clouds and soon we were at our cruising height (whatever that was because the captain was obviously far too busy to tell us).

The beautiful Greek cabin crew girls soon emerged with their trolleys and it was time for a drink. Who could say no to a glass of Greek red wine at 37,000 feet? The empty seat on my right separated me from a lovely English lady called Tess who hailed initially from Sandhurst but was on her way 'home' to Corfu after spending a happy Christmas in England. I am quite happy to drink alone but I was even happier to drink with someone else and Tess was an ideal companion. She now lived between Dassia and Ipsos and loved her life on the island, taking on a little part time work to pass the time and fatten the purse. Tess was a tall and elegant lady and it came as no surprise when she told me she played netball in order to keep fit! (I later found that netball is the top sport of a lot of ex pat ladies in Corfu.) She described an island in winter as I expected to find it. Much wetter and cooler than in the summer months, quieter because of the absence of tourists but still stunningly beautifully and the quality of life was better than ever. It was important for ex pats to have hobbies and interests because it would be easy to sit back into a life of nothing other than excessive alcohol consumption and boredom. I have never hidden the fact that I like a drink – usually more than one, actually – and I could imagine being vulnerable to that kind of lifestyle, so probably not a good idea for me to emigrate to Corfu.

We talked of our favourite places, some of which we had in common, some we didn't. But we both agreed on the wondrous qualities of the small village of Agni on the north east coast. A lovely pebble beach, various landing strips and, best of all, three excellent restaurants from the traditional Taverna Nikolas, Toulas Seafood restaurant and the more international type of restaurant, the Taverna Agni. I had to declare an interest at this point. Although we holiday on the north west of Corfu, we always make a point of visiting Agni and eating at the magnificent Taverna Nikolas, run by the unmistakable figure of the avuncular, moustached Perikles Katsaros. We have been visiting the taverna for well over a decade but the taverna has been there for much longer, serving the best food in Corfu (in my opinion). And the motto of the place, 'Arrive as customers, leave as friends' would not fail the trades description act, which is another reason we keep going back. I had already written to Perikles before I left the UK, hoping to secure a meeting with him, to talk about him for the purposes of this book.

Tess and I were enjoying our second glasses of wine when lunch was served. I'm afraid I am one of that rare breed who enjoys aeroplane food and I was not to be disappointed today as my foil package arrived. There was a small Greek salad with a modest portion of feta cheese, the usual roll and the main course, which was Pastitsio, a pasta and meat concoction, not unlike lasagne. It was most agreeable.

I read my newspaper for a while but as soon as gaps appeared between the clouds, I was more fascinated with what I could see below, which sometimes was land and at other times was the sea. Sadly, the captain was still too busy to make a single announcement – well, it must take all of your time watching the autopilot doing its job – and I had no idea where we were until we finally started to descend. I could see the snow-covered mountains below and mile upon mile of wind turbines. The light was slowly beginning to fade by now as we started to turn for our final approach into Athens. The city looked stunning from around 10,000 feet, gradually becoming more illuminated as night followed day.

The city lights were bright by now, although I had no idea whether we were flying over the city centre or the suburbs, it was probably both. I don't recall a slower landing either and it seemed as if we might somehow stop before we even landed, but we reached terra firma with barely a thump. Stage one over.

We left the plane to enter the terminal building and had to go through security again. Now I am not a seasoned passenger when it comes to scheduled airline services but I would have thought it would not be that difficult to enable passengers to simply go directly to the departure lounge for a transfer flight, but no, we had to go through security all over again. Looking back, it was nothing really, but I was beginning to feel a little tired (the red wine probably didn't help) and it was more an irritation than anything.

Tess led me to the departure lounge where I dreaded we would be catching a small propeller plane for the last leg of our journey. Suddenly, Tess said, "You know who we were talking about? Take a look over there!" And there he was: Perikles Katsaros of Taverna Nikolas. You could have knocked me down with a feather. We said hello and waved and over he came for handshakes and kisses. "I wondered if I might see you here!" he said. He had been to the mainland (obviously!) with his wife and son, to visit a guesthouse he owns and he was on his way home. Talk about small world. For my money, Perikles is what Corfu is all about. We exchanged numbers, had a laugh and a joke about it and suddenly our flight was called. Judging from the numbers in the departure lounge, we would not be travelling to Corfu in the small propeller plane I was dreading and sure enough we boarded an Airbus A320 with every seat taken. I much prefer the idea of flying in a jet with two great big powerful engines than a little rattling propeller plane.

I had the same seat number but as it was a different plane, I did not have the space afforded from Heathrow and I found myself next to Mickey from South (or was it North?) Shields near Newcastle.  Like Tess, he was returning home to Corfu after spending Christmas at home but unlike her he had a business to go back to: the 'One for the road' bar in Kassiopi, in the north east coast of the island.  He only opened for maybe one night a week in the winter, more often if there were good football matches on satellite television.  He enjoyed the winter break because the summer was "full on", pretty well 24/7 with hardly a day off from spring to autumn.  Mickey enjoyed the business, had a large number of returning friends every year and, I suspect, catered for the more traditional British holidaymaker who enjoys Magners rather than a Mythos!  And he had a smoker's cough to die for, which I sincerely hope he doesn't.

It's a short hop from Athens to Corfu – "drives me flipping mad, flying over Corfu and then having to fly back to it" (and he didn't say 'flipping') – and the descent started about halfway through the hour-long flight. I could see land to the left but, thanks to another equally mute captain, had no clue as to which land it was. But then we straightened up and I could plainly make out the south east of Corfu.  We were a lot further from the coast than normal as we flew past a distant Benitses and it became apparent that we were to carry out a rare landing across Corfu Town which came into view to my left.  A tight left hand turn and we were descending over, and it seemed next to, rooftops and TV aerials before a sudden downward plunge and BANG! Huge reverse thrust and soon we were at the far end of the runway, which has the lagoon on three sides, turning round looking up at Kanoni where I was staying and taxiing to the apron, which, unlike summer, was totally devoid of other planes. All this time, Mickey had been in the brace position, head in hands, terrified of landing and refusing to believe me that we had landed across the town! I suspect his first pint wouldn't have touched the sides after that!

In summer you disembark the aircraft, go down the steps and get onto a bus for a trip to the arrivals hall that is rarely more than 50 yards away. This time, there was no bus because ours was the only plane at the airport. There was a strong wind blowing, coming up from the south, which explained why we landed across the town. If we had tried landing from the south, we'd have ended up in the town.

But there was still THAT smell you get in summer when you leave the plane, a mix of airplane fuel and the Corfu night air (this is not a bad smell these days, honest). I walked down the steps, into the terminal building, observed the most cursory passport check in history and waited by the elderly baggage carousel, which eventually cranked into action. And this is another dread for me. I can never remember what my luggage looks like and tonight was no exception. Most passengers did not have hold luggage and went straight through the airport to awaiting cars, taxis etc. I waited for my case, watching a few cases going round and round before finally realising that one of them was mine. I had nothing to declare, but then there was no one to declare anything to. The airport was in as near as a state of hibernation as anywhere else I would see. I was back in Corfu.

I left the arrivals hall and then the airport itself, looking for the taxi rank that, handily, was situated directly opposite. The first thing that struck me was the silence. Not the summer cacophony of heavy traffic, hot and fractious passengers queuing to get inside the terminal building to join still longer queues, raised Greek voices and the continuous sound of jet engines screaming. The Corfu airport I knew was a million miles away from this oasis of calm. The only noise was from the occasional departing taxi and the wind, a cold wind at that. In fact, close your eyes and you might have been in England in late September. The Corfu of January felt like autumnal England.

I hailed a cab and off we went to the Ariti Hotel, Kanoni. I knew the route well. Turn right from the airport, pass the football ground (Kerkyra play in the Greek Super League – more about that later), travel past the village room I first stayed at in 1985, reaching the Bay of Garitsa, turn right and head on the mainly one way road that runs parallel with the airport runway, finally snaking up a steep hill, a sharp left and there it was. I gave the driver his €10, plus an assortment of shrapnel as a tip and made my way to the reception desk.

It is at times like this when my less than basic level of Greek can cause great embarrassment and for this trip it had not even occurred to me to bring a translation book of any description. Quite understandably, the taxi driver's English was not the best, but it was still light years better than my Greek which was limited to 'efharisto' (thank you), 'yammas' (cheers) and, of course, 'mee-a beer-a paraka-loh' (a pint of your finest ale, please, landlord, or words to that effect).

The Ariti Grand Hotel, to give it its full name, is a four star hotel and it certainly looked it as I walked up the steps and headed to the reception desk on the left. Here I was greeted by Helen, a very pleasant Greek lady with long dark hair, and she guided me through the check-in procedure with all the patience you require with a Brit abroad. We had a friendly chat about the hotel, about the reason for my visit and all the usual pleasantries. It was at this point that I congratulated Helen for her excellent grasp of English. Helen smiled, suggesting that she might just have heard this compliment before, and pointed out, in the most kindly fashion possible, that her expertise in such a complicated language might just have been down to the fact that she hailed from Cardiff!

The check-in procedure complete, Helen gave me the card to room 606 which was two floors up from reception. There was an elderly lift that I took and made my way to the room. There was nothing exceptional about the room itself with the familiar bathroom immediately on the right and two single beds pushed together into one on the right. Straight ahead of me were the French windows and the balcony. As I indicated earlier, I had specifically requested a room that overlooked the airport runway and I was not disappointed, far from it. It was a cool, slightly damp and very breezy evening but I stepped onto the balcony and looked out. To the left, looking down, was the lagoon with the runway running right through it. Straight ahead was Corfu Town and beyond that, not that I could see it (it was the middle of the evening, after all), was Mount Pantokrator. The view took my breath away and I breathed it all in. The odd vehicle rumbled along the road to Kanoni but apart from that it was very quiet. The room, like the hotel, was spotlessly clean and I knew I had made the right choice.

I decided to sit on the chair on the balcony for a while, to enjoy the cool Greek evening air and to watch the aircraft landing and taking off. I had always fancied staying somewhere like this. Disappointment soon set in when it occurred to me that the runway lights were off. The last flight for the day had already departed – the return of the plane I was on to Athens – and that was that. I needed a drink.

I started to unpack and soon realised I could not find my passport. Minor panic stations ensued. That was it, then. So much for my tour of Corfu.

I would spend the entire time in the island at the British Consulate, trying to sort out a new passport in order to get home. There might be some light comedy relief in my stupidity, but I didn't think it would stretch into a book about Corfu in winter. I went through my bags and coats several times over but the passport was definitely gone. Only one thing for it: head to reception.

I walked down to reception, down the echoing stairs, and asked Helen if it would be possible for me to get a beer. "Of course," she smiled. "And you might want this!" Relief! I had handed my passport to Helen when I checked in and in my enthusiasm to congratulate her on her excellent English and my anxiety to dump my luggage and get back down for a beer, I had not remembered to retrieve it. "You men," Helen might have pointed out. "You are hopeless without a woman to organise you and point you in the right direction!" But credit to her because she didn't. She was a professional. The customer was always right even when this one was a sandwich short of a picnic. The bar was straight ahead to the left and I thanked her for pouring me a cold one which I took to the side of the bar near the entrance. I sat quietly, looking out of the window facing the gates of the Corfu Palace Hotel, which opened occasionally as vehicles came up to it. The rain was falling heavily by now and the wind howled down the road from Kanoni, down towards Corfu Town. I had envisioned what the weather would be like and this was pretty well it. Piped music was played across the bar and reception area, although unfortunately for me it was Adele. I have nothing against the girl but I'm afraid for my elderly ears her voice is the equivalent of fingernails down the blackboard. I heard a lot of Adele when I was staying at the Ariti, which turned out to be my only complaint about this lovely hotel (and I didn't actually complain – I'm not that petty-minded).

Sitting there, alone in the bar, gazing out on a filthy Greek evening, I could almost imagine myself as a tortured artist, suffering the slings and arrows of abysmal weather in order to entertain readers back at home.

The Ariti has over 150 rooms and a vast array of excellent facilities, including a lovely pool (sadly, but not surprisingly, out of use in mid-winter!) and at warmer times snack bars and a restaurant. It looked ideal for every kind of traveller from the business person to families and couples. I could certainly see myself staying at a packed Ariti in summer but for now it was January and it was understandably far from full. Many other hotels, and just about all other businesses in the area, were closed down.

Before I retired to my room, I decided to go for a short walk. I was wearing three layers of clothing, including a storm jacket, and it was all needed. I left the hotel and turned right towards Kanoni itself. There were street lights but it was still dark. The rain fell mercilessly as I trudged forward and a few hundred yards later I had reached the spot where the road rises from the right and the buses reach their terminus. In front was the Café Kanoni, which was open, and just to the right was the souvenir shop and cafeteria where visitors gather in the summer in order to relax in the sun and, if they are like me, to watch the planes landing and taking off. Below was the causeway that went from Kanoni to Perama, just wide enough for the dreaded motorbikes to pass you by as you watch the planes fly a few feet over your head. And in the darkness it was not possible to see the former monastery at Vlacherna or beyond it the legendary Mouse Island. In the day I would be able to see the view, which is undoubtedly synonymous with Corfu, its most recognisable features. To the south were the flickering lights from resorts like Benitses, the one-time 24 hour party people place.

The wind howled into my face. It was unlike anything I had experienced in Corfu but like just about everything at home, often in August. Unsurprisingly I appeared to be on my own this first evening, locals having the commonsense to stay indoors, probably until the following May.

The local 'Blue Bus' that travels to Corfu Town and back, the number two, rumbled up the hill, depositing a few passengers who appeared to be dressed up like Nanook of the North. The weather was deteriorating and I was half-tempted to take the bus back to my hotel but as it was only one stop, I decided it would be taking the Mickey. Anyway, I didn't know the Greek for,

'A single to the next stop please'. I walked and got soaked.

A few people were gathered by reception as I dripped my way past them up to my room. I should have been tired, I suppose, but I wasn't. Whether it was the excitement, the nervousness or a little adrenaline – or all three – I don't know. I put the TV on and sat up in bed. There were all manner of channels but only one was in English: Sky News. I left the sound on low and tried to read my book, but I could only think of Corfu. I had finally done it. I had been carrying this ambition to visit Corfu in winter for a very long time and here I was, a relative stranger in a strange town, on my own, overlooking the airport runway, or rather I would have been if it was lit up.

I scattered all my maps and guides all over the desk and made a plan for my time on the island. I would travel everywhere, from Kavos in the far south, to Kassioppi in the northeast and Sidari in the northwest. The aim was to visit the resorts rather than the villages, lovely though they are. The villages stay much the same all year round and perhaps that's a tour for another day, another time.

This is not the story of a journey, as such. I did not start in A in order to get to B. I wanted to experience the holiday island – my favourite holiday island – out of season, out of time. To compare the summer experience with a winter experience. To see who was there and to find out what they did when everyone went home. Above all, to get the feel and express the feeling of paradise in the rain.

I had a fair idea of what the various business owners in the resorts would be doing in winter and that would not be a lot, but that didn't apply to everyone. There might be no tourists around – I guessed that I might well be the only one – but Corfu would need to be ready for the time when they were around. The island might be a thing of great beauty but with the ravages of winter, the storms and the wind and the rain, it also needs a helping hand.

And could Corfu become a winter holiday destination, too? The blazing Ionian sun is a key, the key, attraction for many. Did the island have enough to offer when all the sunbeds have been chained up for the winter? I had an open mind, but the very fact that I had taken the plunge, albeit in a semi-working capacity, suggested to me that there might be something in it. There were certainly enough hotels to go round, the sights and sounds were broadly similar, and there were plenty of walks to undertake, albeit requiring wet gear. And there was the sheer novelty of being there.

## 4. Starting Out

I awoke to bright, sharp sunshine, the type you at first blink and wince at as I drew back the curtains of my room. If you had arrived in the hotel lobby, you might have been forgiven for thinking that it was the height of summer, but looking out of the windows, to the north of the island, the sky was black and I do mean black. The mountains in the distance, beyond Dassia, Ipsos and Barbati, slowly disappeared from view as the clouds marched southbound until it felt like it was night time again. It all happened so quickly. One moment, bright sunshine, the next slate grey skies, followed by black skies. And then rain.

I chose a window seat in the breakfast hall, gazing out at the opening heavens above and the small river appearing on the road below. This would not be the healthiest breakfast of my life but it was by no means the worst. It was a self-service buffet arrangement from which you could choose a cold option, consisting of cakes, croissants and more cakes, a cold savoury selection of various cold meats and cheeses (what is it about cheese abroad? I've never had it for breakfast at home, except in McDonalds) and a selection of hot foods including bacon, sausages and baked beans. Indecisive as ever, I had a bit of everything.

Helen, my Welsh/Greek receptionist and guide, was there bright and early. Did she live there, or something? Actually no. She lived with her family at Achilleo, sometimes needing to catch two buses to work. The speed at which Greek buses travel suggested that Helen might just have time to get home from the night shift in order to catch the first bus back the following morning. There is little paid work in any of the villages, so most people travel into town. When your industry is tourism, there is little to do from November until the following May. Given that many people work seven days a week every single week from May to November, that downtime is desperately needed.

I had booked a hire car through Arillas Cars and arranged for it – I had no idea what 'it' was going to be – to be delivered to the hotel. It made sense to use this company because it is run by the Krasakis family at whose apartments, Anna Studios, my family and I have stayed since 2004. Anna and Kostas, along with their two sons Theo and Tasos, have become far more than people from whom we have rented rooms in recent years. I regard them all as friends and, almost, family.

Theo, slim, dark-haired, elegant and unflappable, runs the Arillas Car business which is near to the beach. I have rented from him on many occasions before and I had no hesitation in renting from him this time. I contacted him in September and he replied, in classic Greek fashion, that I should contact him again shortly before I left for Corfu to firm up the details. "No problem!" Calling a car hire company at home was a far more complex and time-consuming business.

Theo was due to collect me at 10.00 am and, typically, I was ready long before then and at 9.40 am I decided to walk to Kanoni to take in the view of Vlacherna, Mouse Island and beyond. I had no sooner walked down the steps from the hotel than a car horn grabbed my attention and there, driving a small white car, was not Theo Krasakis but his brother Tasos, slightly younger, irritatingly slim and very good looking (countless ladies had told me this over the years; it is not my view alone). Normally, Tasos is clean-shaven or has some designer stubble, but today, in midwinter, he had a full bushy beard. Very Greek, I thought. He drove into the hotel car park and we embraced as old friends do.

"Where were you going?" he smiled.
"I was going to Kanoni to see the view until Theo arrived. What are you doing here?"
Tasos explained that Theo had been taken ill and was in Corfu hospital undergoing tests. So far, all the tests had come back clear and it did not appear there was anything serious to worry about but doctors were keeping him in just to be on the safe side.

It is the mark of the family that despite one of them being incapacitated, another ensured that I got my hire car, a white something. In fact, it was a Hyundai something. I am not an expert.

We walked to Kanoni and as we got there, we were almost knocked off our feet with the strong southerly wind. There was broken cloud but mostly the skies were beautifully Greek blue, the abiding colour of the country and her islands. I had been here many times but I had never seen waves crashing into the monastery or the causeway. In the summer, the waves were benign, if there were any at all. The airport, to the right, was deserted with, I soon discovered, three flights a day, all of which went to Athens. I could hear a faint buzzing noise above the gale and observed a man on a moped braving the causeway as he went from Kanoni to Perama. Rather him than me, I thought. One mighty gust and you'd be in the drink.

It felt the same, but very different, which I know sounds like gobbledygook and probably is. But when you are used, over 30 years, of seeing a place in only one way, it is startling to see it in another.

It is the absence of people, tourists, that makes the big difference. Kanoni fairly bustles throughout the summer. It is somewhere people stay – there are lots of good hotels nearby – but it's also a place where people go for day trips. There's a constant hubbub, people on the move, others sitting down to eat or drink or to simply take in the view. But now, there was almost nothing going on and, apart from the Café Kanoni, there was nothing open.

Used to seeing blue skies and scudding thin white clouds, the blackness of the sky to the south and north could not have created more of a contrast. The difference I noticed more was the light, that gorgeous soft, clear light that on a clear day you could almost see forever. You could almost see forever and you wanted to be here forever. Impending old age has increased the need for my needing reading glasses, but not yet in Corfu. At home, I am holding the book away at distance before giving up and putting my glasses on, but in Corfu there was no need. I thought of the history, my history, of Corfu in general and Kanoni in particular. Even today, it represents an essential part of every time I visit the island. To many, the development of the area will be a huge disappointment, to say the least. Kanoni, jutting out to the south and the sea between the island and mainland and looking north to Corfu Town and beyond, is obviously not what it was. Takeaway food, a good kafeneion, a souvenir shop, a quite good one too actually, selling lots of things I don't really need, but that never stopped me buying something.

The airport runway cuts right through Lake Halikiopoulos, home to various types of birds, reaching just short of the causeway connecting Kanoni and Perama and the road south. And the little monastery, Vlacherna, a little souvenir shop in summer, but locked and chained in winter. And the last time I visited Mouse Island you could buy ice creams and drinks whilst admiring the views and ear splitting roar of the passing jet planes.

To some the development of Kanoni is little more than a crime against modern day building standards but on the other hand that development has encouraged business that might not otherwise have happened. Visitors might have enjoyed the unspoiled Kanoni, but they might not have stayed long and there would have been nothing to spend any money on. My feeling was that the area had been spoiled in some ways, but enhanced in others. And the development, because of the geography, was inevitable.  If there are great views, people want to see them and the building work just follows. In the words of Bruce Hornsby, "That's just the way it is, some things will never change." These days, nothing much changes in Corfu.  They've developed as much as they should, although there is no guarantee that someone, sometime, will take the development a step further than it should go.

"That will do," I said to Tasos. "Shall we make a move?" He nodded and we walked back to the hotel.  I suggested that he drive because although I am perfectly capable of driving on the wrong side of the road (bit of controversy there), he would be able to drive that bit more efficiently and quickly.  He suggested we find somewhere to stop for coffee so we drove down from the hotel on the one way system to the Bay of Garitsa, with houses and apartments on both sides before the road briefly became two-way, with the results of a large archaeological dig on both sides by the road to Mon Repos, birthplace of Prince Philip

(THE Prince Philip, I should add, or Sir Prince Philip as he is known in Australia), and then back to one-way again before the bay was right in front of us. There was a nice looking café with protective plastic sheets to keep out the elements and we went in. Tasos ordered some coffees. Across the bay was the Old Fort, looking resplendent in the winter sunshine. The odd small boat tootled by in the middle distance, the magnificent Mount Pantokrator stood proudly beyond.

I asked Tasos what it was like in winter, when all the tourists had gone home.

"The first few months are okay. You work all day and every day through the summer season and it is good to have a rest. After Christmas, you start to think about the new season and there are always jobs to do. You prepare the pool, make sure that everything in the apartments is working and replace things that need to be replaced.

And how about the weather?

"It is not as warm in the winter and it rains a lot, sometimes for many days in a row. Sometimes it gets very cold and you get a frost. But it doesn't stop you doing anything. Once spring comes along, everything must be ready for visitors."

Corfu Town was going to be different from the rest of the island, I knew. People lived there and if they didn't they gravitated there, especially in the winter. Older folk would be happy to enjoy the post tourist peace, but if you are young, what's to do in a closed down beach resort? And Corfu Town is where pretty well everything is. If you want a bank, Corfu Town is where they are. My early research – I actually did some, you know – revealed that only the tourist attractions in the town would be closed.  Life was, well, normal in the winter.

We settled the bill and returned to the Hyundai something.  I got in the passenger side and asked, "Where's the steering wheel?"  Tasos smiled and shook his head.  I think I may have used that line before. I was pretty sure he had heard it before.

We drove alongside the bay and turned left on the road towards the airport.  Soon, we were headed out of Corfu on the duel carriageway past the Port, stopping occasionally for traffic lights with their slightly different sequencing to ours in the UK.  The green to amber to red process is the same, but the red to green process skips the red and amber bit altogether, giving the whole thing a Formula 1 type feel.  Passing the beautiful bay to the right and the resorts of Dassia and Barbati beyond, the skies gradually closed in, that lovely blue being replaced by slate grey.  We drove through Kontokali – at least I think we did: I could barely see anything! -  Because the rain was so heavy.  There was so much rain I couldn't make out any raindrops but then it turned into a hailstorm with golf ball sized stones battering the car!

"I hope you can see better than I can!" I joked.

"No!" replied Tasos and this time I could see he wasn't joking. The rain was coming down in stair rods, bouncing high off the bonnet, the car driving through huge puddles. And of course we were frequently overtaken, usually on a near blind bend, in typical Greek driving tradition. You have to admire the mutli-tasking that goes on with Greek drivers. They are able to hold the steering wheel, change gear, smoke, make a telephone call, eat and argue with other drivers all at the same time. The state of the Greek road is not taken into account, nor are the sheer drops on the switchback roads in the north east of the island. When driving myself, I am carefully edging my way along, barely blinking, never taking my eyes from the road ahead. Driving on the right makes an enormous difference though. I'm sure I'd get used to it, eventually.

And then, as if by magic, the skies cleared and the road was totally dry. We approached a major junction, the turning to the right led to Dassia, Ipsos and Barbati and then up the north east coast and straight on to the north and northwest. There was little traffic and the further we went the less there was. Just before the road split again, straight ahead for Paleokastritsa and the mid west (I made up that term but it sounds very glamorous) and right to the northwest and the north, there was a mid-sized van. In the summer the van is used to sell melons from the side of the road. I asked if that was what the man sold in the winter. "Potatoes," replied Tasos, and sure enough as we passed by there they were, bag after bag of lovely looking fresh potatoes. If I ever moved to Corfu, I knew where I would get my spuds from!

We took the right turn and started to climb towards the Troumpeta Pass. At the foot of the climb there was a huge poster featuring a very beautiful bikini-clad woman. Happily, I was not driving so I could thoroughly examine the contents of the poster and I noted that it was advertising the 'Ammos' bar in Arillas. It was a bar with which I was very familiar, selling as it does excellent meals, drinks and cocktails in the most ambient atmosphere imaginable, as well as a view across the bay at Arillas which is to die for. In all the years we had been staying in Arillas I had not seen her but there was always hope although I didn't expect to see her there in January. Perhaps next summer, although I wasn't sure how she would quite fit in with the atmosphere.

The climb got steeper, passing through the village of Skripero which is so narrow there are traffic lights at each end to ensure there were no traffic blockages, as there were years ago. The main road cuts straight through the middle of Skripero and I well remember the chaos that ensued when two buses tried to pass each other on the impossibly narrow road, watched with disinterest by men in the local kafeneions.

Having been through Skripero on countless occasions, I suppose I should before now have bothered to learn something about the place. It's always been somewhere I have dreaded arriving at because it adds time to my journey, but then I suppose it's even worse for the people who live there. I learn from the internet (so it must be true) the following: "Skripero is a large village located 18 km northwest of Corfu town with rich history and culture, mostly known for its philharmonic society that was founded in 1909 and it still active. Skripero displays old Venetian mansions and an excellent folklore tradition." Well, I never!

That's the thing about going on holiday when you're a lazy, casual, uncultured person, like me. I still didn't get the chance to explore Skripero this time – I was, after all, concentrating on the resorts – but there will come a time.

The climb goes on forever; looking down at the spectacular Ropa Valley to the left and the mountains, everywhere still green, to the right.
Troumpeta (meaning – Surprise! Surprise! – Trumpet) Pass came into view. From this point, if you can be bothered to stop, you get the view to the south and the view to the north. The pass is brief, a small kafeneion is on the left as you drive through and then the descents begin. I say descents because one road takes you to Arillas, Agios Georgios (north) and San Stefanos to the northwest and the one twisting down to the right takes the traveller to the north, Sidari, Roda and Acharavi.

We passed the open-cast quarry, a real eyesore, this, and a reminder of Corfu's careless dalliance with unfettered development. My intention was to travel straight to Arillas but as I had forgotten to bring enough money to Corfu, Tasos took me to Sidari, the main resort of the north, where there was a cash machine. I knew of one next to the supermarket on the edge of town. Now here was something else us Brits take for granted when we go abroad. I inserted my bank card, fully expecting some complex operating instructions – in Greek! – But no, everything came up in English. Phew! This is no accident either. If the holidaying Brits are going to part with their hard-earned cash, it's always handy if they have the first idea how to get hold of it.

Resuming the journey, turning right into the resort itself, we dodged more enormous puddles that at times covered the entire road. By Corfu standards, Sidari is a large resort. On each side of the narrow road, slightly better than a dirt track, were countless restaurants, shops, bars and apartments and almost all of them were closed, as you might expect. I was told that there were 16,000 registered beds in Sidari (although someone else told me there were 'only' 12,000, so take your pick – it's still a lot) but the normal population was around 200. The main beach, never Sidari's main attraction it has to be said, was covered in flotsam and jetsam, but other than that it was tidy enough.

And there were the bars – the Bed Bar, the Calypso Bar, Shaker's Bar – as well as the pubs where you can find, at the height of summer, that essential pint of John Smith's smooth, the traditional Sunday lunch and that Greek staple, bingo! Let me emphasise now that I carry no hint of snobbery about any of this. I have, even in recent years, purchased cider, eaten McDonalds and read English newspapers in Corfu (although I do draw the line at bingo). In summer there are elements of Sidari that really represent a 'home from home' for people who want all the benefits of a Greek holiday (the sun, the beach, the pool) with all the comforts of home. And frankly, if I don't want that kind of holiday, I go somewhere else. After all, not everyone is like me and regards a different holiday experience as being a different beach or sunbed. I can be as uncultured as the next person and on occasions even more so.

Everywhere, almost as far as the eye could see, were empty holiday complexes and apartments, some with empty swimming pools and others with water that varied in colour from light green to dark green. It hardly looked appealing but the rain includes certain nutrients that allow this to happen in any pool in the world. There's no point in keeping the pool crystal clear when no one will be visiting for the best part of four months. On this bright and sunny day, it might as well have been the height of summer, except that everything was closed and no one, bar the odd dog walker, was in town. Actually, I liked it more in winter than I had done in summer.

The beaches in Sidari are, shall we say, quite scruffy. Not dirty, but just a little untidy. To the far end on the right runs a small river where the bars and apartments end. When I was there in 1996, the odour was, shall we say, a little pungent, more down to the non-flowing water becoming stagnant rather than through pollution. Having said that Sidari can be a home from home to some British tourists, but it's still unmistakably Greek. I suppose I have been taken in by the proliferation of English type bars and restaurants, not to mention an Indian and a Chinese, but you don't have to venture far off the beaten track to find Sidari is it used to be.

The waves buffeted the beach, battering the nearby Canal d'Amour (Channel of Love). Despite an over-abundance of development not untypical of Sidari, the area is known for its beautiful rock formations that form some beautiful coves. It is said that couples that swim through the narrow canal will soon get married. I can confirm that this is rubbish. I had swum through it with my friends back in 1985, having been unable to persuade nearby females to accompany me and, to date, I have not married any of them.

We had a brief drive down the road towards Arillas. There were ditches on each side of the road and there were times when I fully expected to find our Hyundai Something end up in one, as various vehicles came from the other direction, seemingly up the middle of the road. Around 300 yards, maybe even further, along the road was Yiannis Village where we had stayed in

1996. With a two-year-old son being shoved around in a pushchair, this was not exactly an ideal location. It was a good (or rather a bad) walk into town and an even further one to the beach but although the apartments were a little dark and dated, we had a pleasant enough break, being royally entertained by the owner's son whose name was Telis. Years after we stayed there I was surprised to see him fighting with a customer on one of those 'Holidays From Hell' shows on television, but from outside appearances in the depths of winter, the complex looked so much better, completely modernised and refurbished. I could only speak as I found and I always found the family who ran the apartments to be incredibly friendly, considerate and helpful and can only surmise that someone had caught him on a bad day!

Going back into town, we took the coast road through Peroulades and Avilotes and eventually to the resort of San Stefanos. I had never been to Peroulades but had been told on numerous occasions I really should do. There is a picturesque bar with a very un-picturesque car park rising above it. At the end of the walkway you can see the rocky cliffs back to Sidari and you can view the beach below through a glass floor. We entered the resort from the north and took the switchback road down the hill, with the bay – and Albania – to our right. And what a view it was. In summer the beach was also an ad hoc car park but today huge breakers were crashing in. No car would park on it today. We drove past the empty shops and bars, turning right to get an even better view of the surf. If you had arrived in Doctor Who's Tardis, your first guess on where you were would surely be Cornwall and as if to confirm your suspicions, the only people we saw were two young men wearing protective clothing, carrying out wind measurements and preparing to remove their surfboards from the top of their car. All you needed was a pasty followed by a cream tea. Quite a contrast from the pedalos of July! I really like San Stefanos. It's not really a 'living' village, as such, and only comes to life as the holiday season arrives but because it has not been overdeveloped it retains its summer charm. It was here that I began to think that Corfu would be so much more than just somewhere to get a decent suntan. It was fabulously beautiful too. All right, in terms of history and culture, San Stefanos might struggle, but then you could say that about many places around the world. Corfu in winter was a bit of a novelty to me but I was beginning to think that Corfu in winter might hold a lot of attraction for a lot of people.

There is little or no noise in summer, apart from that generated by human beings and assorted birds and domestic pets, but there was in mid winter. A strong swishing and whooshing wind, the crashing of the breakers; the sea usually blue was broken up by the white waves, the seas were choppy, even to my uneducated eyes rough. I knew where I was but it almost felt like I was somewhere else. How I could have murdered a hot coffee – yes, it really was cool, to the point of being cold – but there was nowhere to get one.

We got back in the car and bumped our way out of the town, passing my favourite pizzeria (a well known Greek speciality dish) and climbing to the junction that would lead us into Arillas. To my left on the main road out of town were various tavernas and the all-important Corfu brewery where we had the pleasure of touring the previous summer, ahead was Kostas' supermarket where we shopped during our holidays for the last 11 years. Kostas is a kindly old chap whose entire diet seems to consist of cigarettes. I am guessing that this is not the famous healthy Mediterranean diet we keep hearing about! But where the postcards and fresh vegetables once stood, it was all shuttered up. We took a right and headed down the hill into Arillas, giving us beautiful views across the bay. Past Anna Studios and the cake shop, turning right at the bottom of the hill where a lone supermarket was still open, as was the Amourada restaurant. And there they were: Arillas rent a car, the Malibu Bar, the Coconut Bar (where Bumblefoot from Guns'N'Roses played a gig in 2013 and would play again in 2015 – seriously!), the Akti Arillas hotel and then right ahead the sea. And it did look great. The wind was still blowing and the waves were battering the small jetty, but Arillas was a picture. And believe me, I took a good few pictures! For our summer holiday, I didn't bring so much as a pair of trousers to Corfu but in January, I had three layers of clothes on! The beach, such as it was, was a small strip of shingle and rock as a result of the frequent winter storms that ravaged the coastline and to which Arillas was particularly vulnerable.

I looked to the north and could just make out the Akrotiri Lounge Café, which is located at the top of the cape (Akrotiri is the Greek word for cape) run by my friend Nikos Goudelis. It really is the most special of locations, overlooking the bays of San Stefanos and Arillas, and the café itself is particularly noted for it's excellent food and variety of meals (the salads are to die for). The Akrotiri is open weekends only in winter. If I lived in Corfu, I'd make a point of going there as often as I could. It's easy enough to find. As you take the road to San Stefanos from the junction with Arillas, you take the first turning to the left and climb the hill that has houses on both sides. Soon – and not so soon, if you are on foot! – You are looking down on Arillas. Take a right up the steeply inclined dirt track and there is the Akrotiri. You cannot miss it and a highlight in summer is to climb the stairs to the roof and watch the sun set over the horizon.

The winter storms had certainly had an effect on the beach; we had retreated to near the main road. The sand was covered in pebbles and rocks, as it always is in winter. When spring turns into summer, sand returns, not through the wonders of nature but by sheer hard work from the local community.

The contrast with summer, which I was there to observe, was obvious. People wandered past, occasionally, walking dogs or just walking with nowhere obvious to go to. It's what is not there that you notice more. No tourists, next to nothing open with everything shuttered up, no delivery vans bringing urgent supplies of ice cream, alcohol and small lorry loads of live chickens, which would soon not be alive. It seems that certain meat products do not arrive neatly packaged as they do at home.

I could have stayed on the front for hours and just gazed at the swishing waves battering the jetty but time was of the essence and we drove back up the hill to Anna studios. As ever, the small complex of 18 apartments was immaculately clean and well maintained. The bar area at the front was shuttered up; there was washing hanging up and some firewood. It was the first time I had ever arrived at Anna Studios and not ordered a large beer from a frosted glass! The first few times we stayed there were through travel companies. One year, the transfer in the bus from the airport to Arillas took longer than the entire flight from Bristol, crisscrossing as we were to various resorts around the island before ending up in Arillas. Now they were independent and we booked direct through their website. It was almost like being at home. Tasos led the way; we went down the side of the house and went through the front door. Anna Krasaki, always smiling, always bubbly, came over for a welcoming hug. Tasos' girlfriend Elena was there, as was Anna's mother. By the door on the left as I came in was a roaring log fire, something I had never before seen in Corfu. Quite frankly, it was boiling! Kostas was at Corfu hospital with

Theo for his medical tests, I asked them to keep me in the picture as to how he was.

The summer was one hectic 24/7 mad rush. The bar area opened up for breakfast, then lunch and all day for drinks. I could see that the rest had done Anna a lot of good. When the visitors had gone home, it was time to step back, have a break, chill out for a few weeks, to start putting stuff away. Having stayed at Anna's for 11 successive summers, this was the first time I had ever entered the inner sanctum of their home. In common with their business, everything was in its right place. Although most of the businesses, save the supermarket at the bottom of the hill, the Armourada restaurant and the bakery were closed, Arillas was very much a 'live' village, with a population of some 400 people. And it felt like it. There was a sporadic stream of vehicles going up and down the hill. In winter, I suspect the quiet villages and towns like Arillas were fine for those of us who were not in the first flush of youth but for younger people it could get boring, which explained why the cafes and bars of Corfu Town were always busy during the day. What would a young person do in Arillas? Watch TV and what else? There was nowhere to go clubbing in summer, never mind winter (thank goodness).

This, said Anna, was a relatively normal day, except that Theo was in hospital. She would tend to her mother, whose English was as fluent as my Greek (given that she lived in Greece and I didn't, I could hardly be critical), cook lovely meals (there was an incredible aroma coming from the kitchen and I was offered lunch but reluctantly had to decline) and plan for the summer. Oh, and shelter from the endless days of rain. I could think of worse places to spend winter.

Following a life-enhancing double espresso, I made my apologies and left the Krasakis family with a promise to return later in the week to see Theo, assuming he had been discharged from hospital, and Kostas. I drove back down the hill for a long lingering look at the sea. I could never tire of Arillas.

I drove back into the village and headed to Brouklis Taverna. Brouklis is not on the seafront. It's hidden away behind vine leaves – you can't even see the sign at the moment! – but it's worth seeking out. It's a family-run business and has been there for over 40 years. And the family man in charge is Dimitris Kourkoulos. It's very much a traditional business too with recipes and ingredients handed down through the ages. No microwave warmed up food here. Everything is freshly made and when something on the menu is gone, it's gone. And as well as the regular menu, there is a daily specials board. For reasons I do not intend to repeat here, lamb does not agree with me, but my family and friends say the Spit Roasted Lamb is the nearest thing to heaven they know. But then, so are the Stuffed Pork Roll and the Zucchini Balls. And did I mention the sardines fried in olive oil? And the village sausage? I don't think I did.

Dimitris and his wife live at a house high above the taverna and he opened the door with his newborn son in his arms. He's reasonably tall with thick dark hair and, unfortunately, extremely good looking, a cooking, multilingual Richard Gere, if you will. His wife served home grown oranges – sensational! – and we talked about winter.

"I am chairman, if you like, of the local business community, Kostas (Krasakis) is the vice chairman. He was chairman last year. We meet usually every month to plan improvements, to make plans for the summer, to discuss future projects like more pavements. Our aim is to improve Arillas, not develop it.

"The key to the success of Arillas is that many of the key businesses are owned by the people who work in them. It gives pride to the area. We know that parking has been a problem so we are looking at providing clearly-signed areas a short walk from the beach."

The collective effort of the local businesses plainly works. There is usually something new, like additional sea defences for the winter storms or just a new seat at the end of the jetty. The key to Arillas is not to make it different, just to maintain and improve it. I get that. I know there is a danger of my repeating things, but Arillas, like so many other places in Corfu, has so much more than somewhere to lie down on a sunbed. And each resort had something different to offer. I discovered years ago that the northeast coast had a lot of lovely walks, some easy, some not so easy. In many ways, the walks might even be more pleasant, more bearable, in winter than in the hot summer sun. Why had nobody thought it before?

I thanked Dimitris for his hospitality and moved on. I left Arillas and made the short drive to Agios Georgios, via the lovely village of Afionas. I dropped down into the resort. The beach was stunning, all two kilometers of it from Akrotirio (Cape) Arillas and Akrotirio Falikron. The development here has been somewhat crass, but the natural beauty of the area has been maintained. There's an excellent windsurfing centre here too as well as other watersports facilities which include basic scuba diving instruction. I drove up and down a few times, desperate to speak with someone who lived there or was passing by, but this really was a ghost town! I was told later that the winter population of Agios Georgios totaled three! I don't know if this figure is true – I would be surprised if it was that many – but they were all out when I visited.

I could not find the place we stayed at in 1993, but then I can sometimes barely remember where I was yesterday, but I did find Theo's Hotel which was situated on the way out of the town, high above the road. We had been there a few times to use their pool which was open to non-residents and to purchase light refreshments, or ice cold beer as I call it. I'd walked through it a few times and Cath and I agreed that one day we'd stay there. We're still thinking about it but from the outside looking in, the hotel looked excellent.

The hills surrounding the bay are full of tall pencil shaped Cypress trees and groves of olive trees. It is a stunning backdrop giving the impression to the visitor that it is an island to itself. Sleepy in summer, Agios Georgios was positively comatose in winter.

I somehow managed to get lost on the way out of the resort before I found the correct road to Roda, which would be my starting point of the next stage of my journey. I would not be stopping – I had arranged to meet some British expats later in the week – but it would take me back to Corfu Town the long way round. I very much like Roda. The beach is lovely and it's excellent for bathing and whilst there has been a fair bit of development, it is still charming, especially the little harbour within a rough breakwater. I was told that fishermen still work out of Roda. I didn't stop, but this was clearly a real live town, with plenty of local non-seasonal businesses.

The sun shone even more brightly as I drove on to Acharavi, a popular family resort with a long beach a short distance from the main road. We've stopped here many times for provisions, for a snack and/or drink or simply a swim. To the east lies Almiros Beach, somewhat remote but less crowded it is a particular favourite but the shoreline has mudstone reefs which can be slippery.   To the right, high above are the wooded heights of Mount Pantokrator and small villages like Episkepsi and Lafki among the olive groves.  And then, next to a huge hotel complex, the Gelena village, is Hydropolis which, you may not be surprised to learn, is a waterpark.  It is not a waterpark like the gargantuan Aqualand which is situated nearer the centre of Corfu, but it's perfectly functional and acceptable with the usual hydrotube, slides, a lazy river and the 'Space Bowl' where you go down a quick slide, enter the Space Bowl and flop into the water below, often head first, like I did.  As you might expect in deepest winter, the water was an unattractive green colour and the grass, always long and rough even in summer, looked even longer and rougher.

The main road across the north of the island is as good as it gets in Corfu.  It's nice and wide, generally smooth, apart from the odd bone-shaking pothole.  My next stop was Saint Spiridon.  My first visit here was in the late 1980s.  The locals of Kassiopi had recommended it to us as a beautiful sandy beach and very, very quiet and so it was.  The only visitors were local Greeks, reveling in the peace and isolation. Thirty years ago, we made our way there and we could see what the fuss, or rather the lack of fuss, was all about.  There were no facilities whatsoever, nothing to do, nothing to see beyond this beautiful unspoiled beach. If you wanted anything – a drink, a snack – you had to bring it yourself. If you needed toilet facilities – well, do I really need to go into details?

How times had changed. The main change was the Blue Bay Escape resort, a massive 800 bed all-inclusive hotel, which had changed Saint Spiridon forever. Some hated it. When I visited in summer a few years ago - and please don't tell anyone about what follows – I took lunch in this hotel. My family was sprawled on the beach and I went for a walk to see what this complex was like. It should be explained at this point that I did not know that this was an all-inclusive complex. I walked in and was handed a cold beer and some burger and chips. I reached for my wallet and it was precisely at that point when I realised I didn't need my wallet. The hotel staff had not checked whether I was wearing a wristband and had taken me as one of the paying guests. I took my food and drink to a remote table with my towel draped over my arm to hide the all-inclusive wristband I wasn't wearing.

To be fair, the hotel looked all right. The resort was certainly changed forever, but the beach was still good, the bathing clean and safe and, along to the west, was a nature reserve famous, I am told, for it's flora, its butterflies and it's birds (stop sniggering at the back – I was referring to the feathered variety). Now, out of season, Saint Spiridon looked oddly unspoiled, despite the development. The sea had calmed by now and I sat quietly on a seat looking over to Albania. Once more, the potential of Corfu as somewhere other than a sunshine island was writ large. Granted no one would want to stay in all-inclusive accommodation in the depths of a Greek winter, but there was so much more to do and see. The nature reserve was of a good size and would surely appeal to a different kind of tourist. And everywhere there were walks and climbs, some gentle, some tougher. The island was still beautiful and it seemed to me that the winter tranquility only made it more beautiful still. I walked all the way along the beach past the rocks and towards the nature reserve, sensing the possibilities and potential for Corfu. Then it started raining.

I returned to my Hyundai Something on the road at the back of the beach. Obviously, everything had been put away for winter, but there were still the summer shower unit and changing rooms nearby. I could see the showers marching down from the north, the scene ahead of me changed by the second. One minute bright blue skies, the next thick black cloud and rain beating on my windscreen to the extent I could not see out even with the windscreen wipers at full speed. And, almost in an instant, the blue skies returned. Albania, with its snow-capped mountains, would come into view, and then it would disappear again. All the time, contrasts.

Returning to the main road, I turned left onto the road towards Kassiopi. My windscreen wipers still struggled with the returning downpour, but just as I pondered pulling over and waiting for the storm to clear, it did and sun broke through. I took a sharp left turn down to Kalamaki, a very steep narrow road, taken in first gear. A couple of hundred yards later, the road got even narrower and even steeper, passing some shuttered tavernas and I parked up in the sandy car park, which was of course deserted. We have taken a bit of a liking to Kalamaki over the years. It's a small resort with a long sandy beach and the water is incredibly shallow. When you walk out to sea, it is possible to imagine walking all the way to Albania. To the left, there is an elderly, rickety wooden jetty and when I was there it was covered in birds (hooded crows, I was later told). In the summer, there are a couple of beach bars and, heading to the east side of the beach, some great looking apartments. I walked out on the jetty which seems to have a life of its own, moving back and forth with the waves. If it had deserted its moorings, I wouldn't have fancied my chances. The birds scattered – sorry about that, ornithologists – and I made my way to the end where, in summer, boats full of tourists disembark to enjoy the beach facilities.

In the distance, towards the east, I could see what appeared to be fishing boats, bobbing up and down seemingly equidistant between Corfu and Albania. There is a small wooden walkway at the back of the beach leading to some private villas and little hotels with stunning pools. Isolated, for sure, but ideal for a winter residency of R&R.

Back in the car, I switched on the radio. Now I am not entirely stupid, so I knew that the odds of me finding a radio station that satisfied my musical taste were long. I didn't really understand the mechanisms for changing stations either so it was a question of knob twiddling and button pressing until Bill Withers informed me it was a lovely day, which it was now becoming. I managed to make out the station was called something like 'Radio Albania'. Perhaps Bill was as popular in Tirana as the late Norman Wisdom, who found unlikely superstardom there in old age? Driving out of Kalamaki always fills me with dread. It was so narrow that if anything came down the hill towards me, I would have to reverse back down to the bottom again. The slightest misjudgment would see me fail to ascend the hill and roll gently back onto the beach cum car park. I wouldn't have wanted to do this even if the driver's seat was on the right, but sitting on the 'wrong' side filled me with dread. I roared up the hill in first gear and made it, just, skidding a bit and almost panicking. I have had enough trouble driving up that incline in summer, never mind when the road, such as you can call it a road, is slippery and wet.

I barely saw another car on the road as I approached Kassiopi. What was a small fishing village is now a thriving resort. The main street has countless bars, shops, clubs and cafes and it is hard to detect evidence of the prehistoric settlement that was once here. I knew that Kassiopi was a 'living' town so I expected to find some signs of life and sure enough, just down on the left, was a supermarket. I was by now in need of urgent provisions (the usual flavoured croissant and a sugar free drink so I didn't feel too guilty) and I went to park just past the entrance. As I went to get out of the car an elderly man approached me and waved me on. Once again, my failure to learn a few basic Greek words, or bring with me a Greek phrase book was not helping my cause. I am guessing the man was saying something along the lines of, "You can't park there, guvnor. It's more than my job's worth" although it could have been "Go down there and park, mate". I smiled politely and drove past, unable to find anywhere suitable to stop! I was on a one-way street that led to the harbour and I couldn't be bothered to drive round the entire town again. Thirsty and croissant-less, I drove down towards the harbour.

There is a small road junction about halfway down and to my left I could see the 'One for the road' bar run by my fellow Aegean Airways passenger Mickey. I had stayed in Kassiopi three times in the 1980s, but could I recall the name or location of any of the places in which I had stayed? Of course not. To the left hand side, just before the road sloped gently down to the harbour, was 'Kostas Bar'. I was pretty certain that this was the same Kostas who we got to know well back in the 1980s when he ran the Wave Bar in the harbour. A small bearded man with thinning hair, I knew I would have recognised him instantly. I had the feeling that some 28 years later, he might not recognise me, especially as back then I had long flowing (dyed) blonde hair and a substantial moustache, which I would rather forget about. I got out of the car and walked to the door but like everything else, Kostas Bar was closed for the winter. Just before the harbour, on the left, was Illusions, where in 1989 I had watched Michael Thomas do his best to ruin my holiday with a late goal for Arsenal at Liverpool handing the league title to the Londoners.

The last time I had driven to the harbour, I had struggled to find anywhere to park. Today, I was spoiled for choice. I drove to the middle of the parking area where not a single other vehicle was parked. To the left, on the narrow road to the rocks and beach was the Wave Bar where we would sit into the early hours, watching the fishing boats bob up and down. At the back of the harbour were bars like the Cocktail Café, the Passion Club and the Dolphin Café bar. Two elderly Greek ladies stood chatting at the far side of the harbour and a young man scuttled by on a moped, walking his dog, but that was life as we knew it in winter.

I walked up the hill past the Wave bar. There had been a fair bit of development since I had first stayed in Kassiopi and it didn't exactly enhance the surroundings of the remains of the 13th century Roman castle above the headland. But the flat rocks on which we sunbathed were unchanged. Albania is only a couple of miles away at this point and today stood under a massive dark cloud. During my early years in Corfu, Albania and its people were met with suspicion, but times had changed.

Despite the development, and much of it was away from the harbour area, the feel of Kassiopi remained. Whilst it could not be regarded as a traditional Greek village, it had not been completely spoiled either. A lot of people returned to Kassiopi, as I had done, and it was easy to see why. Much of the accommodation has been built behind the harbour and you can't actually see much of it from the harbour itself.

In the summer, the harbour is the focal point, where everyone meets and nearly everyone eats and people watches. It positively buzzes with chatter, laughter and Greek music from every bar. The boats in the harbour bob gently up and down, life can't get any slower than Kassiopi. In January, it couldn't be any quieter either. There were no boats left in the harbour, not a single business around the harbour was open because there was nobody at home.

Following the one way system, I rejoined the main road. My next stop was Kalami where Lawrence Durrell lived for a time in the famous 'White House' and where he wrote the epic book Prospero's Cell. It was obviously a great place to write in winter because there was no one in town. The deep blue bay with its amphitheatre of olive and cypress trees captures the essence of old Corfu, even if the clumsy development of the town with modern apartments and roads gouged into the hillside do their best to spoil the view, happily without quite succeeding. The winter waves obscured the small pebble beach but the view across the bay was still stunning. I drove along the narrow road, just beyond the 'White House', which these days is a taverna with apartments on top. Orange and lemon trees, full of fruit, swayed in the breeze. Kalami doesn't need any more development but as with so many places, I could see a market for winter breaks. Who would not want to enjoy the views across the bay, the seaway separating Corfu from the daunting mountains of Albania? Just because it wasn't sunny and warm surely didn't mean no one would want to come here?

I assume most of the properties in Kalami are lettings because I never saw a single other person as I walked the length of the village. No one seemed to live there, apart from at the White House where there were washing lines full of clothing. The contrast between summer and winter could not be greater. A large ferry made its way up the channel in the direction of Italy, creating a large wave that nearly took the water over the beach and onto the road. It was the only thing of note that happened in all the time I was there.

I drove back up the hill to the road and continued to drive around switchback roads through small towns and villages which all looked the same. Driving was relatively straightforward but it was always worth remembering that there was a constant sheer drop to the left until the coast road went down to Barbati and Ipsos. On a blind bend to the right, I took a left turn towards the small bay of Agni, which is off the main road near Kentroma. The steep road down has been improved over the years – it used to be terrifying, especially if something attempted to pass by from the opposite direction – but the sensible driver crawled down the bendy hill in second gear. At the bottom of the hill, the road heads toward the small pebble beach with small areas of land set aside for the three tavernas that are found at this most picturesque of places. The jetties were not in use, the tavernas were all closed. Only Taverna Nikolas immediately on the right looked anything like it did during the summer whilst the excellent Troulos didn't look like a restaurant at all and Taverna Agni looked half-demolished, as builders crashed away, punctuating the afternoon calm. The population of Agni is 10, apparently. I know a good few people who would be happy to personally make it more than that. Agni is completely unspoiled, apart from the two new tavernas that have appeared and grown in recent years and a few holiday apartments away from the pebbly beach. There are no garish developments and the recent coming of the road has not removed the need to bring in many of the goods to the restaurants by boat. Indeed, in summer a good number of visitors arrive by boat to take lunch and dinner. I saw one old lady, pottering around in her garden, but no one else was at home. Just beyond Taverna Nikolas was a herb garden with which this wonderful place garnishes its incredible food. I was meeting Perikles Katsaros this week, having already had the unplanned meeting with him at Athens airport, something to which I greatly looked forward.

I got back in my car and roared slowly up the hill. The hard yards were in first gear, which tells you how steep the road was, but it's more manageable than it used to be. A long wall now, thank goodness, blocks the sheer drop to the sea. I rejoined the switchback road, passing Nissaki and Barbati and down the hill into Ipsos. Radio Tirana became theme time radio as a series of songs with the name 'friend' in the title were played, including ditties by Andrew Gold, Mark Knopfler, Randy Newman and Weezer. Gene Pitney explained that something had gotten hold of his heart as I drove along the dead straight road in Ipsos that separated the sea from the shops, bar and apartments. At the best of times, the beach at Ipsos is nothing to speak of and today it was nothing at all. I remembered the place as a non-stop party resort, second only to Benitses, in terms of youthful merriment but on a winter's day, Ipsos was home to a few dog walkers and that was it. I stopped at a café and ordered a Nescafe, which is what they call pretty well any regular coffee you can buy in Corfu. For those of you who know Ipsos (and I know this is of little use to those who don't) I was near the Dassia, south end, of the resort.

There were a few people in the café, an old couple who were, I reckoned, German and two late-middle aged men who were conducting the traditional Greek blazing row, which is to say a normal conversation. With my coffee, I ordered what I guessed might be a cake of some sort. I asked, in my seriously fractured Greek, what was in the cake and I didn't understand a word of the waiter's reply, but I nodded as if I understood all of it. And sure enough, a cake arrived, the size of a medium-sized plate, enough to feed a small family. It tasted of lemon, although I had no idea what was actually in it. Nonetheless I struggled through it as best I could. You don't want to offend the locals, do you, and it certainly negated the need for lunch and quite possibly dinner too.

This was the first time in 30 years I had ever set foot in Ipsos and on foot the resort was much longer than I realised. And it was surprisingly busy, not just because the main road went through it. Then a man dressed in what appeared to be Lycra came up to me and said something in Greek.

"Sorry – no speak Greek," I explained in a kind of Pidgin English.

"Ah, you're English!" exclaimed the man, in perfect estuary English "I wonder if you can help me?"

"Go ahead."

"Do you know how to get to Kassiopi?"

Phew, what a relief. I knew that bit. I was worried I might be asked directions to some mountain village.

"Just stay on this road," I said, pointing to the north and you'll find it in about half an hour."

"That's not too bad then, especially as I am on my bike. Thanks a lot."

And he was, a smart racing pedal cycle. Unless he was Sir Bradley Wiggins, my estimate was probably a little on the generous side. Half an hour of driving at a sensible speed would probably do it, on a bike maybe six or eight times that. Then he put on a helmet, mounted the bike and wobbled off towards the end of the sea front to begin the endless climb to Kassiopi. I would describe this as a mountain stage.

The journey south goes through Dassia, with the imposing Chandris Hotel to the left, Gouvia and then left on the road to Corfu Town. The traffic was heavier now and of course everything was overtaking me on the dual carriageway. There are traffic lights every few hundred yards which seem to amuse themselves by going red just as you have gathered speed from the last set. The road from Gouvia through to Corfu Town is developed pretty well all the way at least on the right. It's a dual carriageway all the way in too.

After the resort of Kontokali, the bay to the left opens right up, leaving the driver seemingly at sea level. Mount Pantokrator, with its TV and radio masts plainly visible from many miles away, towers over the island; across the sea is the Greek mainland. Gradually, the town comes into view. Once you reach the port, you either take a left turn to go into Corfu Town, or straight ahead for everywhere else. The road changes from a dual carriageway into a big wide road with virtually no road markings and whatever time of day you are there, it's very slow, almost gridlock. Motorbikes and mopeds dart in and out of the traffic, suddenly emerging from lanes and roads and car parks, angry drivers hoot their horns at drivers who, like me, don't really know what they are doing.

The airport runway suddenly comes into view and then it really gets fun if you need to do a left hand turn. This is not difficult if you are driving on the left and your hands and feet are naturally co-ordinated. Here, your hands are in the wrong place for gear changing and opening windows and you are on the wrong side of the road. It is so tempting to just put your foot on the gas, close your eyes and hope for the best.

From here, you can see down the entire runway from Corfu Airport, separated from the road by nothing more than a fence topped with some barbed wire. I looked in vain to see if there was a plane about to be landing or taking off.

I took the Kanoni road towards my hotel but turned off to the right on the small road that leads to the Causeway to Perama, to the right of which is the airport runway, a charming café (closed of course), the monastery at Vlacherna and, across the sea, Mouse Island (Pontikonisi). Mine was the only car in the vast car park, although a few people were wandering round the small harbour where, in summer, a succession of boats ferry visitors to Mouse Island and the tiny Byzantine church that stands between it's thicket of trees (and landing lights). I walked towards Vlacherna, which is now a gift shop for the summer. A middle aged Greek woman, the roots of her hair unaccountably dyed white, tried to engage me in conversation. I nodded, smiled and walked off to the short causeway. She carried on talking which seemed odd since there was no on else near. Maybe she was talking on a mobile phone, perhaps? But she wasn't, bless her. She just wanted to talk, even if it was a somewhat one-sided conversation with herself.

I walked down the little causeway to the monastery and noted there was a man walking round dropping something. I got nearer and saw that he was actually dropping food for four cats and a dog who were busy playing together. They were plainly strays – four cats and a dog would not have come from anywhere else in the locality because there isn't anywhere else in the locality. As my winter time in Corfu went on, I noted that various people were bringing food for the animals who lived here.

With no aircraft landing or taking off at the airport runway to the right, the only significant noise was from the waves battering the rocks around Vlacherna and the wind that was bringing them. On the main causeway to Perama were two men fishing. I walked up to one old man, who was wearing a dark waistcoat and a black cap. Next to where he was fishing was a bucket in which a number of small, rather limp fish, gasping for air, swum around slowly. He reeled in his rod and put the fish into a bag, stood up and walked off. These small fish were his dinner. They could not have looked any less appetising.

I am not convinced the winter water at Kanoni is the cleanest on the island. There is a small harbour where numerous boats are moored. Various types of debris, including cans, bottles and, I'm afraid to report, condoms, washed up to the harbour walls. The smell is not the best, either. It is not dirty or polluted enough to kill off the local marine life – there were crabs and fish galore – but it did Kanoni few favours.

It is easier to get into Corfu Town from Kanoni by bus than by car and the number two service runs like clockwork. You literally could set your watch by it.
The fare is €1.50 and it takes you right to the Liston in Corfu Town. (I had somehow remembered this from 1985. Impressive, eh?)

Down the one way system once more – this was encouraging – stopping, I reckoned, at every single stop to pick up a solitary passenger, almost all of whom seemed to be beautiful young females, most of whom were old enough to be my granddaughters, but almost certainly weren't. Then, as we reached the Bay of Garitsa, we turned in land and I was immediately lost, though not catastrophically so, yet. The bus made its way through the busy streets of Corfu Town, somehow not clattering into pedestrians and motorcyclists alike. When we approached junctions, the bus simply called the car drivers' bluff. 'I'm going down there and you will get a large dent on your car. Make my day.' Nobody did make our driver's day but after a few further seemingly impossible manoeuvres, we suddenly pulled up where I wanted to be, the Esplanade and the Liston.

I have never pretended that this book will educate and inform on the history of Corfu. It's one man's occasionally chaotic, and always disorganised, journey round an island paradise out of season, but it is worth briefly referring to the history of this part of Corfu. It was the Venetians who cleared the medieval town that lay in front of the fortress to ensure the line of their buildings along the western edge of this open ground thus enabling straight alleyways to allow direct line of fire against any attacks from the landside. Happily, the buildings survive along Kapodistriou Street but on the Platela, the arcaded buildings today known as the Liston were built by the French in the style of Paris's rue de Rivoli. So nothing too Greek about the Esplanade with its fountain and flowerbeds and bandstand where brass bands perform on Sunday afternoons. In front of the Liston is a cricket pitch, largely overgrown, and an artificial wicket in the middle, which was covered in huge puddles. The restaurants and cafes are not cheap, but they are stylish and usually well-populated. Oh, and there's a McDonalds.

There's always a McDonalds, everywhere you go in the world. Nowhere is exempt. I remember as a child visiting Rotterdam in the Netherlands, seeing these giant 'M' signs. McDonalds were in the Netherlands and elsewhere in Europe long before the reached the UK. I assumed the 'M' was for Metro, the underground railway. The one in

Corfu Town, right next to the legendary Liston, appears to be within what we might describe as a listed building. It's not as obviously a McDonalds as you might see elsewhere because it is not a new build, but it's still rather obvious what it is.

There is one thing that every tourist and visitor does in Corfu Town: they walk up and down the narrow streets, usually for ages and to little constructive purpose, other than for the sheer pleasure of it. The backstreets are mostly flat, with the gentlest of gradients, until you get down towards the harbour. In winter, it's more bearable to walk around although there are fewer shops open to browse.

However, on my first evening there was a problem. Horror upon horror, the emergency services, all three of them, were out in force. A huge crowd stood by, held back behind huge amounts of yellow tape. The police, routinely armed in Greece, barked out orders to each other. In retrospect, my question to a young police officer (he looked about 12 years old, I swear) – "How long will Corfu Town be blocked off?" - was perhaps not the smartest. "I don't know," he replied, in excellent English. "We have a jumper." "Blimey!" I said to myself. I now had a choice. I could either take a long walk to the Port Area and find a grillroom or some such authentic Corfiot eatery, or I could go in McDonalds. I have thought long and hard about whether I should confess to this since I am always the first person to say, 'When in Rome' and all that but – I know, I know: this is no real excuse – I was very hungry. I hoped that no one I knew was watching and walked slowly, almost shame-faced, into the 'restaurant', ordering a Quarter Pounder meal. I could have ordered a McGreek meal, I suppose, offering at least a token sop to the fact I was actually in Greece, but when in McDonalds, I had might as well play safe. And, I am even more ashamed to say, I enjoyed every bite of this high fat, high salt, heart-attack-in-a-box.

There must have been in excess of 100 people standing outside, presumably waiting for the jumper to jump. From what I could tell, he was at the top of one of the buildings down a side street off the Liston. An ambulance backed up next to the 'restaurant' and an officer told people to get away from the window. I was sitting as far away from the window as I could get so it didn't affect me, but there were plenty of people who were and what's more they weren't eating anything, which was probably a wise move. I don't know if the jumper jumped but as I left, an ambulance pulled away and slowly the police cordon disappeared, apart from down one of the lanes where people in fluorescent jackets were gathered in earnest thought.

The lanes off the Liston are truly beautiful. The cafés and bars were all open, packed with young people drinking coffee, as were many of the shops, but only the shops that would be frequented by the locals. Those selling inessential tourist tat were all closed, to my disappointment, as were the plentiful shops you could go into, take your shoes and socks off, put your feet in a bowl where fish would eat your skin. I have not researched the reasons why people want to have fish eating their skin, but whatever floats your boat, I guess. It certainly doesn't float the boat of Corfiots. Some of the little lanes were dark and deserted but at no time did I feel unsafe. On the contrary, just wandering the lanes was as relaxing as it got. It's much darker in winter, partly because it's usually cloudy, but also because so many shops are closed down.

Having walked up and down all the lanes behind the Liston, often more than once, one arrives at the main shopping area. Now here was a revelation; it was dramatically busier than it was in summer. And almost everyone was young. Just along from Marks and Spencer (I kid you not) there was a stall from which people were handing out leaflets in respect of the impending general election. Given that there were so many different political parties standing, the only stall was that of the radical left wing party Syriza and the only posters I saw showed the face of its smiling leader Alexis Tsipras. I do not have any great understanding of Greek politics, but it was rather obvious the way this election was going to go.

Passing the street sellers, mainly grilled corn cobs doused in salt, Corfu did not look much like part of a country that was an economic basket case. I can only speak as I find, but I did not find poverty on the streets of Corfu Town. It may have been there and I am not pretending that everyone was incredibly wealthy, but it did not look like the media reports I saw from 1000 miles away.

The Greek winter is not the British winter. As long as it was not raining, people still sit outside in a coffee culture kind of way. One evening, I chose to join them. My lack of English held no problems for the café. I pointed vaguely and the assistant spoke immaculate English. Everyone did.

I sat outside on the end of a high table with six stools round it. No one batted an eyelid. There were four young Greek lads sitting there so I decided to risk embarrassing myself by talking to them, hoping against hope they could speak my language. Of course they could. Two of them were called Spiros which was not surprising since every other person I met in Corfu shared the same name.

They all loved Corfu, but feared what the future might bring. As we have seen, the problems afflicting the mainland were not as keenly felt as they were on the islands. Something like 25% of the workforce was unemployed on the mainland and 50% of all young people. Corfu benefitted from tourism which boosted the island economy and provided seasonal work from the beginning of May to the end of October. If you were lucky, you might earn a few extra Euros getting things ready for the summer season and taking things down at the end of it, but then that was the end of the working year.

The summer season was an almighty slog, a 24/7, work till you drop with barely a day off to speak off. This was where the money was earned so you could survive in winter. Corfu had a tourist economy and, mainly in Corfu Town, a service economy, but there was not enough work to go round.

Please do not misunderstand, people were not moaning and complaining about the situation. They were smiley, happy people who were just getting on with it, but always in the knowledge that the future was uncertain. Some talked of moving abroad, maybe to London, where they knew the streets might not be paved with gold but there might be work. Others had parents who ran small seasonal businesses which they might one day inherit. Until then, what was there to do apart from living their lives in the best way they knew how?

Syriza, the far left party went on to take power. Corfiots voted in far greater numbers for Syriza in the subsequent election than folk on the mainland. A country that has been reeling under a massive debt and subsequent austerity, with catastrophic levels of unemployment. There were demonstrations and riots on the Greek mainland, policed by officers whose pay and pensions had been dramatically reduced. I had no idea about the percentages of unemployment in Corfu but I did not see any beggars on the streets. I had been told on numerous occasions that what happened on the mainland, in terms of economic crises, did not affect what happened on the islands. On the basis of my own observations and upon hearing anecdotes from locals, I saw no reason to suggest this wasn't true. The truth is that Corfu always feels the same to me, it's just a bit dearer than it used to be when they had the Drachma, but that's another story.

The magnificent Liston still buzzes in winter, but where in summer it is thronged with tourists, in winter Greeks occupy the bars. There are many seats outdoors, across the Liston, but they are empty. The people walking up and down are not relaxing and taking in the views. They are purposeful, the Liston takes them to wear they want to go. The hubbub is of Greek chatter, no thumping music and people come and go in roughly the same condition, which is to say sober. Just round from the Liston, a loud brass band played in one of the first floor buildings. The sound was terrific although in the room it must have been absolutely deafening. No one walking past batted an eyelid.

The number two bus back to Kanoni is suitable for watch-setting too. You board it at the same place you depart on San Rocco square. It trundles through the narrow streets of the town, somehow, I don't know how, not hitting or scraping anything or anyone. The most popular store along the way appears to be the many chemist shops, open, it seems, all hours. Hardy souls sit outside the kafeneions, usually hidden within the plastic sheet outbuildings, unconcerned when it rains and when it rains in Corfu, it rains, hard enough to drown out all but the loudest Greek conversation.

I wore the kind of clothes I would wear in a British spring or autumn. Jeans, a jumper, a raincoat and some sturdy trainers. Corfiots clearly felt the cold much more. Whenever the bus stopped, Nanook of the north lookalikes would board, wrapped up in thick coats, scarves, warm Cossack style hats and thick boots. The buses were strictly non-smoking, except for the drivers, that was. Helpful no smoking signs were everywhere and everyone obeyed them. At one stop, a man who appeared to be a Blakey style inspector (ask your parents, kids) got on, went through the bus, studying everyone's tickets with a stern expression before sitting down next to the driver who continued to puff merrily away, engaging him in a deeply serious conversation, punctuated by violent hand signals and loud laughter.

I tended to leave the bus some way short of my hotel, to visit the local supermarket and stock up on non urgent provisions, the type of which would necessitate a diet when I got home. Biscuits, croissants, a bag of Babybel cheese. beer, crisps – all healthy eating.

Eventually, I would make my way to the Café Kanoni, situated at the top of the steps down to Vlacherna. It is the only café that remains open all year round and that's good news because it's excellent too. The plastic shutters are down for most of the winter and for good reason. I made my way to the seating area and ordered a large Ionian Pilsner, brewed at the Arillas brewery. Most evenings, there would be anything from two or three people, to maybe a dozen, enjoying the ambience. As with everywhere else, I would be the only person drinking beer.

The co-owner was Spiros, which was hardly surprising, given that almost everyone else is. Unlike many businesses, his did not go into hibernation throughout the winter. Tall, dark and handsome, Spiros said the Café Kanoni was open from 8.00 am to midnight every day. I do not know whether he was there throughout that time, but every time I went by he most certainly was. He has a lovely menu too, with all manner of delightfully tasty snacks and meals. My preference, I might as well admit, was the cheese and ham toasties. I had one on my first visit and enjoyed it so much I had it a good few more times when I called in too. But don't worry. Sometimes I varied my meals by having a plate of chips with the toastie.

There was no Greek bouzouki music in the café. Instead, played on an endless loop was the laid-back cabaret drawl of Michael Buble. If I stayed there long enough, as I usually did, he would cry me a river on three or four occasions. I would also sit in the corner, utilising the Wi-Fi, to travel the information superhighway and to write up everything I had learned during the day. And it was an excuse, if ever one were needed, to have another pint.

It was a bit of a jolt to remember that Greece does not have a smoking ban in public places, or if it has it doesn't bother to impose it. Given that almost everyone who visited the café seemed to smoke, I began to wonder if it might be compulsory. "Sorry mate. You can't sit here and not smoke. Either you light up or I'm going to have to tell you to leave."

If I was lucky, a plane would land. The evening flight from Athens arrived sometime around 8.00 pm and, if it wasn't raining too heavily, I could watch the plane emerging from the gloom to the south and thumping onto the runway. Otherwise, it was Michael Buble, some unintelligible (to me) Greek conversation and Michael Buble. Just occasionally, a madman – and he just had to be a madman – would propel his motorcycle across the narrow unlit causeway. You could occasionally hear the spluttering, roaring engine between the whistling winds.

## 5. Fall out zone

On 26 April 1986, a catastrophic nuclear accident occurred in Reactor 4 at the Chernobyl nuclear power station.  It was the worst nuclear accident in history and the radioactive leak spread throughout Europe.  The nearby town was hurriedly evacuated and remains abandoned and preserved in time like a post-apocalyptic horror film.  The town is known to all the world as Kavos.  Well, not really.  Kavos isn't a nuclear wasteland, abandoned by locals, looking the same as did before radioactive fall out but without human life. It just looks like it.

Turning right at the traffic lights that weren't working and passing a number of locked up apartment complexes, the road then opened up.  And it went on.  And on.  And on.  There was a proper road now, not the dirt track I recalled from almost 30 years ago.  There is what is known as "the strip", with mile upon mile of traditional Greek bars, shops, nightclubs and chemist shops.  There was Bulldog Tattoos (why else would you go to Kavos?), the Greedy Guts takeaway and Lap dance Disco, not to mention Scorers, 'Kavos' only sport bar' (I would definitely dispute that: there seemed to be loads of them), 'Rolling Stone' ('outrageously strong cocktails and cheesy tunes') and the timeless charm of Buzz Bar ('dancing on the poles and tables is encouraged').  Those poor Poles get a bum rap everywhere these days.  And how about 'The Stake House'?  What on earth were they selling?

My Hyundai Something gave out a temperature of 17c now and I decided to leave the car behind and walk the streets of Kavos. Occasionally, a car flashed by – there was no reason to drive slowly, believe me – but generally the only sound was from a creaking sign above one of the endlessly boarded up and shuttered bars. I started this chapter in very poor taste, with a jokey reference to the town next to Chernobyl that was abandoned after the nuclear disaster in 1986. Kavos really did feel like it had been abandoned, which it certainly had been for the winter. Pripyat, the city next door to Chernobyl, was probably no less quiet than Kavos, but probably had slightly more radiation. And people would be returning to Kavos.

Along the main drag, you pass Barry Sheene's motorcycle rental shop. It is possible that this was not the same Barry Sheene who won the world motorcycling championship, especially since he tragically passed away back in 2003 and the name is designed to attract people to hire bikes to travel the island. I see a potential problem here. Your average Kavos punter is likely to be aged somewhere between 18 to 30, probably at the younger end too, if you think how old someone who was 30 looked when you were 18. Barry Sheene is probably not a name that resonates with young people but as I said, it could be there's another Barry Sheene. At least it proves there is some history in Kavos.

Corfu's great love of chemist shops is certainly shared by Kavos. There are chemists and medical centres all over the place, incongruously housed next door to some of the more popular drinking holes in the resort. Holidaymakers can purchase items to deal with the variety of injuries you can acquire by falling off a motorcycle or simply by falling over after an arduous night of tattoos and shots. Visiting some months later, at the very height of summer, you could see the medical staff had been hard at work, with large bandages, slings and even plaster casts in evidence.

The walk along the Kavos strip is not exactly thrilling. As well as resembling Pripyat (the abandoned town next to Chernobyl) the place had a touch of the Wild West about it too. The cool wind blew down the road, gusting and throwing dust into the air. On both sides of the road were wall to wall, entirely unspoiled British themed clubs and pubs. And, like you find almost everywhere in the world, here was a branch of Subway. I tried hard to imagine being the lone gunslinger, strolling through this lawless town, waiting to be ambushed by angry locals, but it never happened. There was nobody home.

There are numerous roads and lanes that lead to the beach. Down one that had particularly tatty, dilapidated apartments on one side and the delightfully named 'Sex Club' to the other, which is famous for 'the best foam party on the island'. I am guessing that the club looked a little more exciting inside than it did outside, but then I am rather nearer to my bus pass than many of those who will be foaming themselves this summer.  It had all the charm of a small warehouse, if I am being honest.

The beach certainly lived down to my expectations.  Mainland Greece looked stunning in front of me, but the beach didn't.  There was flotsam and jetsam, mixed with bottles and cans by the water and an interesting and substantial collection of black bin liners by some of the beach side clubs, many of which were leaking their unpleasant contents onto the damp sand.  I will not go into the contents of some of these bins but let's put it this way: you would not want to see them on a beach at any time.  Some apartments looked tired, dated and tatty, but many were far worse than that.  I concluded that it would take an enormous effort to get the beach habitable before the summer season and although I knew the locals would, I am not sure all that many of the 18-30 guests would care either way.

Then, as I turned to walk back down the lane past the 'Sex Club', I saw a homemade poster that had been blown around in the wind.  It said, 'Kavos – where ugly people go to have sex with other ugly people.'  I was in no position to judge but I picked it up and put it in one of the many black bin liners.  Sadly, I had to abandon my litter-picking because there was so much of it and the odours were sadly reminiscent of a gentleman's urinal that had not been cleaned for a good while.

I soon determined that there was little point in me tidying up. I could have spent a month there and it wouldn't have helped much. However, I can report that I did pick up some ugly, sharp slivers of glass from the sand. I would like to think someone would carry out a thorough examination of the area before the tourists descend on the place.

Down a road leading to what in summer is a water sports centre, it appeared to be situated next to a sewage outlet which is not normally ideal. Before the end of the road were a number of holiday properties with dark green water in their pools. Not only were the gates to the property locked, there was barbed wire all round the walls. I could not help wondering if it was there to try and keep people in than to keep intruders out.

Kavos had certainly been an experience. Not necessarily a life-enhancing experience but, from my point of view, much better than it might have been during the summer, or perhaps not quite as bad. There were two good things that came out of Kavos. One was obviously the road and the other was that it provided summer jobs for the locals, especially from nearby Lefkimmi. In a country that's still embedded in a deep economic crisis, that's a good thing, but nothing can change my mind that Corfu could do without Kavos. The island has already moved the party capital out of mainstream Benitses to as far south as it's possible to go without putting it into the sea (not a bad idea in my opinion).

Many islands have their Kavos. Cyprus has Ayia Napa, Zante has Laganas, and Crete has Malia, but does Corfu really need Kavos? I have seen the enormous changes to Corfu in 30 years and in so many ways it is better than it was. There was a time when development threatened to overwhelm certain parts of the island and arguably that has happened, but if it hasn't stopped, it's certainly slowed down. Dimitris Kourkoulos in Arillas always emphasises how the business community of the town seek to 'improve not develop' and I sense Corfu has now got a handle on that. If change had carried on as it threatened to do 25 years ago, it would not be the paradise it is today. I was without doubt the only tourist in Kavos on that January day and for the most part I was the only person in town, too. And that was not without reason because there is nothing to see and nothing to do, other than to satisfy a curiosity and see it for yourself. And, remaining as it was, Kavos would always resemble a nuclear fall out zone for half the year.

Finally, I found something in Kavos that was open. A small supermarket, more a grocery store really. It was open but it was so dark within I really didn't fancy it. I wondered who the shop was serving. Perhaps some people lived in apartments off the strip. God knows there were enough of them.

Kavos serves a purpose, more than one, actually. It keeps the young Brits all in one place, which in my experience is no bad thing and it provides a lot of jobs for the locals, horrendous though some must be. I am told that people go to Kavos "to get ratted" which is a particularly British thing to do. Now I like a drink as much as the next man (or woman), and I certainly like a drink when I'm on my holidays, but I cannot quite understand why you would want to spend a fortnight in one of the grottiest places I have ever seen. Perhaps that's why people get so drunk?

The day I visited, in January, was as good a day as I experienced in the Corfu winter. The sun shone brightly, it was T shirt weather and Kavos looked every bit as enticing as the local council tip. When I left, I realised why the traffic lights on the edge of town weren't working: they weren't needed. No one lived in Kavos, no one really needed to be there, except one particularly stupid Englishman.

I wasn't sorry to leave Kavos, even as the sun shone brightly and the temperature reached a balmy 19c. It didn't look any better and I soon reached the crossroads, navigating the traffic lights that still weren't working.

## 6. South from Corfu Town

The journey south by car from Kanoni is not straightforward and it certainly doesn't start by travelling south. A long drag south of Corfu Town, passing the end of the runway (almost every route out of the town passes the runway), and then a large arc around the heavily built up surroundings. Eventually, the road straightens up with the sea to the left.

First you pass through Perama, which is described by my guidebook as a "laid back village on Corfu's east coast on a hillside dotted with olive and cypress trees. Here you can live life in the slow lane" and so on, failing to add "as long as you are not staying anywhere near the very busy main road that cuts it in two. The causeway from Kanoni reaches Perama so if you are a motorcyclist you would save yourself a lot of time and petrol by using it, and all the locals do. Things to do in Perama include, continues my guidebook, snorkeling, hiking and exploring Corfu Town, which suggests there is not very much to do at all. For the plane-spotter there is much to do. From any one of the many hotels and apartments by the sea you can watch the planes come and go to your heart's content, with Mouse Island adding to the view, right ahead of you. It is worth adding that Corfu airport does not shut at night but as long as you are not bothered by the sound of roaring jets at virtually any time of the day or night, Perama is for you. I exaggerate here, but only just. Away from the road, it's actually quite nice. In winter there is nothing.

Next on the journey south comes the formerly lively resort of Benitses, where it was party-time 24/7. I had heard of Benitses before I had heard of Corfu. In 1985, as referred to earlier, this was the place to go if you were aged between 18 to 30 or if your IQ was in the same bracket. It had gone from being a sleepy village into a relative madhouse. Although Benitses has long shed its party image, it has not returned to its former self. The fishing village did not and could not come back to how it was and instead it has evolved into a bustling mid-market resort, with plenty of wining and dining, a pleasant man-made beach and a new marina.

These days Benitses is famous for the Corfu Shell Museum where you can see an excellent collection of, well, shells, although obviously not in winter. And there was a faded poster advertising (and I am not making this up) a Sardine Festival that took place in the previous August. After driving past the modern new marina, I noted the village square restored to its pre-party island splendour where there were numerous cafés and bars. There was also a sign pointing to the ruins of a Roman villa which, I suspect, was of minimal interest to the tourists of the 1980s. They certainly never told me about it.

The road narrows and on both sides there are countless bars and restaurants. Now that bit did remind me of the 1980s where you would drive through, carefully avoiding those for whom excess meant Benitses, lying in a heap next to the road. I thought Sex On The Beach was a cocktail until I visited Benitses. You could tell that the community and businesses had worked hard to rid the town of its past reputation and by and large it was succeeding. I would never had dreamed of stopping in Benitses in the old days, but now I would recommend it as probably the most improved resort on the island. The big hotels which once shook as the 18-30s partied towards and often beyond the dawn, had been reclaimed and renovated. With the mountains on one side and the sea on the other, the whole place had changed dramatically and for the better. I walked the entire length of Benitses and, apart from where I was jaywalking out of necessity because there was no pavement and the road was narrow, there were some distinctly appealing places to eat like Lotza Luxus Café, Taverna Zorbas (Zorbas in Greece! Who'd have thought?) and the Argo Taverna Benitses. Well, I am guessing they would be appealing places to eat but of course they were closed! Other tavernas and restaurants are available, but not that many in January. Some places were open, though, and in the evening it appeared that a good number more would be open, all with appealing looking menus.

It's a real live town, boasting a Shell Museum and a primary school, the pupils of which made enough noise to make up for the general quiet of the village. It's not far from the lovely village of Gastouri and the legendary Achillion Palace.

Down the coast to Moraitika which is a combination of the old Ano Moraitika, a complex of old houses, modern tavernas and apartments and the resort proper, so to speak, which is a sand and shingle beach just off the main road on both sides of which lie a vast array of shops and tavernas many of which will appeal to the British desire to buy tat. The main road itself isn't exactly picturesque but the beach is good with decent watersports, all of which were tied up and weren't going anywhere in midwinter.

It is worth pointing out at this point that I alleviated the boredom, as and when it occurred, by listening to the radio. I did not quite grasp the complexities of actually setting the car radio so I twiddled the dial until something listenable came along, in this case Kiss radio to which I became rather fond. I did not understand anything the presenters were saying but that in itself is not unusual. Have you ever listened to commercial radio in Britain? But the music was good enough. 'Hey Jude' accompanied me for most of the journey from Benitses to Moraitika, followed by 'Satchmo' himself, Louis Armstrong, who reminded me what a 'Wonderful World' it was. Stuck in a traffic jam on the outskirts of Moraitika did not seem all that wonderful to me as I waited for a large van to unload what seemed to be several hundred bottles of water.

Taking the left turn after Moraitika is Messongi, home of the Messongi Beach Hotel which observant readers will have noted that I assumed was somewhere in the Caribbean! The coast sweeps away to a gentle curve to the south and the horizon is filled with tree-covered hills. The sea was more still by now as I walked by the flotsam and jetsam on the beach. I said hello to a fellow beachcomber and it turned out he was English. His name was Mike and he hailed from – and here my sense of geography lets me down again – the north of England. I may have asked him but I was so anxious to hear what he had to say, I probably didn't. He was about 6 feet tall, wearing dark ankle length trousers (like a sailor might have worn in days gone by), moccasins, a cotton shirt which looked like a table cloth design and a tattered panama hat.

Mike, who came from London, was retired and lived near Argyrades, a large village about halfway between Messongi and Lefkimmi. He had lived in Corfu for many years (he was not clear how many!). He had settled with his wife and bought a small property in which they intended to spend a long, happy life together. Sadly, she died little more than a year after they arrived and he had spent a decade living there on his own.

"Winters can be a bit lonely," he said. "But I'm used to it by now. It doesn't cost me a lot to live so I manage easily enough with my pension. Where I live, it's a proper village and almost everything is open throughout the winter and I can get what I want easily enough."

But what was the difference between winter and summer and how did it affect his life?

"Where I am, tourism doesn't really affect me. Most of the resorts are to the north of where I am.  All that's near me is Lefkimmi, which is another real life place, like Corfu town. It's where all the farmers go.  And a lot of the locals get summer work just down the road in Kavos.

"In many ways, the winter is better.  I know a few of the Greek chaps in Lefkimmi and I might go and have a coffee with them.  And I might go to Corfu (Town), calling at the 'British Corner Shop' on the way."

I was intrigued.  "The what?"

"It's up past Benitses.  It sells all the stuff from back home.  HP Sauce, Hobnobs, and Hartley's Jam – you name it.  They even sell frozen food from Iceland, the British supermarket, that is.  I don't use it for everything because I don't live in the UK anymore and anyway it's not cheap, but sometimes you have to, don't you?"

Well, I would use it if I lived in Corfu, probably far more than was good for me.  Obviously, it wouldn't be cheap to buy all your stuff there, because of the cost of importing it, and why would you buy everything anyway?  You might as well live in Britain if you wanted to live a totally British lifestyle.  And besides, you can't just abandon what or who you are.  If you loved, say, HP Sauce when you were at home, you wouldn't just stop liking it when you arrived in Corfu, would you?

"So, what's a normal winter's day like for you, then?" I asked.

"This is one.  When it's raining in winter, it can rain for days on end.  And I'll stay in, not seeing anyone.   I keep a diary but it's not very interesting because nothing much happens.  And I might write a letter to my kids."

Wow, I thought: letters. People still write letters?

"I don't have a computer, never got on with them. I write letters which can still take over a week to reach England.  I get books, read one every couple of days.  In the resorts, many of the hotels and apartment complexes have unofficial libraries.  At the end of the season, I'll go to a few of them and if I'm lucky I'll go home with maybe 20 of them.  I'll read anything, me."

"You should get a Kindle," I suggested. "You can download as many books as you like then. Many for a few pence – or in your case cents – and some for nothing at all.  You really should try it."

"Do you?"

"No. I prefer books!"

"There's your answer."

"Do you know the Messongi Beach hotel?" I asked him.

"Never stayed there, wouldn't want to. All Russians and Poles. Bit faded too."

I moved on. "Do you ever return home, or does your family come here?"

"I went home in 2010, haven't been back since. My place is small, one small bedroom and a broom cupboard sized bedroom. My son came over a couple of years ago in winter. I think all the hassle of flying to Athens and then Corfu put him off. Maybe if there was a direct flight in winter from the UK..."

But there isn't a direct flight in winter from the UK. And the 'hassle' for me was getting a flight from Heathrow, instead of Bristol, and then getting two flights to Corfu instead of one. My flights were as cheap as chips and they were scheduled flights from Heathrow Airport, too. Much, much cheaper than Thomson and Thomas Cook in the summer and depending on when you booked and the dates you were travelling, cheaper than some easyJet and Ryanair flights too. I enjoyed and embraced the inconvenience, which made the experience more of an adventure. But if there was a direct flight in winter from the UK, there would surely be people who used it.

"So for you, the main differences in winter are a bit more traffic going through Argyrades and the weather. That's it?"

He nodded slowly. "That's it."

And what about media, what's going on in the world?

"I don't care what's going on in the world. I'm in my world. Listen, it's been nice to talk. I have to go."

And with that he was gone. Strolling off to the road, slightly bowlegged, very stooped. I hadn't learned anything much from Mike, other than his existence seemed very basic and not a little sad. I certainly learned little about Corfu in winter. His life was probably the same whatever the season. Maybe that was kind of what the ex pat's life was like. It was like everyone else's life, anywhere in the world. As my journey went on, I certainly got the feel of the ex pat lives, but they were never the same. None was as dispiriting as this one. I never expected to feel sorry for anyone who had emigrated to this paradise island, but now I did. Mike's was just an existence, not a life. I guessed there was probably a lot he didn't tell me and why should he?

I made the point of exchanging email addresses with some people I met, to get in touch after my visit, to ask the questions I might have forgotten. But I had gone as far as I could with Mike, not that he had an email address anyway. He was an open and closed book all at once.

Leaving Messonghi, the road heads inland, cutting a swathe across southern Corfu. It's a good road, too; wide enough and with far less potholes than some places you could name. Once again, as I headed south, it could easily have been a summer's day, but for the temperature and even that was more than bearable, rather like a more than half-decent early summer's day at home.

After Messonghi, there are but a few small villages before arriving in Argirades, a "proper" Greek village, too, by which I mean one that was all but impossible to navigate at anything above a snail's pace, at best. One travels at a good lick until Argirades, but once you enter the village, the wide road turns into a very narrow one. In England, the local villagers would undoubtedly demand a by-pass to alleviate the bottleneck, but here no one seemed to care. Old men sat in the kafeneon, watching the world go by very slowly. If I had possessed the ability to converse in Greek, I could have wound down my window, engaged the locals in conversation and left as old friends, so slow was the traffic. Two lorries, one from each direction, squeezed slowly past each other as I waited behind a bus that rattled and hummed and belted out thick black smoke every time the driver put his foot on the accelerator, which wasn't all that often.

I am at my worst at times like this. At home, you just wait for the traffic to clear, maybe let your thoughts drift to other things. In a gridlocked Corfu village, you find yourself losing concentration, forgetting where the gear stick is, revving the car unnecessarily when you are trying to move up a slight gradient and, of course, stalling, usually right in front of the locals. I worked up a mean sweat crawling through the village. Some 2000 people live in and around the village and most of them, it seemed to me, were out driving when I struggled through.

There are basically two industries in the area: tourism and agriculture, the former being absolutely essential for the latter. The people normally work in the quieter resort of Agios Georgios (South) which is only a few minutes away and Kavos. I know which one I would rather work at!

The road after Argirades really opens up. Toni Braxton warbled on my radio that she required me to unbreak her heart. In normal circumstances, I might have been more sympathetic but not today. I had places to go to, people to see. This was basically a dual carriageway with no road markings at all. It would have been wide enough for a dual carriageway and even a motorway, but the authorities had left it as a very wide road. Nearing Lefkimmi, a variety of stores appear on each side of the road, but never close together. The turn for Lefkimmi comes and goes and I carried on to my main destination, the holiday hotspot of Kavos, to which I refer elsewhere. And somehow I missed it. Before I knew it, I drove into a small port beyond which, and not far beyond which, was the mainland. There were signs for Igoumenitsa and Paxos but I didn't want the ferry, which was just as well because there wasn't one. In fact, there was nothing resembling a boat, nor a port official for that matter. The mainland was incredibly near, seemingly little further than a stone's throw, with a channel of choppy water glinting in the morning sun.

Returning to the crossroads, navigating the traffic lights that still weren't working (not that it mattered since there was next to nothing on the road) I was able to make another toe-curling mistake. I pulled over at a large supermarket helpfully called 'Market' in order to buy some sugar-based confectionary products and a soft drink. Except that 'Market' wasn't a supermarket at all, something I only realised once I had walked through the entrance and saw a fascinating selection of furniture and rugs. I caught the salesman's eye, which was the last thing I wanted to do. I nodded and he nodded back, uttering some Greek which was probably something like, "Can I help you, Sir?" What do you do at a time like this? Ask the gentleman whether he speaks sufficient English so you can explain that you don't actually want to be there at all? Or do what I did which was to say my goodbyes by saying, "Yammas!" which in Corfu refers to the glass-clinking cheers and not the one we use at home, at least in the west country.

Passing Perivoli, I soon found my way meandering through Argirades again, just as slowly as before and stalling the car twice before roaring off towards Agios Georgios South. I turned left at the sign and drove down the narrow road into the resort itself. I passed Eleana's apartments where we had stayed in, gulp, 1992 before passing 'Mad Mike's' bar and turning right past Hector's very closed looking supermarket, the excellent Balcony restaurant (well, it was when we last ate there in 2002) and then the small, not particularly sheltered harbour before the road ended by the Palm Beach hotel complex that sprang up in the early 2000s. It was padlocked shut so there was no possibility of my walking the path into the Corfu Plaza for old time's sake. The good news was that the resort had not extended beyond the Palm Beach and the gorgeous dunes beyond remained untouched. And of all the places I had so far visited, it was the one which looked like it did in summer, albeit without any people. The beach as largely intact, the streets were clean and tidy; it was a very good place to be. I could read and write books here.

I sat on the wall by the small harbour and thought to myself how mad was this? 1000 miles from home in a holiday paradise, out of season and devoid of any local people, apart from the lady in the local supermarket where I groped my way through the darkness inside to buy yet another croissant and an ice cold Coca Cola. Here was the prime example of Corfu in winter, one that I had imagined, and it looked exactly as I expected. There was no real live community in the resort, the road which leads to the dunes was empty, the only sounds were the wind, the gentle splashing of the waves and some distant clanging wind chimes.

In summer, this is a bustling resort with sun beds as far as the eyes can see. The towels are over all the sun beds in the Palm Beach, music plays from many of the bars. But when I was there, the resort was in hibernation.

I walked past Mad Mike's where we had been almost 23 years before. I knew it was Mad Mike's but for some reason – and this is very hard to explain – I didn't recognise it. I had not thought about it for many years either so maybe the memories somehow managed to fade out altogether. I think I remembered what Mike looked like too, the wrestler Mike Marino (ask your grandparent's children) who once graced ITV's 'World Of Sport'. Or did he? I wasn't sure now. Maybe I was imagining that was what he looked like. There was a lot of washing hanging up outside so I supposed I could knock on the door and find out, but what would we talk about? "Remember the time I had the Full Monty breakfast here back in 1992? You must remember me." Later that evening when I was back in the hotel, I Googled Mad Mike's (other search engines are available) and the man in the photographs wasn't the Mike I remembered from way back when. It was best to leave it at that and hope he was still with us. Or maybe the man who ran it wasn't actually called Mike at all?

There was barely a cloud in the sky by now and I decided to visit a few other places before I returned to Kanoni. I drove back to the main road and cleverly stalled the car at the junction right in front of the small Kafeneon which, sadly for me, was packed with men who found my lack of clutch control highly amusing! Well, I'd have laughed if I had been someone else! Why does it take so long to start the car again and then turn the engine into a snarling monster, merely adding to one's embarrassment? I joined the main road for a few hundred yards before finding a small turning marked Issos Beach. This, as I instantly recalled, was not a road at all, it was a dirt track between the grassy background to the dunes. There was a reasonably sized car park at the end where the path rose to the top of the dunes and then down the other side to the water. In the summer, the beach is alive with customers spilling our of the excellent Issos Beach Paradise Bar, just beyond are usually temporary beach volleyball courts and various watersports. Today, all that remained of the Issos Beach Paradise Bar was, essentially, a roof. The whole thing had been completely dismantled for the winter. And there was something else that had been dismantled here many years ago: James Bond's beach villa.

Yes, the James Bond as played by Roger Moore in For Your Eyes Only, where he made love to

Countess Lisl von Schlaf (and who would blame him?), only to see her mown down the following morning in an unfortunate beach buggy accident. Way to go. This was in 1979 and whilst the beach hadn't changed much, the background certainly has. To the naked eye, it rather looked like St George didn't exist at all. Strangely, even though everything had been packed away for the winter, Issos was still a picture. Whilst there was nothing to be gained by sunbathing, there were some lovely walks, especially behind the dunes and, to the north, Lake Korission. The lake is man made and is home to a wide variety of birds. I will not attempt to list the birds available for 'twitchers' because you would know full well that I had Googled it. So, if you are that keen to learn, there's what to do.

It's quite fiddly to get to the lake and I am always better with a seasoned navigator to my side. That rarely happens: my partner is usually the one carrying the ancient map, which to be fair is all you need seeing nothing ever changes. I had purchased a large map which told me everything I need about the lake:

"Korission Lagoon is situated on the south west coast of Corfu. The lake is the largest of three on Corfu and covers and area of 6000 acres. From its sand covered dunes on one side to the soft sands of the sea on the other, this area is both beautiful and wild. The wind swept dunes covered in Juniper bushes meet the beaches of St Georges, Issos and at its far end separated by a small inlet channel the beach of Halikounas.

Along the lagoon's shores you can find an ancient rare cedar forest, 14 different species of sand orchids and the rare sand lily Pancratium maritimum

"This is a protected area in Corfu and is abundant with flora and wildlife and the area is listed on the European Environment agencies website and is a protected area categorised on the European Nature Information System (EUNIS) under Natura 2000.

"In 1992 legislation was introduced to protect the most seriously threatened habitats across Europe and Natura 2000 was the result of this legislation bringing together special areas of protection and conservation.

"It is an important stop for migrating birds on their journey from Africa to Europe and at certain times of the year, over 2000 birds seek refuge in the Lake, including a wide variety of water birds, flamingos, swans and falcons. This is a beautiful and largely unspoilt region, with great walks, long soft sandy beaches and great scenery."

Getting to the north of the lake was, to say the least, quite fiddly. I had gone so far from where I believe the lake to be I wondered if I had missed the turning altogether, but no. A good standard road soon turned into a smaller, pot-holed road and soon I rolled into Halikounas, passing the inevitably closed taverna on the way. As views go, they don't get much better than this anywhere on the island. Mountains to the north, the rippling lake to the south, separated from the sea by the beach, and the Ionian Sea to the west. And there is enough to keep the average naturalist and "twitcher" enthused probably for life, never mind a long weekend.

The added winter attraction is the lack of anyone else being there. If I had collapsed in a heap, I might not have been discovered until the first tourist arrived in May! Nothing had changed here for years. Whilst the island itself had been developed in many places, some things stayed the same. Lake Korission is worth a visit anytime. In winter, it was almost magical.

Driving back through Moraitika and then through Benitses, I reached 'The British Corner Shop' mentioned to me by Mike earlier on. And sure enough, there was a great big sign advertising the Iceland food products. I did pull into the car park and thought about seeing what was in the store, but then thought better of it. I had no doubt that a shop would not sell this stuff if there wasn't a market for it so there was no story there. They could only tell me what I probably knew, that there was a significant ex pat community that liked to live abroad but rather than eat local food, they would prefer to eat frozen processed meals from the UK. Whatever floats your boat. I'm afraid I am one of those for whom my boat would have been well and truly floated. Fussy eater, as I may have already mentioned, does not do sufficient disservice to my eating habits.

I restarted the engine, Debbie Harry sang 'Call Me' (if only) and I made my way back to my hotel. The sun was still shining, it was still bright and warm and I had covered a lot of miles, or at least it felt like it. I suppose in reality, I had probably driven as far as Bristol to Chippenham, but island driving, especially Corfu driving, is a constant exercise in gear-changing, slowing down, stopping and, worst of all, driving on the wrong side of the road. It's never boring but it can get tiring, what with all the concentration required to avoid cavernous pot holes and sheer drops at the side of the road.

Upon returning to the Ariti Grand hotel, I caught the 4.00 pm bus back to Corfu Town. The weather forecast was for severe storms, so I packed my storm clothes into my rucksack. The bus trundled down next to the Bay of Garitsa and through town. I was wearing a pair of jeans and a T shirt and I was pleasantly warm but no one around me was! Everyone else was wearing huge overcoats, Tom Baker sized scarves, woolly hats and gloves. You'd have thought it was the middle of winter. "Turned out cold again, Spiros!" But it wasn't cold, certainly not by English standards. I decided to get off at the next stop and walk into town. I took the airport road and after around 80 yards there it was: the place where I had stayed when I first visited Corfu in 1985. The house looked slightly disheveled now, overgrown with foliage but still there was the 'Rooms To Let' sign, although whether there actually was would be a moot point. Turning right and heading into town via a road called

Alkinoou, I noted on the right the little café I had visited, run by the late Agoris, the silver haired old guy who was there from dawn to dusk and beyond.

I walked past a bar where a couple of men were standing outside, smoking cigarettes and the music that was belting out – and I do mean belting out! - was Hotel California, as surreal as anything I saw and heard during the time I was there. Every other shop again seemed to be a chemist shop. I remembered visiting one in 1985 when I was suffering from 'holiday tummy' and was recommended some tablets by the pharmacist. I was in no position to argue (don't worry: I'm not going to elaborate) so I paid my drachmas, swallowed and hoped. And yes, they worked all right. In fact, they worked so well I did not, well you know, for almost a week.

There were no 'jumpers' tonight so I decided to find somewhere other than McDonalds for my evening meal. I found a very tidy 24-hour takeaway not far from Marks and Spencer and ordered, by way of pointing to and waving at, a savoury crepe. I sat on a stool by the road and watched the world go by, as well as enduring some second hand smoke from a Greek woman who, very impressively, multi-tasked by eating her pizza at exactly the same time as she drew on her cigarette which had the charming aroma of a damp carpet. This is similar to the tradition of my home city of Bristol, where residents have become extremely competent at smoking, eating a Greggs pasty (other pasties are available, but not many quite so good) and conducting a messy conversation.

Licking my lips, the (highly attractive, it has to be said) female assistant brought me my bag of goodies and off I went to the Liston to eat it.   I found a park bench which I discovered, by sitting on it, was very wet. A wet bum would not deter me. Bring forth my crepe.  But it wasn't a crepe; it was a burger with soft cheese running through the middle and an industrial portion of skin-on chips next to it.  It was quite nice too, although a little disappointing because burger and chips was becoming my staple diet. And just to annoy me still further, there were several gherkins, which as everyone acknowledges, are disgusting. Why restaurants serve these things is totally beyond me.   My meal was very good and I couldn't really complain.  My inability to speak Greek was now being matched by an equal inability to point at a menu.

It was time for a beer.  There is only one thing worse than drinking on your own and that's not drinking when you're on your own so it was to the nearest bar, the Libra d'Oro that I headed.  I went inside where there was a gentle hubbub of chatter. This was the coffee culture I had heard about and I went up the stairs where I grabbed a chair and small table.  I had barely sat down when a young waiter turned up.  I ordered a large beer and was offered what appeared to be the full range of Ionian ales and beers, as well as one or two imported beers.  I chose the Ionian Pilsner, which I had drunk many times at the

Akrotiri café at Arillas. I looked around the café and quickly realised that I was the only person in the upstairs area who was drinking beer. Everyone else was drinking various types of coffee, typical Brit abroad, eh? This one barely touched the sides and I ordered another. I got my book out of my rucksack and read a few chapters.

No one bothers you in the cafés. The only person with whom I spoke was my friendly waiter when he brought be a new beer. There was a hubbub of conversation and the thick smoke from cigarettes, which wasn't quite so nice.

The weather forecast was right after all as I left. The thunder rumbled overhead, punctuated by huge forms of lightning above the Town. Great. The route to the bus stop, around 50 yards, was guarded by large trees. There was no bus yet which meant, according to my calculations, that the bus would leave pretty well as soon as it arrived. I would have to walk beneath huge trees in an electrical storm to get home. And the rain started as my bus rumbled to a halt. A huge flash then, 'Kerboom'! Exactly on time, the bus departed to Kanoni and the streets became a lake! We sploshed our way through the town, with assorted bedraggled passengers getting on and off the bus. The windscreen wipers were in fast and furious mode and I just hoped the driver could see better than I could. The other thing about the bus was that all the signs were in German, suggesting that Corfu had probably bought a job lot, possibly as part of the financial bail out, but hadn't had the time or perhaps inclination to change the signs to Greek.

The bus reached its terminus and this was where I made my first major mistake of the day. I disembarked, after doing up my storm coat, and immediately realised that this was not my stop. All right, my hotel was only maybe 200 yards down the road but the heavens had well and truly opened now. There was only one thing for it: I couldn't bring myself to get back on the bus and attempt to speak to the driver in heavily fractured Greek words, so I walked. I reached the hotel reception in the knowledge that I could not have been any wetter if I had stood fully dressed under a shower on full power.

I have always enjoyed a decent Greek storm and I was not going to pass up on this one. My balcony had two chairs and fortunately the wind was not blowing the rain onto it. In summer, the storms usually come and go quite quickly and soon it will be like it hasn't rained at all. It would not be like that tonight. The airport runway lights were off, the terminal building was lit up like a distant Christmas tree and beyond that Corfu Town carried on as normal beneath the storm.

I sat on the balcony, Metaxa in hand, hoping that a stray lightning bolt wouldn't land next to me. The bolts were landing everywhere else, including in the hotel pool. It was as if the storm was stuck above Kanoni, but it seemed that actually it was a very wide storm. The rain became so heavy it was hard to see anything. The road below became roaring rapids. I decided to stay out there until the storm ended, but it just went on and on. I awoke in the early hours to distant rumbles and "kerbooms" and the rain was still coming down when I awoke the following day.

## 7. Go West

And so to the west. The storms had long gone, blown away by a strong southerly wind which now encouraged scudding high clouds to pass quickly by.

The breakfasts of cakes, cheese and ham was a little wearing by now.  Not that there was anything wrong with them, just that I had the feeling that they might not be doing my weight-loss programme any good.  Before the next adventure, a morning filter coffee was the ideal next step at the Café Kanoni.  Spiros, for it was he, delivered it to me in a cafetiere then took pity on my inability to pour it out properly and did it himself. The mild weather of the days before had gone.  An icy wind blew into the plastic awning of the café; the sea was more rough than choppy. Replacing the storms were short, sharp showers. And you could see them marching up from Benitses and beyond and as they moved north the villages disappeared from view.  They then reached Kanoni and it was night time again.

Having downed several life-affirming coffees, I decided to have yet another cup at the Café Kanoni.  Spiros took my order for a filter coffee and then returned with it a few moments later. Humiliatingly, he had to return to my table because it was obvious I was struggling to pour it again. Winter had returned to Corfu, though, and you could see the showers advancing from the south as the resorts began to disappear from view, as eventually did Mouse Island.  The waves

194

were crashing onto the Causeway and to the monastery where I could see some of the cats on the roof, sheltering from the elements. A lone motorcyclist crossed the causeway to Perama, trying and sometimes failing to avoid the waves. Where there had been puddles the day before, there were now small (very small!) lakes in the big car park below and it was much colder. Once again, Michael Buble's dulcet tones came over the music system and confirmed, yet again, that he just hadn't met me yet. I returned to my complimentary biscuit.

I waited for a gap in the rain and walked back to my hotel, in the rain. I got in my Hyundai Something and headed off towards town, turning left, passing the end of the runway and then a right turn towards Pelekas. I had a moment's panic when I noted that all the traffic on my road, except me, was coming towards me, but it seemed that very few vehicles were going in my direction. I took another right turn following the signs for Agios Ioannis, my first destination. Well, that's not strictly true: my first destination of the day was Aqualand, which isn't actually a place at all. It's a water park and a closed water park at that.

Ah, Aqualand. Allow me to quote from its website, 'Aqualand – a unique and unforgettable experience of joy, happiness and endless fun'. Well, having been there many times over the years, and thoroughly enjoyed the experiences, then fair enough: it's a cracking day out at a big waterpark.

I am not in the first flush of youth, or even the last flush for that matter, but I do enjoy some of the rides at Aqualand. The Crazy River, The Lazy River and the Black Hole being among my favourites, along with lying on a sun bed with a cool drink and a high calorific snack. The Hurricane Twister and Kamikaze slides are not exactly my idea of fun. I'll leave those to the kids, as I have always done. If Aqualand was not massive enough in itself – 57k of square feet, I believe – there is the Aqualand Resort next door, a monstrous collection of apartments the needs of its occupants being met by the all inclusive holidays on offer. If Corfu was a dartboard, Aqualand would be the bullseye, so if you were to book a holiday at the Aqualand Resort, it would be an advantage if you liked being next to a very noisy waterpark. If not, be prepared for plenty of bus travel if you wanted to see a beach. I would say that just about everywhere in Corfu is equally awkward to get to from Aqualand!

The resort has sprung up during the time we have visited the island. It still looks fabulously new and modern, but out of season it looks very odd. There is nothing to do and nowhere to go if you are staying at the Aqualand resort, unless you hire a car to travel elsewhere, in which case why don't you stay somewhere else and travel to Aqualand for day trips? I would not describe holidaymakers as being imprisoned, but it's not far off.

Today, I drove into a car park that was largely empty, save for a number of buses with

'Aqualand' written on them. These had probably been there since the end of October. The wave pool, 'the third largest wave pool in the world' is its selling point, was a dark green colour (as I keep saying, this is normal and doesn't indicate a lack of hygiene) and of course deserted. I will not use the exact words a friend of mine used to describe Aqualand in the context of where it is based, but let's say she regarded it as somewhat worse than a blot on the landscape. With all it's gates closed, it's fast food outlets boarded up and the attractions without running water, the place had the Chernobyl feel of Kavos. The rain fell steadily and the wind made a few things creak inside the park as I walked alongside. Just by the Caribbean Pirate Adventure Pool stood a group of four men, smoking profusely (this was an indication they were probably Greek) and not doing very much. As I reached the bottom of the 'Crazy River' and the Hydrotube, I noticed the side gate was open, so I let myself in and had a look around. To be fair, it was actually quite clean which was impressive since I doubt that they had had a customer since October. It was just the silence that struck me. No loud music, no sound of water rushing down the slides and no screams from people like me whizzing down them. Just the wind from the wires around the side of the park and the rain beating down on it. No one was around to stop me, so I just carried on walking, looking at nothing in particular and getting increasingly wet!

No one seemed to care when I walked in at the side of the Crazy River. An old friend of mine said that if you were going somewhere that you shouldn't really be, then walk in a brisk, business-like manner, looking straight ahead. It worked a treat that day.

Running through the heart of the waterpark is the "Lazy River" where people float around on rubber rings, driven slowly along by carefully created currents. It was very odd to see it with nothing in it, other than rainwater. Similarly, the splash pools at the bottom of the rides were empty too.

I left the park and walked back down to the car park. The four men were still standing around chatting and smoking, completely oblivious to this trespasser, but this was not Aqualand as I knew it. The rain was coming down even heavier now, the wind a constant "whoosh", and I broke into a trot before leaping into the car. But I couldn't drive anywhere. Not for the first time, I had jumped into the passenger seat of the car, temporarily forgetting that the steering wheel is on the wrong side in Greece. Happily, there was no one around to watch because if there were, I'd have had to wait patiently in the pretence that the real driver would be along soon!

Leaving Aqualand, taking the road towards Pelekas, I drove through the thickest drizzle I had ever come across. It was as if the windscreen wipers were merely there for show because they certainly weren't displacing water at the rate I required. Suddenly, out of nowhere, came a mature lady bounding towards and then past me, wearing a bright orange top and white trousers and a huge baseball cap. From what I could tell, she was power-walking, although there did not appear to be much power going on. And she was very, very wet. I started the drive up to the hillside village of Pelekas which, though relatively unspoilt, has certainly evolved into something of an inland tourist resort since the nearby resort of Glifada has gained in popularity. It's still a charming little village, although I am not going to pretend it hasn't changed since 1985, though happily not to destruction. The water was flowing down the hill as I drove past the cafés and tavernas and the one little supermarket which was open. I carried on driving to the other side of Pelekas and the road became still narrower. I had to admit to myself that I was in danger of getting lost, so I executed a less than subtle six point turn (at least) on a small road and headed back to the village.

I decided that I might as well drive up to Kaiser's Throne, so I took the tight left hand turn, passing the whitewashed church and arrived at the parking area next to the Sunset Restaurant. I walked through an archway, through the trees and up some steep steps to the Throne (or Lookout or Tower as it is sometimes known). The Kaiser concerned was Kaiser Wilhelm II who frequently drove from the Achilleion Palace to see the sunsets of the west coast. And who could blame the old boy? I had been here in the summer and the views were stunning and even today, dodging the showers, they were no less stunning. To the east, you could see Corfu Town and Vidos island; to the northwest the Ropa Valley; south to Mount Mattheos and west through the trees to the sea. And beyond Corfu Town was the mighty Mount Pantokrator. The clouds bobbed and weaved across the skies, the rain came and went, the wind blew continuously. And once again, there was that light; the clear light of Greece, even when the sun is behind the clouds everything is so clear. And from so high up there were the contrasts between the areas where the sun was breaking through and the darkened areas where it wasn't. You could see the showers marching up the east coast as the picture changed all the time. I could have stayed there all day. Then a huge rainbow appeared, adding still more colour to a colourful scene.

The weather by now was so awful that I abandoned my plan to drop the car off and walk the streets of Pelekas. As the saying goes, the weather had 'closed in'. I drove back down to the main road and set off towards Paleokastritsa. But first some golf.

I made a point of stopping off at the Corfu Golf Club in Ermones and drove in to find it closed. (A cursory browse of the website clearly stated that the club closed in the winter, but I didn't check until I had arrived back at my hotel. Another big fail.) The website blurb stated that the course was one of the finest in all of Europe, which is some claim indeed. I had no idea whether this was true, because when I called by it was more than somewhat overgrown and unkempt, and that was just the greens, or rather the browns, as they appeared to me. There was also a driving range 'Proudly sponsored by Coca Cola', which to my uneducated eye looked like, well, a field. I crossed a bridge across a babbling brook and the course stretched out before me. Overgrown, yes, and definitely out of season, but it seemed to me, a golfer so bad that I don't even have a handicap, apart from golf itself, that this course probably did live up to its self-billing, in season.

I definitely want to play the Corfu course sometime but have always been slightly put off by the weather. Not the weather in winter, which struck me as perfect golfing weather, but the weather in summer where, it appeared, you might need to set off with a dawn tee time in order to avoid sunstroke. And was this, I wondered, developing my theme, another winter attraction? What golfer would not want to fly to a beautiful island like Corfu and spend their time thrashing around this golf course? But no one was here. I assumed there was little enthusiasm from the local population but I'll bet there could be abroad. Well, I'd go.

I had driven past the club many times before but had never ventured in. The clubhouse and facilities, the ones that I could actually see, looked terrific. From the road, you wonder how on earth there could be a full-length course at all, but once inside it looked rather impressive.

What I feel the course needs is for a little known British author to be commissioned for a modest fee (plus flights and accommodation) to write a short article about the course for publication in the media. Feel free to contact me...

I had strayed well beyond the car park and onto the fairways when – yes, you've guessed it – the rain returned. In traditional British style, I had decided that the sun had now come out and there would be no further requirement for my raincoat. I made my way back to the clubhouse, bidding 'Yammas!' (again) to a man who was driving a tractor and returned to the car. I would now visit Paleokastritsa.

At Paleokastritsa, or Paleo as us Brits call it, the tree-covered mountains give way to the sea. The views here are truly spectacular, despite much of the utterly crass development that has taken place in recent years that has done so much to detract from its natural beauty. Paleokastritsa is very much the end of the road, literally, and there is a real sense of arrival. There is a small monastery up the hill on the far side of the bay but even in summer I can't be bothered with it. Yes, I know that this classifies me as an out and out philistine, but once I have seen one monastery, I have seen them all. I have feigned interest in the past to keep the family in good humour, and to maintain my happy marriage, but the truth is I could not be less interested. The best bits of this particular monastery for me are nothing to do with the spiritual side of life, but the views across the Bay of Liapades to Cape Agios Liodoros.

Paleokastritsa isn't all 'spiritual' though. Beaches of varying quality offer sunbathing facilities of varying quality, there is the usual plethora of 'water sports' and there are organised boat trips and scuba diving. In the summer. For all its spectacular viewing, a damp, overcast day did the town no favours. My driving did me no favours either as I twice left the main road and headed down lanes that led to hotels and apartments, one of which took me up an absurdly steep and twisty hill which led to nowhere at all, necessitating a painfully slow reversal down the same road.

I have never been a fan of Paleokastritsa if I am being honest, but that's me and no reflection on the resort itself. With the possible exception of Kavos, it's perfectly normal for people to find things to love and admire about anywhere in Corfu. With the rain in freefall under slate grey skies, I suspect nowhere on earth could have looked particularly nice that day.

But since I had first visited Paleokastritsa new villas and hotels had mushroomed as far as the eye could see. The olive trees by the sea had mostly gone. I stopped by a couple of boarded up tavernas and restaurants and the menus were mainly in German and Russian, the latter unheard of in Corfu until in more recent times. And of course souvenir shops with low grade tat for the less discerning visitor (like me).

Perhaps I had just caught Paleokastritsa on a bad day. Perhaps it was because I was as damp as the gloomy grey atmosphere? Or perhaps it was because Paleokastritsa and I were incompatible? I suspected it was probably the latter when one considers how busy and thus popular it becomes in the summer. A glance at Trip Advisor provides the answer: people love it and it's hugely popular. What did I know? I turned the car round and headed to Corfu Town. And the sun came out.

Mick Hucknall's Simply Red came over the airways singing about a Fairground and I was on my way. I passed Aqualand again and got stuck behind a learner driver with a dodgy offside brake light. Now, I rarely get stuck behind anyone whilst driving in Corfu but a learner driver was another story. With any luck, the driver would not be going in my direction for long and I could resume at my normal speed. But he didn't. Every time a decision needed to be made as to whether he would be turning left, right or going straight ahead, he made the same choice as I did. If there had been nothing behind me, I would have been fine about it and just crawled into Corfu Town, but there was something behind me. In fact, there was a rather long convoy behind me and I felt under a little pressure to get past the learner, not least when drivers came up from behind to carry out four or five car overtaking manoeuvres, but only when approaching a blind bend or when the driver could not be sure whether there was something coming the other way.

Garitsa Bay was now bathed in sunshine and the sea was nowhere near as rough as it had been. Arriving in the car park by the boundary of the cricket pitch, it was clear that the wicket itself would have been unplayable with at least an inch of water on the artificial pitch. The cafés and bars were all open for the young people of Corfu, who sipped lovingly at their coffees. Having eaten nothing since breakfast, I decided to find somewhere, not McDonalds which was depressingly busy, for a nibble. I'd have really liked a sandwich but they don't seem to do sandwiches in Greece but I did find a very nice looking takeaway place that sold all manner of baguettes and rolls. I settled for a Brioche type concoction, which featured a lot of meat (obviously), cheese and assorted vegetables. I suspect it would not be conducive to a calorie-controlled diet but my god it was tasty. It had given me an appetite, I'm afraid, so I stopped by another takeaway and bought a Gyros, a delicious wrap with pork, chips, tzatziki and assorted other bits and pieces. Well, that was healthy, wasn't it?

With some time on my hands, I decided I would pay a visit to the Old Fortress. You reach it from the east side of the Esplanade. To the right, the main gatehouse incorporates the Byzantine collection of Corfu with mosaics and sculptures from the Basilica of Palaiopolis. Impressed by my knowledge? Of course, you're not. It was all in the small guidebook I picked up. You don't think I'd have known detail like that, do you? Anyway, I crossed the bridge and I observed a middle-aged couple walking past some rickety old shacks. They couldn't live there, could they, I surmised, and they didn't. As they walked along by the water, a seriously large number of cats and kittens appeared. It was feeding time for the waif and stray cats of Corfu Town and didn't they look happy as they followed the two kind people who scattered offerings as they went along? I made the steep climb past a Venetian clock tower and took in the view over Corfu Town and Mount Pantokrator. Pantokrator certainly looked spectacular, standing as it does 906 metres in the air. I have driven there before and it's a feat of endurance and downright terror at times. At the top, there is a small church which is dedicated to Christ Pantokrator (The Almighty) and a small café. You cannot see the church from a long way off but on a clear day you can see a huge radar mast and a variety of aerials and beacons which, when you are actually there, you can hear buzzing away merrily and noisily. There is something a bit mad about having these eyesores at the top of the mountain but somehow the view is not totally spoiled.

At the top of the fort, I looked out to sea and was surprised to see an aircraft coming from the south, banking slowly across the bay before straightening up to land across Corfu Town, skimming the rooftops as it passed by. And then nothing, not a sound apart from the wind setting off some clanking wind chimes.

This was such a fantastic place. Not just the Old Fortress or Corfu Town. The whole island and, apart from the beaches which were entirely redundant this time of year, there was so much to see and do. Unarguably to me, the Old Fortress was more suited to a winter visit since my previous summer visits were carried out in draining heat and once I had got to the top I wanted to get back down again. Today, unusually for me, I was looking at the history of the place, thinking of so much more than where my next sun bed was coming from. As I have said before, this is not a book in which you will learn a great deal about Corfu's history but I was showing far more interest in it than I had in the past 29 years. In summer, if I go anywhere, I simply must take in the sun's rays every single day. If the day involves sightseeing, I will ensure time is made for sunbathing too. Obviously, out of season there would be few opportunities for sunbathing so the sights and the history came into their own. I could stop, admire and learn, not wishing I was somewhere else.

I walked past the Museum of Asian Art and down towards the Old Port. The afternoon sunshine flickered only briefly as some fluffy clouds scuttled by. The tree-lined island of Vidos was across the bay; the odd small boat chugged away from the Port. There were none of the giant ferries of the summer in Corfu apart from one large cruise ship which did not appear to be going anywhere anytime soon. And just out to sea there was a warship. At the foot of the hill was a small café and I decided it was time for a coffee. I ordered in my usual painful badly fractured Greek and sat down. As luck would have it, I was sitting next to a Scottish couple of middle age and a bit. I engaged them in conversation.

Dave and Janet had been living in Corfu for five years. They had been to Corfu many times on holiday and had decided to escape the rat race. He had worked in finance and she was a teaching assistant. Things had "really gone to the dogs back home" and they wanted to escape from it. Dave was a big man, over six foot tall and stout in build, wearing brown combat type trousers and a checked short-sleeved shirt. He had thinning red hair with a bright red face to go with it. Janet was the opposite, pencil slim, her hair a short dark bob, wearing a neat knee length floral dress. The Glaswegian twang was a little tough to deal with at times, as no doubt my Bristolian burr was to them, but we got on well enough.

Dave explained how they had ended up in Corfu: "We had been coming to Sidari for many years and we made plenty of friends there. Back home, everyone is on the make, rip off Britain and all that, and everyone is in a hurry. We liked the easygoing lifestyle and no one was in a hurry to do anything. As the years went by, we decided that we wanted to make the move before it was too late."

"So, how did you did you decide to buy a property and what happened next?" I asked.

"It was quite easy, really," said Janet. "We knew where we wanted to live, somewhere in the north west of Corfu, in easy reach of Sidari, Roda and Arillas.  Soon we settled on a small house in a village just outside San Stefanos.  As soon as we saw it, we knew that was where we wanted to be. All we had to do was sell the house back home and move over.  Well, it wasn't quite that easy."

It certainly wasn't that easy and eventually they decided to rent out their modern semi to the west of Glasgow, rather than sell it, and use the proceeds of the rent to pay the mortgage they had taken out in Corfu.

"It was a bit fiddly, to say the least," explained Dave, "Because there was tons of paperwork and red tape – I thought Scotland was bad enough – but there were a million and one things to do. The house needed some work on the damp, some plastering and the drive had several bomb craters on it.  That took forever to sort out.  In fact, even now the plastering is only half done, but that's Greece.  Everything is no problem."

"What's it like now?" I asked.  "How does your life compare with life at home?"

"It's a home from home really, " said Dave. "We've got a lot of home comforts like satellite TV so we can keep up to date with what's happening back home.  Friends send us stuff that we can't get over here and there's a shop by Corfu Town that sells a lot of British stuff."

"How is life over here?  Are you involved in any of the Greek customs?  Do you feel like you've fully integrated?"

Dave laughed: "Well, we drink Ouzo and Metaxa! There's a little café about five minutes drive from ours.  It's not exactly lively but we'll have a pint with the locals, not that we really know what they're saying.  They don't speak much English in the old villages, except for the people who live in the villages and work in the resorts in summer."

I wasn't really in much of a position to be critical, since I had arrived in Corfu with – literally – a handful of Greek words to aid my journey.  But it didn't sound much like integration to me.  I said so.

"Don't get me wrong", continued Dave, warming to his theme. "We get on well with the locals, they do their thing and we do ours.  We buy stuff in the local shops when we're in town – we've got a car full of shopping today – and we say hello to everyone.   To be honest, we keep ourselves to ourselves.  We've got some British friends over here, though, and we see them for drinks from time to time.  There's a few places we can go to, some places stay open in the winter, or we'll go to each others' places, crack open a few bottles and that."

"What about the local traditions, like the Easter festival in Corfu Town, all that plate-smashing?" I asked.

"We've been meaning to go for years. We'll do it one day."

I said that I knew what summer was like for the tourist and I was beginning to see what winter was like for the Corfiot and the ex pat. "What's winter like for you?"

"Wet!" said Dave. "It rains and rains and then it rains even more. There are days on end when you think it's never going to stop. Massive great thunderstorms that go on for hours and it can get very cold at night. We have a log burner downstairs but upstairs we rely on an electric heater, none of that central heating! We might drive down to Kassiopi if we're really brave (laughs) and have a coffee. I have a mate who lives in the village.

"Winter can be a drag, but it's like that wherever you are, isn't it? We went back home for Christmas – what a palaver that was, I'll tell you. We had a flight to Athens, then another flight to London, then a bus to Glasgow, all that just to get home for a week with the family, my kids and grandkids and all that.

"At least coming back we had something to look forward to. Get away from Britain. It's not like it used to be."

Did they have any hobbies or pastimes?

"He plays a bit of darts now and then," replied Janet. "And maybe a bit of boules if there are enough ex pats about. There are a few things we could do, I suppose, but we're here to enjoy ourselves. We mostly potter about. We had a little garden but that's overgrown now. It's hard work maintaining it in the summer because of the heat and in the winter it's chucking it down.

"The long winter nights can be a bit depressing, when we're on our own night after night. But soon enough it will be spring and you get some nice weather from April onwards. Sit out the back, have a glass of something cold."

"And then another glass," roared Dave. "It's a hard life, but someone's got to do it."

"What's the plan for the rest of the day?" I asked.

"We'll drive back to the house," said Dave, "Cook up some pork chops we've bought with some spuds, have a glass or two of something and watch the box. You can English TV over here via cable. I don't read much – actually, I don't read at all. When my eyes are going, I'll stagger off to bed."

I wondered if there was anything that distinguishes summer from winter in their lives.

"The weather mainly," said Dave. "And there are beachside bars open where we can meet our friends who come over. There's loads in Sidari, cheap booze, good atmosphere. It's party time all summer. We can eat out a lot more too. Some cracking restaurants in Sidari. There's even a decent Chinese. It's a bit wild with all the tourists but we like it that way. It's weird when they go home and most of the resorts shut down completely. Some places really do shut down completely."

I had enjoyed meeting Dave and Janet, but it was time to go. As I was to discover, theirs was not the typical ex pat existence but they were pleasant enough people.

"I've got one more question," I said. "Are you here forever, or do you plan to go home one day?"

"We're here to stay", said Dave, firmly.

"Or until our health gets worse," intervened Janet. "We'd go home then. I mean, the hospital here is good, don't get me wrong, but it's not the NHS. But we're not planning on leaving anytime soon. We love it here."

I had wondered about that. It is one thing retiring to a Greek island, but quite another to grow so old that things start to go wrong. We will all need more than a little luck to avoid the unpleasant things that go with the job. Increasingly frailty is a certainty, what if a partner gets ill and dies, what if you develop one of those horrible incurable conditions like Alzheimer's? The sunshine islands of Greece and Spain house over a million, mostly older, Brits. Where would you want your life to start falling apart around you? You are not meant to feel that way because you dream of the time when you don't have to work anymore, at least not full time. It's something I'd think about though. Sitting in a perfect Greek village in the depths of winter, a thousand miles from my family and friends and the public services I had probably taken for granted all my life. I guess you balance it all up in the end, perhaps you hope for the best or put the negative thoughts as far from the front of your mind as possible. It is not so much a question of where you would want to be as you got old, it's where you would want to be if and when things started to go wrong. A big question I decided not to ask. It's not why I was here, I suppose, but I couldn't help thinking about it.

I shook hands with them and left them to it, as Dave ordered more coffee. It was late into the afternoon and it was gradually getting darker. Having walked round the side of Corfu Town, I decided to walk back to the Liston through the town. I never tire of these lovely lanes and streets. I'd love to be able to say that I know my way round all of them, but that would be a terrible lie. I still get lost, although never for long.

This time, I took a slight detour and walked past Agios Spyridonas, or the Church of St Spiridon, the tall red-domed bell-tower being a landmark of the town. I'd like to say that I went in to pay my respects but even God needs a holiday and it was closed. That was a shame since St Spiridon was quite a lad and is fondly remembered for expelling the plague from the town. He is affectionately known as 'The Keeper of the City' and it is because of him that something like half the men in Corfu are called Spiros. St Spiridon's casket is kept in the church and exposed annually on various dates, including at Easter. You don't have to be religious – and I am anything but religious – to enjoy the history and traditions of Corfu. One day, I shall have to make a serious attempt to improve my ignorance of the island which, I suspect, shows through on every page!

After calling into what we would call an off license to buy a large bottle of 7 star Metaxa, I returned to my Hyundai Something in what can only be described as heavy rain. Once again, I dropped the car off at my hotel and braved the elements for a couple of beers at the Café Kanoni. Spiros, who seemed to work 24/7, and maybe even more than that, had guessed by now that I had coffee in the morning and beer of an evening and he soon returned with a cold bottle of the latter. Not wishing to be seen as some kind of ignorant British tourist, I ordered a traditional Ham and Cheese toastie to go with it.

The lights to the south flickered in the wind and rain and the wind battered the windows of the café. There was a steady hubbub of chatter from the customers, all of whom were smoking, as remains the tradition in Corfu. I am far from convinced that if smoking was banned in Greek bars and cafés that anyone would pay attention to it. I just about tolerated the smell of smoke, which I suppose I had to since I was stinking of it myself.

It was time to go. I gathered my bits and pieces, left my Euros on the table and Spiros came over to say goodnight. I offered him my hand and tripped over the step by the exit door and found myself on my knees, looking up at him. 'These English,' I wouldn't have blamed him for thinking, 'Can't hold their drink, can they?' Well, I can actually, but I staggered back to my feet, mumbled something and left. I got outside into the open air, stood up straight, closed my eyes for a moment and cringed. Then I walked back to the hotel.

Once again, the wind howled up from the south as I made my way back to the hotel. It was a strangely novel experience, of cold, wind and rain in this island paradise – and it remains so, even in the so called depths of winter – but it was not an unpleasant experience either. The maritime climate of the UK, in particular the south west of England, Cornwall, Devon and the like, did not see the end of tourism just because the calendar moved on. As with those places, Corfu has so much more to offer.

## 8. North and north east

This travelling about malarkey really did make me feel like a proper explorer, albeit exploring and discovering things that many others had come across before me. After countless visits to Corfu in the previous 24 years, this was the first I had done alone. I was responsible for getting from A to B, I was the organiser but I also had the flexibility to change at short notice. This being winter, I knew this might just happen.

The next touring day meant an early start and – praise be! – the sun blazed in a clear blue sky. There was a slight chill breeze but the view across the lagoon from the hotel and north to Pantokrator was stunning; crystal clear. I was convinced, by now, that the blue sky was not as blue as it was in summer. This was probably nonsense, but it seemed a lighter, milkier blue to my uneducated eyes.

Stuck behind the number two bus on the one-way street, which as usual paused to pick up a single person from each bus stop (I swear this happened!), the initial part of the journey was slower than usual, but when the Bay of Garitsa, the town and the Old Fortress came into view, it was worth waiting for. A solitary fishing boat chugged across the bay in a northerly direction, there were white flecks from the gentle waves but peace had descended on Corfu. Cars parked on both sides of the road as I drove past Corfu Town and the Esplanade. The car park was fairly full too and it wasn't even 9.00 am. Down to the old harbour once more and once the road had opened up and widened, I began to relax. I was remembering now to look in my rear-view mirror which was, of course, above me to my right and there was nothing behind me. I took the right turn to the north. Except that I didn't. This was not the first time in my Corfu driving experience that I had made a directional error and whilst this was not exactly a major incident, it was embarrassing. I had driven into the Ferry Port where a large ferry was waiting. I then managed to compound the situation by somehow joining the queue, albeit not a long queue, nine or ten cars at most, to board it. As soon as I was able I swung to the right and found myself facing some huge pallets containing large boxes. A port official, resplendent in dark uniform and cap, approached.

"English!" I announced, as if this would explain everything.

The official looked bemused. "Are you catching this ferry?"

"I'm going to Arillas," I replied, unhelpfully.

"You are in the Ferry Port," he said, unsmilingly, pointing to a large exit sign. "For Arillas, you go that way."

"Efharisto," I told him. "Kalispera!"

I zigzagged my way to the exit, realising that I had, early in the morning, wished the official

'Good afternoon!' It was a slight improvement on 'Cheers', I suppose.

The first point of call was Kontokali, which is the first resort north of Corfu. I had not visited for the best part of 28 years and my memories of the place were not exactly flattering. It was in 1986 or 1987 when my friends and I called by. It had just rained, there were huge puddles everywhere and the Kontokali I saw was a bit of a shanty town, resembling more a Brazilian favela than somewhere you would want to spend a holiday. To say the beach was unappealing was an understatement. Why would anyone want to stay here? But today it was unrecognisable. Far from being a tatty shanty town, there was now a staggeringly good and large marina, albeit scarcely populated on a stunning winter's day. There were facilities for hiring yachts and the beach, which was once a bit of a pebble and stone shambles was now an attractive pebble and sand beach, albeit a narrow one.

The little roads of Kontokali were now the home of attractive looking restaurants and tavernas, some decidedly upmarket, and some fabulous looking hotels. It even looked good in winter, which surprised me a little since on my last visit it didn't look too good in summer. There was a signpost to the north, which led to a 'Venetian Boatyard'. It was not hard to find. I am no expert on architecture but the skeletal arches were stunning and it was not hard to imagine how this would have looked in the day. I should have visited before, had I bothered to learn about it. In winter, there was plenty more time to seek out the rich history of this summer island. In short, Kontokali was a real surprise. It surely had to be worth a visit in the summer and it wasn't a John Smiths/Sunday Roast resort either. There were lessons to be learned, certainly by me. I had lived with the view that Kontokali was somewhere worth avoiding by dint of a fleeting visit over a quarter of a century ago and when discussing Corfu with others I had persisted with that view. And that view was so wrong. The view across the bay was delightful, it was clean and tidy and looked an ideal place, and base, for a nice holiday.

I took a detour and stopped in Dassia through which the main road to the north east runs. The resort is dominated by two big hotels, the Corfu Chandris and Dassia Chandris and its lovely shingle beach with its wooden jetties that cater for visiting boats. Like many places in Corfu, Dassia is buzzing in the summer, especially around the big hotels and around the beach, but what is there for winter? The initial reaction is not a lot. But then, there is not a lot anywhere unless you put you put your mind to finding things to do. There is not too much history in the Dassia area and the main road is not exactly picturesque, but there are still lovely walks, through Gouvia to Kontokali to the south, to the long strip of Ipsos just to the north. I wasn't there for more than half an hour, I suppose, but I was beginning to like nothing as a pastime.

Down the hill to the long strip of Ipsos and up the other side towards Barbati, a small village where I had never once stopped in nearly 30 years. To the left was a scattering of bars and tavernas, to the right a series of small roads to the sea. I took one of them down to the beach and as soon as I reached the bottom it occurred to me that I had missed out on something. The shimmering blue sea separated Corfu from the border separating Greece to the south and Albania to the north. It always struck me that, on the face of it, Albania had not come out of the border separation too well, much of the land appearing bleak and mountainous.

To the south was Corfu Town looking stunning in the morning sun with just a gentle breeze coming in from the sea. It went without saying that I was alone on the immaculate pebble beach with all the summer sunbeds and watersports attractions under lock and key. There was not much else to say about Barbati, to be honest. Like many other resorts, there was nothing going on in mid winter (not that this day felt like winter at all) and the resort which is basically either side of the main road is not picturesque at any time of year, but off the beaten track – well, Barbati, like so much of Corfu, was a winter break just waiting to happen.

I drove very slowly back up the hill to the main road, dreading *that* left turn which would see me on an incline, trying to judge traffic coming from the left on my side of the road. Inevitably I managed to stall, twice not once, before roaring back towards Ipsos, Dassia and then a right turn towards my eventual destination. The traffic lights at Dassia, a significant junction, were out of order, or maybe made redundant for the winter but the right turn north was much easier for a confused, disorientated Brit.

Once again I passed the summer melon, winter potato man and turned right, passing the highly distracting advert for the Ammos Bar in Arillas which, as you may recall, featured a bikini clad female, and commenced the long drag up to the summit at the Troumpeta Pass. I was in no hurry and made plenty of room for locals who were, although as ever they tended to wait for blind bends to carry out what appeared to me to be extremely dangerous overtaking manoeuvres. After passing through Skripero and its traffic light controlled one way system, I found myself trundling behind an extremely elderly small truck which belched out thick black smoke from its exhaust pipe. It made quite a lot of noise too, drowning out the music on Kiss radio. It would have been nice to get past this truck, not least to preserve my lungs, but the final stretch to the summit was not the best for overtaking, especially not for me. This did not stop various motorists and unhelmeted motorcyclists tearing past in what appeared to the naked eye as being suicidal overtaking!

By the time we breasted Troumpeta, the line of traffic behind trailed back a very long way. Hopefully, the driver would be taking the right turn to Sidari and the north, but it was not to be.

I carried straight on at the virtually unmarked junction and managed to get past the truck. The road was clear from hereon in and I found myself driving through the pretty village of Dafni listening to what sounded like an appalling Bryan Adams impersonator on the radio. On closer aural inspection, it turned out it *was* Bryan Adams. The next song, which was classic Europop, included the epic words, 'Making love is magic, breaking up is tragic'. I felt these words were a bit of a generalisation, but I could see where the singer was coming from, in between bouncing in and out of potholes which closely resembled small craters.

The knowledge that Arillas is not far away comes when you pass the 'Olive Wood' shop. This is not a lady called Olive Wood, I hasten to add, but a lady who makes the most incredible things out of olive wood. We toured the studio a few years ago and some of the stuff she sells is incredible. It's in the middle of nowhere and quiet as the grave apart from the passing vehicles. The sheer size of some of the things she makes mean you can't buy them because you wouldn't be able to take them home. I think we might have bought something we didn't need – maybe some wind chimes or something, but I wouldn't bank on it.

I love the drive down into Arillas. You have already seen the sea low down to the left, through the trees, before the descent and there is a certain excitement, born I suspect from familiarity, as you near the beach. Except that I always seem to think the beach is around the next turning and it isn't.    There's another landmark I seem to have forgotten. And like Paleokastritsa, there is a sense of arrival because Arillas is the end of the road, unless of course you turn right and go on to San Stefanos!

Today, this lovely little resort was stunning.  I approached from the road at the southerly end, passing various shuttered apartments and hotels and some excellent restaurants.  The waves were slight this time, not battering  the jetty.  A long line of lovely restaurants and tavernas were on my right, like Kostas on the Beach, Thalassa and Horizon. I took a right by 'Sharon's Pool Bar' and headed away from the beach, once again passing the Coconut Bar and the Malibu Bar which seems to have grown yet again in advance of the summer season.

I took coffee with Anna Krasakis at her studio apartments and, mercifully, Theo Krasakis who had been discharged from hospital, something that was not entirely surprising because he looked a picture of health.

Theo is a model of calm.  His English, like that of the rest of the family, is excellent and he runs the family car hire business which is situated on the road to the beach.  He had enjoyed the break when the summer season had ended but now he was bored. "Sometimes, I drive to Corfu Town, maybe twice in a day to see friends," he said.  "At this time of year there is nothing to do.  I drove over 1000 km last week just driving back and forward to Corfu Town."

So was that it? They wind down after a hectic 24/7 summer season and get bored all winter?

"Oh no, " replied Theo. "Soon there will be plenty to do. There are always improvements to make in the apartments, some painting to do, perhaps. In a few weeks, we shall be putting down a new floor in the car hire shop. And then there are the cars. They have to be in good condition for the new summer season. That is a big job."

And of course he was right. Anna's always seems to have some improvements with each passing season, but to be fair much of Arillas in particular and Corfu in general seems to do the same. No one stands still for very long. Whilst the tourist can grill under the Ionian sun, Corfiots are already planning their next move. As Brouklis Taverna owner Dimitris Kourkoulos said elsewhere, they seek these days to improve, not develop, what they already have. Corfu has been down the road of developing and it didn't always work. There was a danger that they would develop areas so much that they could become unrecognisable to the people who came to stay and so drive them elsewhere. If you fall in love with a place, like so many of us have with Corfu, then they turn it into something else, you may go somewhere else. As Mike Love from the Beach Boys once said, "Don't mess with the formula" (except that the word he actually used was not 'mess', but this is a family book).

We took a walk outside. The sun shone with just the occasional cloud drifting by on a gentle breeze. The sunbeds were piled up by the bar area to my left, the pool itself was about half full, but even in the depths of winter the whole area was remarkably clean. I say remarkably but perhaps I shouldn't. It was typically clean. My travels suggested that Corfiots had enormous pride in their island, always wanting it to be at its best. In the sun, I could picture myself seven months hence, lying on my sunbed, reading a book, occasionally making the long two yard walk to the pool and the much longer 10 yard walk to the bar. Occasionally a moped or a car would roar up the hill, but generally it was very quiet.

I asked Theo if he was looking forward to summer now.

"Yes. I am bored with winter now, I am looking forward to the start of the season," he replied. But he didn't look bored. Theo is not a book, he is not easy to read. When you talk with him, nothing seems to be too much trouble, he knows what's going on, there's no problem. Never a problem. The previous winter, he and some friends had flown to Milan for a holiday ("very expensive") and they had also been to Thailand. It was nice to get away from the island for a while, but I knew they also loved to come back. Mr Laid Back is the deeply unimaginative nickname we have for him. His mother suggests the nickname may not be entirely accurate.

I had missed Arillas on my first visits in the 1980s, not actually discovering the place until

1992.  My memory is not up to recalling whether anything much had changed been 1992 and today, but somehow I doubted it.  Nothing had changed since the early 2000s, that's for sure and that was undoubtedly why people kept coming back.  The more I travelled round the island, the more I realised that this was true for most of the rest of the island too.  In fact, some areas, like Benitses and Ipsos, had dramatically improved in all sorts of ways.

From Anna's there is a beautiful view across the bay and to the right the long cape.  I bade farewell to Theo, pleased that he had recovered from his illness which, according to doctors, was nothing (!) and drove back to the seafront where nothing much was happening.  The beach was awash with rocks and pebbles that been brought in by the winter storms (worse storms followed after I left).  It still looked picture-postcard pretty – Arillas always does – and I knew that by the spring evidence of the winter weather would have long gone.

I walked to the north end of the beach and joined the cliff path which seems to get more inland every year, thanks to the erosion of the cliffs.  It was roped off to ensure that half-witted visitors (like me) didn't take their eyes of the path and plunge to an unpleasant end. I doubt I would have been found until the first naturists descended on the beach below.

For all the development, Arillas remains unspoiled.  Behind the beach lie houses and apartments and areas where locals grow various products. Apart from the sound of the waves and the wind, there was nothing. Every so often, I came across stray cats and tiny baby kittens, often with pathetic, patchy coats. I always wonder how many will make it through the winter. I walked to the top of the path where, to my right, was a small taverna (closed) and to my left was the Akrotiri, the literal one (the cape) and the magnificent Akrotiri Café (also closed). If either had been open, I would of course have paid a visit. The Akrotiri, it seemed to me, would be a good place to visit whatever the weather, whatever the season. In the summer, all the doors are open, but in winter, well, just close them, like we have to do in England. I could see the odd car driving along the front in Arillas, a small bonfire burned in the hills opposite. Aircraft left their vapour trails five miles high, obviously passing Corfu by, unlike in summer when they flew down the west side of Corfu in the final stages of their descent, before sweeping left over Lake Korission and then along the east coast. Without direct flights to Corfu, Akrotiri would remain open weekends only.

I walked back down to the front, passing beehives on the way, to my Hyundai Something, which was parked just along from the excellent Ammos Café.

What were the differences between Arillas now and Arillas in summer? Obviously, there were no tourists, except me. The beach was all bashed up after the winter storms (there would be more),

228

although by May you would never know and everything on the front was closed down. But where Arillas was different was that there were people and a good few of them. Where the traffic in resorts like Agios Georgios (north and south) was non existent, here whilst it wasn't exactly the M25 there was the regular buzz of a car of a motorcycle.

On the road away from the beach, the popular Malibu bar was yet again expanding, the little supermarket at the bottom of the hill towards San Stefanos was open. Asleep on a chair outside was a contented tabby cat and people were taking coffee in Amourades.

My next stop was Roda on the north coast. I was to meet Mike and Jackie Connors, two ex pats, whom I had never before met. We had a mutual friend who put us in contact with each other. I wanted to speak to all sorts of people about what Corfu was like in winter and that included ex pats from the UK who had not only fallen in love with Corfu, they had moved there, lock, stock and barrel. Not only had they fallen in love with it and moved there, they had also made substantial efforts to integrate with the local community. They met me at the crossroads in Roda, I jumped in their car, launched into a whistle stop tour of Roda, more whistle than stop. As guided tours go, it was second to none.

Now I am an unashamed Roda fan. For me, it has everything. It is a proper 'living' village with local businesses and local people. There's plenty going on. The tourist bars and restaurants were obviously closed, but there were plenty that weren't. And strikingly, little or none of the development is tacky and gaudy. Read this description of Roda:

"Once a quiet fishing village, Roda has become a favourite holiday resort with families who delight in the long sandy beach and safe shallow water. Roda is on a fertile plain at the base of olive-clad hills & surrounded by the verdant hills and valleys of Pantokrator, Corfu's highest peak."

You've probably gathered that I didn't write that bit. It's the introduction to Roda on the excellent www.rodaonline.org website and, from my limited experience of the place, it's a very accurate description, too. In fact, my experience is largely driving through the town on the way to somewhere else or stopping for glass of something cold on the way back from somewhere. What it did appear to be was a real life 'living' resort that scaled back for winter, like everywhere else, but had a beating heart throughout the winter. That could be seen just driving through the place prior to visiting my next ex pat 'victims'.

It was just the sort of place I would love to stay at. There was plenty to do, a good number of highly rated eateries and a good range of accommodation, but it was relatively peaceful, certainly compared to its noisy neighbor, Sidari. If we had stayed at Roda many years ago, I can imagine we would have completely fallen in love with the place. There's still time!

I had arranged to meet Mike and Jackie Connors outside the Tropicana café where, I am led to believe, drinks are not free and it's not a club, either. Jackie had sent me a message to say that they might be a few minutes late because they had a dental appointment in the neighbouring resort of Acharavi. As ever, I was early for our engagement and sat on the wall near the café, watching the world – and the traffic – go by. I was by the main crossroads and facing me was the road leading to the beach. And then they were there. Mike, silver-hair, tanned and an unmistakable Welsh accent, Jackie from Suffolk, attractive, slim, a picture of health, in their little orange car. In I climbed and off we went. And we had company. Following close behind was another car, also negotiating the narrow streets, the sudden turns, the occasional three (or more) point turns. It was driven by, I soon discovered, Rick and Debbie Mansell from Leeds, but now from Corfu. Rick, slim, depressingly so for me, a man still suffering from post Christmas over-indulgence, but with as much grey hair as Mike, and Debbie, blonde, bubbly, attractive, again a picture of health and, I speculated, the potential life and soul of anyone's party.

I spent a couple of joyous hours with all of them and when I left it was as if I was saying goodbye to much-loved old friends. And they were all so generous with their time too, both during my trip and after I returned to the UK. Their stories, their account of life, were fascinating and I have written about them separately.

Mike and Jackie met at the Roda Beach Hotel in 1975. They had both travelled with their own friends and they fell in love (all say, Ahhhhh)! A year later they were back in Roda for their honeymoon. Jackie explains.

"We didn't come back for another 10 years. With three children, we only managed a couple of visits because of the cost, but it became our dream to one day retire and live here. When the children were independent sixth formers and University students, we were able to come on our own again. To our surprise, Roda had not changed much during the intervening years and it remained a wonderful resort. In 1975, there were only a couple of tavernas and one hotel along the beach, apart from the larger Roda Beach Hotel where we met and stayed."

I was very interested in how the move to Corfu came about. Jackie continued.

"Before we moved to Corfu, Mike had taken early retirement from his job as a group worker for adults with learning disabilities. I had been a qualified midwife although my last job was with HMP Prison in Bristol in the healthcare department.

"At first, we rented a small apartment near the village of Sfakera on a yearly basis. We would fly or drive over at different times of the year just to make sure we were certain about the move. We did look to buy an existing house and indeed we looked at a good few of them but the actual process of buying from Greek owners was fraught with problems. These included taxes, parts of some buildings being illegal, major damp issues and some places had more than one owner so it was next to impossible to get all the signatures on a contract, as some of them now lived abroad! We concluded that the best way to acquire a house which we knew had no hidden issues was to buy the land ourselves.

"We bought the land and were told of a Greek/Italian building company who wanted to start building on Corfu. Unfortunately, due to a split in the partnership, it took three years to get it finished!"

Mike drove us to the local Kafeneon, the Kafe Neon, known locally as Hectore's, the owner and father of Spiros who runs it, where we settled down for drinks and a chat. It was a traditional village establishment. Incredibly friendly and it was at this point I realised how firmly the four ex pats had integrated into Corfu life. They knew everyone and everyone knew them. There was plenty of friendly banter and, joy of joys, it was in Greek too!

"Mike and I have been learning Greek for two years now," said Jackie. "It is something we wanted to do. It is not the easiest language to learn but we have two two-hour sessions a week."

This was the direct opposite of me, who barely bothered to learn any Greek over the years and, I'm afraid, some of the people I met later on. I asked Jackie and Mike about the actual process of moving. What happened with their house at home, was it problem free?

"Well, no it was far from problem-free," said Jackie. "We both had elderly mothers so we decided to stay home with them a bit longer. We sold our large house in Bristol and bought an apartment, putting our belongings into storage before we could move. It turned out to be a wise move because Mike managed to contract a massive infection of his knee following a knee replacement and he had to spend the next year attending hospital for countless appointments. So it was just as well we bought the apartment. We've kept it too should we go back to the UK for any reason – not that we intend to! – and we rent it out on a short term contract."

I could happily have stayed in Hectore's all afternoon. The man himself turned up with pockets full of walnuts which he shoved into Jackie's handbag. He is in his eighties now but he doesn't look it and sometimes he will crack the nuts open with his bare hands!

"Hectore has a lot of land in the village with orange, lemon, koumquats and walnut trees, as well as chickens roaming free. Sometimes he will hand me what appear to be a pile of tissues but inside will be fresh eggs. Just the other day, he sent one of the villagers to our house with a big bag of lemons and koumquats. We will have to make some liqueurs as we have so many. I will save some for you!"

We all went back to Mike and Jackie's house just outside the village. The drive went up a slope and there it was: a magnificent, custom-built property overlooking the bay and the hills, the most amazing panorama you could imagine and perfect for quaffing that Metaxa nightcap. I will not attempt to describe the house because I would probably do the Connors a massive injustice but it was spotless, airy, atmospheric and, above all, it felt like home.

I asked about winter in Corfu. On the day we met, the sun shone brightly, it was around 13c, but felt much warmer. A gentle breeze came up from the south which meant you could barely feel it in the north.

"Since moving here, we have made many friends. Of our English friends, some live here all year round, a few go back to their UK homes for the winter. The first year we moved, I did have a slight panic attack and a feeling of isolation when the last flight to the UK left Corfu. I was missing our youngest daughter who was in Cardiff, I worried about ill health – what if we needed a doctor in the middle of the night, bearing in mind the nearest hospital is a 45 minute drive across the mountains."

"I don't think there's anything unusual feeling like that," I replied. "Moving house is one of the biggest and most stressful things you can do in life. Moving house to another country is something else altogether."

"No, that's right," nodded Jackie. "But it was shortly after that when I heard on the grapevine that people wanted to form a netball team in this part of the island. I met a lot of English ladies who live in Corfu, Debbie being one of them. Some of the younger ladies are married to Greek men and work in the tourist industry in the summer. We held a social night too so that all the men could come along and get to know each other and the lads played cricket for a few years too. I also do a 'bootcamp' at the gym and Mike plays every week for the local pool team. Also there is a sports bar open all winter with several (pool) tables open for use in the evening."

"I can see that you have made great steps to integrate with the local community, not least in learning Greek," I continued. "Do you participate in any of the more traditional activities?"

"Oh yes," replied Jackie, smiling. "Debbie and I joined the traditional dance group in Platonas two years ago and we dance in the amazingly beautiful Corfiot island costumes. We've done major festivals too. This year, we were invited to the Karousades and Sfakera groups, so that keeps us busy three nights a week.

"We try to be part of our village and attend religious festivals in our church, especially Easter, although the ceremonies can be lengthy and involve a lot of chanting! We love our village and the local people enjoy us being part of their lives too. They welcome us with hugs and kisses every time. They were very proud of me when I danced at the Sfakera Panagyri last year, dressed in the traditional black and white costume."

I was interested in the transition from the summer season to winter. What was it like?

"It's lovely when the tourist numbers start dwindling at the end of October and everything is winding down," said Jackie, warming to the subject. "By November, places are closing down, the roads are quiet again, with no tourists in hire cars, oblivious to traffic, stopping in the middle of the road to look at maps. Oh, and no Quad bikes!"

I could certainly imagine how that felt and Jackie's words described it perfectly. Knowing that the last tourist plane had flown and you were left in peace for the best part of six months. It wasn't difficult to see the attraction.

"How about shopping though?" I asked. "I am a fully paid up nightmare when it involves staying abroad, never mind living abroad. When I think about it, I'd miss so much! You can integrate into a new life and be part of a new community but you can't surely change what you are or what you eat?"

"We mostly buy and eat local produce, but we will go to Lidl and AB in town maybe once or twice a month, " smiled Jackie. "Mike likes the beer at Lidl!

"There are a couple of 'English' shops close to us in the north who get the things we miss from the UK, like decent teabags, HP Sauce, English mustard etc! We actually managed to get some Old Rosie Cider once! We tend to give our summer visitors shopping lists of what to bring with them – extra mature Cheddar cheese is right up there!

"And we miss cheap clothes too, like you get at Primark, Asda and some other department stores like M&S. There is an M&S here too but it's mega expensive.

"And there are things like the lack of items from a female point of view, like the lack of hair products. Deodrants and face creams are very expensive over here. I think the ladies in Corfu miss a good shop!"

But I'll tell you what: they don't miss much else! If this reads like a whinge, then it's my poor writing that has given a false impression. They are simply observations. As a mere male, I would probably think more down Mike's lines: where could I get some decent beer? But having lived with a woman for more than a quarter of a century – and that's a longer sentence than the Great Train Robbers received, I'll have you know – I suspect Jackie's comments are hardly unique.

"The only thing to dislike about winter is the rain," continued Jackie. "Sometimes it rains for days on end, often torrential. But we do understand that it keeps our island green, although it isn't good for the olives and grapes. There were no crops this year and the islanders are suffering. At least our ducks are happy!"

I wondered about Christmas too. I'll bet that was a lot of fun.

"Christmas here is great, apart from missing the kids," said Jackie. "We have started a tradition of Beach Boules on Christmas Eve with our friends. We wear Christmas hats, take a picnic and drink mulled wine. Then we sing carols, much to the amusement of passing Greeks!

"Christmas Day will be spent in a local taverna who will do turkey or a selection of meats with the roast. It will last all afternoon with a biggish group, lots of food and drink! Boxing Day is much the same and we all try and get together. Greek people tend to celebrate more in the New Year, but they love their decorations."

Mike piped up, "When summer ends, that's when our social life begins. The people who tend to enjoy their lives in Corfu are the ones who have hobbies to keep them active."

I had no doubt that was true. As you will read later on, I met people who lived a very different life in Corfu and, if I am being honest, whilst I liked them, their love of the island was, in my opinion, a little superficial. Mike and Jackie were undoubtedly part of the village they so adore. Of course they enjoyed some of the trappings of where they used to live because that was what they were and will always be, but the integration was, so far as I could tell, at an advanced stage or quite possibly complete.

On the subject of winter flights, Jackie could see the attraction. "From a personal point of view, it would be good to have direct flights to the UK in winter, but the flights would have to be cheap.

"Corfu is a beautiful and deeply cultural place to visit with many hidden treasures to find, amazing little museums and architecture. We are still exploring and finding these things ourselves. The carnival season in February is wonderful – everyone dresses up, there are bands and people dancing. The Greeks absolutely love their festivals before the solemnity of Easter begins.

"There are also many ancient Roman and Greek ruins around every corner, not only close to town but all over Corfu. We have the site of the ancient Temple of Apollo in Roda and more in Acharavi. The gift shops in Corfu Town close in winter but the streets are a joy to walk down."

My thought was this: the gift shops were indeed closed but would they remain closed, at least some of them, if there was a winter tourist trade? Perhaps it wouldn't matter anyway. Perhaps a winter tourist might be interested in things other than trinkets and souvenirs?

Rick and Debbie Mansell followed us on the all-too-brief tour of Roda until we ended up at Hectore's. Rick, silver-haired, slim, cigarette at the ready, Debbie, bubbly, smiley and an obvious example of that well known truism blondes have more fun. Rick was manager of two amusement centres – that's a lot of amusement! – for some 30 years before being made redundant. Debbie was manager of a café within one of them, which cooked homemade food. They first visited Corfu as recently as September 2004 on the recommendation of friends who were having a house built in Almiros, which is basically an extension of Acharavi.

"Our first visit to Corfu was to Kalami on the north east coast," explained Debbie. "We first visited Roda in 2006. After coming on holiday several times in the following years to stay with our friends we fell in love with the island. They took us to all the lovely hidden away places you would probably never have seen as a tourist.

"When Rick was made redundant, we made the decision to come and live in Corfu, maybe just for a year or so. First we had to find somewhere to live so we got our friends Pete and Karen to see if there were any places to rent. They were kind enough to look at a few places and came up with what we call our little house on the prairie. And we're just 100 metres from theirs!"

Ah, the little house on the prairie. Immediately, I had visions of that TV series from the 1970s starring Michael Landon who had previously been 'Little Joe' in Bonanza and later became Jonathan Smith, a real life Angel in 'Highway To Heaven'. One for the kids, there. Having carried out in depth research, I discovered that Little House on the Prairie was set on a farm at Walnut Grove, a minor coincidence given the heavy consumption of said nut product by British ex pats in Roda!

They finally moved to Corfu on 23 February 2012 – no approximations here, then – getting the boat from Hull to Zeebrugge, a mammoth drive to Venice, 26 hours on the grand canal to Igoumenitsa and then a short hop to Corfu.

"We found that arriving in winter made it easier to meet and introduce ourselves to the locals," continued Debbie. "We had already got to know some people from our friends who had been coming here for 30 years. We joined the local darts team, watched the local football teams, joined the pool league and I joined the netball team, which was where I met Jackie Connors. And I started dancing too which led to dancing in Corfu Town and in Sidari.

"The first years we were here, I worked at the airport as a travel rep., the following summer I worked at private villas, one in Nissaki, another in Kassiopi.

"We have struggled with the language though. We've attempted to learn but both of us have struggled. We find that we can have broken conversations in Greek/English in a kind of hybrid language we call Greeklish! We've certainly learned a lot from our Greek friends, like how to cut and prune Olive trees, how to clean the wood burner and to drive on the 'wrong' side of the road!"

I asked what the transition from summer to winter was like.

"In the summer, we are working like the Corfiots. Friends and family come to visit, we have barbecues, we go to the beach, we take our friends to the places where we were taken when we first came. But when the clocks go back, the direct flights have ended, all is quieter and cooler and our social activity comes alive.

"There is much more to do than you might imagine. We spend a lot of time in the garden planting things. The summer is very dry and the ground can get bare, but everything grows rapidly through the winter and into spring. We'll travel the island, always finding things we never saw before. On a good day, you can easily sunbathe. Maybe we'll go walking on the beaches, collecting driftwood for the fire. And of course, we visit the local tavernas which remain open in the winter. Our social group includes Greeks, Russians, Germans, Albanians and even some Welsh people!"

I'm sure Mike Connors would appreciate the last bit!

It surprised me to see just how much people got up to in winter. It's retirement, but not as we know it. There is always time to sit around and do nothing – it is my specialist subject – but could you do it all year round, and would you even want to?

"That's right," nodded Debbie. "We're used to working all our lives. We now have six months to do what we want, when we want and you can always find things to do. In the summer, we look after some properties on the east coast which keeps us busy, but winters are all ours. And whilst the touristy shops close for winter, the local shops are open all winter."

"And it's not long from the end of the tourist season until Christmas," I said.

"Less than a couple of months," she replied. "But the build up to Christmas is a much shorter build up. And it's a whole week of celebrations up to New Year's Day. Christmas seems to be celebrated a little more than it was when we first arrived three years ago. Some things are more expensive out here but you can get a Christmas lunch for €15!

"Easter is far bigger though," Debbie pointed out. "There's a massive build up from February onwards – carnivals, parties, kite flying day – and the pot smashing in Corfu Town is a sight to behold. Huge Greek urns are thrown from five, six storey buildings, half filled with water! They are painted in bright colours and covered in ribbons. It's supposed to bring you good luck if you pick up the broken pieces!"

Debbie doesn't think it would be worthwhile the airlines starting winter flights.

"It's probably not worth it for the island and I don't see Corfu as a winter destination. Winter tourism wouldn't really affect us, but remember it is a very small island.

"Not having direct flights can make it difficult," adds Debbie, "But having Skype, Facetime and the internet in general keeps you in constant contact with your loved ones. And if you do need to get back to the UK, you can do it, although not with a direct flight."

I haven't seen Rick and Debbie's Little House on the Prairie yet, but I am hoping to take a trip to Walnut Grove in the very near future.

I have no personal inclination to emigrate to Corfu, much as I love it, but it was not hard to see how someone could.

I had the road to myself as I headed, once more, along the north coast road to visit some places I had missed on my first adventure. The fishing village of Agios Stefanos is just past its busier neighbor, Kassiopi. It is not difficult to locate the steep road, down through the olive groves, but I somehow managed to miss it, turning round at one of the wide areas on one of the many switchback bends. The last part of the drive into the village is particularly steep and winding but then the lovely bay opens up. Here Albania seems but a stone's throw away, here at its closest point to Corfu. Behind the beach lie some white-walled buildings. Wooden jetties project out into the bay and in summer excursion boats in and out of the village vastly outnumber the fishing boats. The beach is nothing to write home about, but head north and the isolated beach at Avlaki is worth a walk, though it can be a tiring walk in the summer heat. Head south and you reach the very long beach at Kerasia. This is a favourite for excursion boats in the summer.

I had not been here for many years but my reaction was that little had changed. There were more residential properties in the hills – the area is not called Kensington on Sea for nothing and you would not expect the Rothschild Estate to resemble a sink estate – but for all that Agios Stefanos had undoubtedly retained its charms, even though there was no one around, save a solitary dog walker who had arrived by car. By now, it was early afternoon and whilst the sun still shone, the wind was beginning to get up and the mill pond nature of the sea to Albania was, as we inexperts say, choppy. I noted the Gallini restaurant where we had eaten contentedly in the past and there were three or four other shuttered tavernas along the front and just up from it. There was something very relaxing and appealing about sitting by the front with no noise apart from the swishing wind through the trees and the waves gently washing over the pebbles.

Why was no one else here? Well, the main reason was Corfu remains hard to get to in winter. I had met no one, so far, who didn't think the island wouldn't benefit from out of summer season visitors. I would have loved a coffee now. It was still plenty warm enough to sit outside, albeit not in summer wear.

The Verve's Bittersweet Symphony accompanied me as I drove back up the hill and then Lenny Kravitz joined me for my next stage, a short hop to Agni. I had arranged to meet the ever helpful, incredibly generous Perikles Katsaros, owner of the magnificent Taverna Nikolas later during my stay. Today, I would carry out a recce because I could. I have devoted space elsewhere in this book to Perikles, to talk about his life in Corfu, the history of the taverna and life out of season. As I have said in other chapters, he does not regard himself as being in competition with the two other restaurants in this tiny picture postcard village (Population – 10), and genuinely believes they all bring things to the (dinner) table.

The Taverna Agni looked like a bomb had hit it, with workman banging away at the shell of the building. Toulas, the seafood restaurant, barely looked like a restaurant at all with everything put away. Only Taverna Nikolas remained completely and adorably intact. All the tables and chairs had been put away in storage, probably inside the restaurant itself. The gentle breaking of the waves over Agni's pebbles was accompanied by constant banging and drilling from the Taverna.

At the top of the narrow road from Agni, the driver – me – has to join the main road on a switchback bend, which is blind from the left, and just hope nothing is coming up the hill. Of course it was as I went, kangaroo style, cutting in front of a large ice cream delivery lorry, the least likely vehicle I would have expected to see in Corfu in mid January. He was in a bit of a hurry too.

My radio didn't let me down, even if the weather began to. The Scorpions warned me of a wind of change – well, it had suddenly got very dark and it was raining – before the Manic Street Preachers said that if I tolerated this, my wife and children would be next. I'm afraid I sang along at the top of my voice, although I suspect the top of my range was not at the same level of clarity as James Dean Bradfield's!

What an experience this was turning out to be. I had prepared for Corfu in winter, planned in advance where to go and had a clear idea who I wanted to see and talk to. But it was turning into something else. Anyone who asked me about the project was told that it was to see what Corfu was like in winter but being there in winter made me wonder why no one else was there. I drove along the strip at Ipsos, heavy rain now beating on the windows of my Hyundai Something and, despite this episode of inclement weather, or maybe even because of it, Corfu had so much more to offer. It was not just sunbeds and swimming pools, certainly not in January, but it wasn't any less beautiful.

Where had the time gone? I edged my way back to Corfu Town and ordered a crepe from a creperie and this time, thanks to an English-speaking Corfiot, it actually contained everything I ordered. And it was absolutely delicious. I had given up trying to shelter and scoffed the crepe whilst walking the dimly lit, heavily puddled little streets. The locals had more sense and stayed in coffee houses and bars but, soaked to the skin, I was as happy as a pig in...er...excrement.

There were very few people around, except for large groups of police officers. My uneducated and wildly inaccurate guess was that the impending Greek General Election was the reason for their presence. They were there to deal with riots, that would be it. Arriving back at my hotel room, I could see that the football ground floodlights were on. It was then that I realised the awful truth: Kerkyra were entertaining AEK Athens in the Greek Cup and I knew nothing about it. A golden opportunity to engage in genuine Greek winter culture and I, a seriously fanatical football follower had not done my homework properly. I had checked the Greek Superleague fixtures prior to arrival and found that Kerkyra had no games whilst I was there. But it didn't occur to me to check whether there were Cup games. Grr! I didn't dwell on things for long. What was the point? But it was a little frustrating. Not for the first time, I headed up to the Café Kanoni for a few Pilsners. And not for the first time, everyone else was drinking coffee!

## 9. McGreeks

"We'll meet you in McDonalds" came the voice down the line, as I sat on the balcony of my hotel room, enjoying the mid morning sunshine.

"McDonalds? Are you serious? I've come all this way and you want to meet in McDonalds?" I replied, almost incredulous.

"They do lovely coffee and anyway, I fancy a McGreek!"

I had known Dave Chalmers, not his real name, for a very long time. I first met him in a Bristol pub back in the 1980s through a mutual friend. We hadn't kept in contact, save the odd exchange of risqué jokes by text and the odd email. He and his wife Tina (you guessed: not her real name) had come to live in Corfu in the late 1990s and settled in a small village near the west coast. I have to be careful what I say because, after all, he's an old mate and he will read this, even though I have preserved their anonymity. He's a Scot, Tina is from the north of England. He worked for a government department, she worked for a different government department. Both on the wrong side of 50 now, they, like other people I had met, had taken the plunge.

I parked up in the large car park which has now pretty well taken over the boundary of the cricket pitch. The skies were slate grey and a drizzle hung over the town. Reluctantly, with the Liston and all its stylish cafés to my right, I headed to the world's favourite fastfood entity. Dave was waiting for me, tall, slightly overweight, grey thinning hair and wearing a short sleeved checked shirt and some light three quarter length trousers.

"What are you going to have?" he asked, in his broad Scottish brogue.

"Coffee is fine for me," I replied. "Where's Tina?"

"Back home!" he snapped.

He made the order in extremely broken Greek, which was really the art of speaking English, but much louder with a Scottish inflection, with the emphasis on certain words, and returned to join me.

"Why here?" I enquired. "This is an odd choice for someone who lives in Corfu."

Dave smiled. "It's easy to find and anyway, I like a bit of a heart attack on a tray sometimes. How's things with you?"

I replied that I was fine. I had finished work the previous June and was between work. I was more interested in what he was up to.

"Oh, a bit of this and a bit of that. I did a bit of work repairing lawnmowers last year which was surprisingly busy. I'd always had this thing about lawnmowers. And when someone said theirs was broken, I said I'd have a look at it. Then one thing led to another."

"I never had you down as a handyman," I said, very surprised as this unusual turn of employment events.

"It didn't last," he replied. "Before that, we 'd done summer work with the rental companies – you know, maintenance, cleaning. I even did some airport transfers for a while. That sounds nice until you're taking knackered Brits to the airport for the 3.50 am flight to Stansted. At least the airport runs used to be on a Monday and a Friday but these days they're all the time now that easyJet and Ryanair fly virtually every day of the week.

"Summers became a real drag after a while. We were just working through the best months, not seeing the very things we had come out here to do and doing nothing in the winter. It can get a bit boring to be honest."

Dave's McGreek with added large fries arrived and he tucked in.

"Once we knew we were coming out here, we sold our place at home," he continued, in between mouthfuls. "We wanted to be somewhere relatively quiet but near enough other English people. We settled on a small house near Pelekas. All the legal stuff was a real pain and so was getting here. I had to drive all the way to Corfu and back twice.

"It was a novelty at first. I don't think we gave it all a lot of thought when we decided to emigrate. It was almost a whim. We sort of made it up as we went along. The first few summers were great. We had some money left from the house sale and from a pay off I had from work. We would go the beach by day and go to the bars and tavernas by night. I think we expected it to last forever and I don't think it occurred to us that the money might not last forever. We knew we would have to work for a living someday. It was a bit of a shock to the system. The summers were what it was all about and then we were working all the way through with barely a day off."

"So what's your village like?" I asked. "Do you have friends there?"

After a short pause Dave replied: "Well, sort of. There are some British couples we meet around the area, although none of them live in our village. There used to be, but they've either died or gone home. There's nothing in our village other than a small kafeneon, nowhere to socialize. We have to go elsewhere to see people."

"So, when everyone has gone home in early November, what's it like?" I asked.

"Quiet," he said, firmly. "Where we are nothing much changes but the resorts nearby, like Agios Georgios, are just dead. There's nothing much to do either.  We live off the money we made in the summer, like the Greeks do really.

" We've got grown up kids now.  They usually come out in the summer, although they didn't this year.  Obviously, we miss them.  We've flown home every year for Christmas.  They don't really celebrate it here.  And we like to be with the family."

It seemed a bit of an isolated, almost lonely, existence to me.

"It can be, I suppose," replied Dave.  "But we've got cable TV so we get all the programmes from home.   There's shops to buy British stuff, although it costs an arm and a leg.  I don't know whether it's the Euro, but everything is expensive here.  It was cheaper when Greece had the drachma."

I agreed with that, although there was little evidence that Greeks now wanted to return to it.  I wondered what an average winter day was like for him.

"A lot of the time it's chucking it down.  Sometimes for days on end and when it rains here, it really rains.  You might be stuck in the house for days on end, not seeing anyone. We have to travel a bit to see anyone, visit a bar.  There's quite a culture of Brits abroad, having drinks parties, basically sticking together.  I can't be having that."

"Isn't that a bit lonely," I asked. "It seems to me you're detached from almost everyone, local Greeks and British ex pats."

"Well, that's true," said Dave, warming to his subject. "We have got friends and we'll get together for a few beers from time to time, but we're not social animals."

"Well, you were back home!" I recalled.

"We wanted a different kind of life when we came out here."

"But you don't know what it is yet?"

"Look – I'm happy with what we've got. I don't want to go home to all that weather, the strikes, the crime, the dog eat dog. Britain's a mess these days."

We agreed to disagree on this one.

The McDonald's gastronomical experience over, we took a walk down the damp streets of Corfu. I pointed out to Dave that I probably knew more about the town than he did, and he lived here. He acknowledged that was probably true. He won't mind me saying that he doesn't share the love I have of the town, or of the island itself. He said as much. It was more the lifestyle that appealed. I asked whether he would ever return home.

"What would I want to do that for?" he responded. "There's nothing left for me at home, apart from the family. I don't own anything back home. I still feel Scottish and all that, but I don't want to live there anymore.

"See that?" he said, pointing at an old man selling food. "Disgusting!"

"I love Corn Cobs!" I replied, laughing.

"What – cooked on coals, poured half a ton of salt on a corn cob? What's that all about? Do you see those blokes in that hut by the road? That's Syriza, the lefties. We've got an election next Sunday. That lot are going to win. Frightening really."

I did see the hut with the people from Syriza and they were the only political campaigners I saw throughout my entire visit. It was as if either no one else could be bothered or because the political parties knew the result in advance. We were approached by a Syriza person, which Dave dealt with in the traditional manner by saying, "Me no speak Greek."

As we walked on I pointed out that living here he should learn Greek.

"There's no point," he said, shrugging his shoulders. "A lot of the locals speak good English, with the rest a few words is usually all right. Up in the hills it can be a pain, mind!"

It felt to me that they'd not really integrated into the Greek community.

"No point," he said, shaking his head. "I feel like a tourist who lives here all the time. I don't feel Greek, never will. I mean, good luck to them and all that. They've got their ceremonies and festivals. They're not for me, but then I'm not Greek, am I?

"You'll write all this, won't you? Make me look a right one."

"Don't worry, I won't use your real name!"

"You'd better bloody not!" he roared, except that he didn't say bloody. I haven't changed anything else.

I was curious. "Are you really happy here? Is this really what you wanted, what you expected, when you decided to come and live here?"

He shook his head. "I don't know what I was expecting. We've just made it up as we went along. It's not perfect, but I'm not going home, certainly not for a while."

That was a bit of an admission. "Not for a while? So it might not be forever?"

More shoulder shrugging. "Who knows? You never know what tomorrow might bring. At the moment, it seems to bring a whole load of rain."

We emerged onto the Liston. It was even darker now, the grey clouds had given way to black, the drizzle had turned into proper rain. The streets were even more empty than before. A few noisy mopeds whizzed by, ridden by callow youths wearing imitation leather jackets and of course no helmets, a group of police officers stood sheltering next to one of the cafés, drinking coffee and laughing uproariously. I thanked Dave for his time and wished him luck.

"I don't need luck, son," he laughed. Maybe see you in the summer? Do that brewery tour."

"You never know!" I replied, shaking hands, before I returned to my Hyundai Something.

I am not sure whether I learned a lot. I left feeling a little vacant, a little empty, in two minds as to whether to include this bit in my book. Dave knew how I felt about his life in Corfu so reading this won't come as a surprise to him. I think he was happy – there were no signs that he actively hated it in Corfu – but there seemed to be little purpose to it. But perhaps some people don't need a feeling of purpose in their lives. Living their lives might just be enough.

And another thought went through my mind: I am not sure I would be much different from him. I am not naturally a socialite by any stretch of the imagination, I am a horrendously fussy eater and, on a bad day, I do enjoy a McDonalds. These are some of the reasons I live in England and not Corfu.

# 10. Perikles and Theo

I never promised that this book would be anything than a haphazard travelogue of my winter visit to Corfu. There are numerous excellent guides that will provide all the information your average tourist will need. But as the project developed, I became convinced that there was an opportunity for Corfu to expand its tourism, in addition to its entirely justified reputation for being a paradise island. This was due to a couple of things. Firstly, the evidence of my own eyes. It became apparent very quickly that Corfu still had potential, not to develop, but to expand its range of tourism to include the winter. Later, I shall expand on this idea. Secondly, I did not meet a single Corfiot who didn't think Corfu wouldn't benefit by direct winter flights from the UK (and possibly other places too).

Integral to my ideas was Perikles Katsaros, owner of Taverna Nikolas at Agni. I had written to him before I left the UK to arrange a meeting but I had still not heard anything when my plane landed in Athens. The rest is history and, of course, recorded earlier in this book. There he was, as large as life, with that unmistakable (now greying) moustache, in the departure lounge. We exchanged telephone numbers and actually met on three occasions. "I am here to help you," he told me. "You tell me what you want to do and I will help you." And help me he did, over and over again. Although Perikles is not getting any taller, there was certainly less of him. "I have lost several kilos!" he announced proudly, and it showed. It must be all that healthy eating! I didn't have the heart to say that if I went to his amazing taverna on a frequent basis, I would gain several kilos in a very short space of time.

We met at the Libra D'Oro café and another day at the Taverna. On my last night, he drove to my hotel and took me to one of his favourite eateries. I'll come back to that later. We spoke for hours at our two meetings and rather than confusing the reader (and myself!), I have combined my notes for the purpose of this book.

As you arrive in Agni and park in the small field with the sign post Taverna Nikolas (the other tavernas have their own parking areas appropriately signed), the pebble beach is only 40 or 50 yards away at most and Taverna Agni is further to the left. Nearer on the left is Toula's Seafood Restaurant and immediately on the right is Taverna Nikolas. Each taverna has its own jetty for the visiting boats of which in summer there are plenty. In summer, there are sunbeds aplenty in front of each taverna and the tavernas buzz with activity. And you can smell the beautiful foods being prepared long before you get to the beach.

Taverna Nikolas was built in 1892 by Perikles' grandfather who was also called Perikles. It started off as a kafeneon and the family lived upstairs. It survived two world wars, despite Agni being occupied by Italian and German forces in world war two. As a teenager, Perikles went to school in Corfu Town where his mother rented a house for them to live in, there being no school in the area. Every Saturday they would take the boat back to Agni. And wisely, given what the future would bring, he learned English at a foreign language school in order to communicate with halfwits like me who turned up in Greece with the ability only to use a handful of Greek words. He got his first job at the giant Nissaki Beach Hotel in 1970 (you still can't miss it when driving down the north east coast) where his English improved still further.

Then, in 1973, after having spent some time at a tourist school, he said to his father that he wanted to take over the running of the kafeneon. But he didn't want to run it like it had been run: he wanted to turn it into a taverna. It is hard to imagine now what hard work it must have been to change from a kafeneon to a taverna with no money and no road down from the main road. Everything they needed was brought in by boat from Kouloura. But on 1 May 1974, Taverna Nikolas opened. The absence of a road meant that visitors would either arrive by boat or on foot from nearby Kalami or Nissaki.

"Sometimes the weather would be very bad, too bad for the boats, and people were stuck in the taverna," recalled Perikles. "I would get a torch and lead people back to their hotel. They would then thank me and give me drinks and I would get back very late! The next day I woke up very early to go to Corfu Town to go shopping and when I got back, the guests would be at the jetty helping me to carry it into the taverna. They were the good old days."

Perikles talks a lot about "the good old days" and he would return to them in a heartbeat. In the 'Brief History' booklet available from the taverna, he says, "Relationships meant more and there was a great deal of honour and hospitality extended to one and all." You get a further glimpse into what he means when it describes the death of his parents, tragically in the same year. 'It was a huge loss for him. He sees his father's boat but he is not on it. He looks for his mother in the kitchen but she is not in it.' He didn't talk to me about them and I respected him to not press him on the subject, but their influence on his life and the success of the taverna are in no small part down to them.

Of the two tavernas that have arrived more recently, Perikles is relaxed. "The only competition I have is with myself. I get on well with the other owners and we all share the same belief which is that Agni should stay exactly as it is. Anyway, I love what I'm doing."

Perikles asked me what I thought of the taverna being very traditional in terms of food. I told him that this was what brought us to the taverna in the first place, as well as the fact that the food is always good. Oh and the hospitality, too! He nodded, "Good, good. It is important to me that the taverna continues the way it is. It will be handed down to my son."

He took me inside the taverna and it bristles with history. There are countless photos from "the good old days", amongst which are those of celebrities. James Bond (Roger Moore) ate at the taverna every day when filming 'For Your Eyes Only', eating trout served without olive oil. He became a firm friend of Perikles, as did Jon Pertwee, my favourite Doctor Who, who stayed in nearby Kaminaki. "Lovely man"" said Perikles, reminding me that Pertwee was a keen and adventurous watersports enthusiast. Princess Margaret ate there too, with her friends from the Rothschild estate high in the hills. And Toyah Wilcox became acting manager of Nikolas for a BBC show called Fasten Your Seatbelt back in the 1980s. Perikles appeared frequently in the show which is available on You Tube and he smiled at the memory. All these old photographs, and many more, cover the walls. I have spent many a happy hour reading each and every one every time I visit.

Winter is not a time for standing still though. Whilst time goes slowly in Agni, the taverna needs careful attention and maintenance. It has to be 'aired' on a regular basis, which was why there was no musty smell when I went inside, and there is always something to do, whether that was planning for the new season or general work.

"In winter, I go to Corfu very often," he told me. "I could do my banking on-line but I prefer to do it in person, to meet people, to find out the news. And I travel often to my guest house on the mainland.  Normally, I go with the ferry although not the day I met you at Athens!"

I asked him what he felt about Corfu as potentially being more than just a summer sun island.  "We need winter flights, " he said.  "Without direct flights from the UK, nothing will change.  But there is a chance that there could be holidays for people.  Perhaps we could open the taverna at weekends where visitors would come to the taverna and cook the Greek food.  They would buy it, then cook it."

"There was talk, wasn't there, about direct flights in winter?" I asked.

"Yes, but there was nothing serious.  Business people worked very hard to get Ryanair to fly to Corfu in the summer and we succeeded.  No airline will fly here in the winter unless they can make money."

It was interesting to listen to Perikles.  He remains passionate about the taverna, cares deeply about serving traditional food and takes genuine pleasure from returning visitors, of whom there are many!  He is pro-active too, not sitting on his laurels.  I won't bore the reader with what went on in getting Ryanair to fly to the island but it didn't just happen and it cost money too.  It was an investment.  A Corfiot sprat to catch a British mackerel (my words, not his).  Yes, he does talk a lot about the old days but he knows how to separate them from the here and now.  His attitude reminded me of that of

Dimitris Kourkoulos from Arillas, who wanted to improve the resort, not develop it. And again, if you developed Agni, the reason for going there would be gone. More than anyone, Perikles gets that and so do the owners of the newer tavernas in the bay.

On the face of it, in summer, Agni does appear to be an upmarket resort. Huge sea-going yachts moor in the bay and their occupants discharge themselves to the beach by the way of small dinghys. And the well-to-do occupants of Kensington On Sea make their way down from the hills to while away the hours under the Ionian sun, eating and drinking some of the best fare you can find on the island. But Nikolas is not a class-based taverna. The food is always good and fresh but crucially it's affordable. You really do meet the world and his wife (and her husband). And Perikles welcomes them all.

So winter in Agni is very quiet, apart from the odd crash from the Taverna Agni where the building work continues apace (or at Greek pace, anyway). An old lady tended her garden but nothing else was moving. With only 10 residents, there was no one moving apart from Perikles and me.

A few days later, Perikles arranged to collect me from the hotel to go out for something to eat. Now this was good news since he was bound to know somewhere very tasty! It was just after 6.00 pm when he arrived in his tiny little van, which he pointed out was perfect for negotiating the road down to Agni. I squeezed myself in and off we went. He took us to the harbour area and parked up. We went into a few places where the owners were still firing up the coals and food would not be ready for a while. Whilst both grill rooms were of excellent quality, we rather needed to eat now. "I know the place," said Perikles, and off we went up the hill. And soon we found it.

It was a classic grill room (The Three Pigs, I think), well away from the tourist trail, run by a family. We went inside and took a seat. It was a takeaway and an eat-in establishment, with a home delivery service too, by way of a man on a small motorcycle who was clearly a very busy man. There was no written menu as such. Perikles asked what I would like. On the grill were two goat's heads, a line of chicken, pork and beef, grilling gently over the simmering coals. The smells just made me hungrier. A young lady came over to take our order. Perikles suggested we get a variety of meats and some salad. Oh and a beer for me, but not for him, the responsible driver! It was the old adage: go where the locals go and you will not be disappointed. I certainly wasn't disappointed.

A steady stream of customers came and went, greeting the tall, balding owner in the hearty and friendly tones of people who had been there before. And then our meal arrived. Wow! There was nothing fancy about the large plate in front of us, but it looked terrific. Great lumps of beef, pork kebabs and chicken pieces, an industrial portion of chips and, of course, a classic Greek salad with large chunks of feta cheese on top. It looked enough to feed a small army. My plate groaned with exquisitely tasty meat – what a surprise in Greece! – and anything else I could put on it. Seriously, it was as good as anything I had ever eaten in Corfu. I told Perikles he should watch out or I would eat here instead. That was assuming I could ever find it again without his assistance.

Utterly satisfied but more than slightly bloated, I had to submit with at least half a composite animal remaining on the plate. Despite the rapid rate of customers coming and going, the staff remained in typical laid-back Corfiot mode. The delivery man came back and forth at a rapid rate of knots, carrying out vast quantities for those who probably didn't fancy venturing out in what had become a very wet evening.

"That was great," I told Perikles.

"Would you like anything else?" he asked, with a mischievous grin. "I am going to buy something for the family." With that, he made his way to the counter and barked out an order which would soon be arriving at one of the best tavernas in Corfu. What a compliment this was. Here was a man who prided himself on serving the best food he could get for his taverna, getting a takeaway from this modest grill room in Corfu Town. They always say 'Follow the locals' when it comes to eating out and you couldn't get a better example than this. I suspect I was the only foreigner visiting that evening but I figured that if word got out, there might be a whole lot more visiting in the future. There was not a great deal in terms of vegetarian options, other than the traditional Greek salad, groaning with house brick sized chunks of Feta (I am exaggerating, but only slightly) on top of the crispy crunchy vegetables. I could have filled up on that alone.

Perikles was given his takeaway and we returned to his little red van in driving rain. It was a Corfu with which I was unfamiliar. A cool winter's evening, the rain was falling, the wind was brisk, but if I had somehow been placed here as if by magic, I would have still known instantly where I was. We drove down by the port, splashing through huge puddles along the way. One large boat appeared to be boarding as he drove past, rather than into, the port itself.

"Will you be visiting the taverna this summer?" asked Perikles.

"Oh yes," I replied, not adding that I would probably be lynched by my family if we didn't. "Taverna Nikolas is a very important part of our holiday. Shall I call you when we are here to reserve a table?"

He nodded. "Many days we are full at lunchtime. Telephone me and I will reserve a table for you. You have my number!"

Perikles Katsaros has a motto. 'Everyone who comes to Taverna Nikolas as a customer, leaves as a friend.' I wasn't going to argue with that and I felt, as we shook hands and said farewell, that I was his new best friend in the whole world. I wasn't, obviously, but that's how he makes you feel. I had learned so much about Perikles, his magnificent taverna, the tradition and I knew now what happened in winter, which wasn't a lot but could be so much more.

"I'm here for you, to help in any way I can", the man had told me and he was more than true to his word. Not only had I enjoyed the chance meeting at Athens airport, he had gone out of his way three times to see me. If I am being honest, his company was so engaging, his enthusiasm boundless, I forgot on more than one occasion the reason I was seeing him in the first place. Perikles even talked about Bristol where he had been and we talked about a Greek restaurant in Clifton with which he was familiar but I knew no longer existed. If nothing else, I now understood the feel of Corfu in winter and I liked it. And what's more, I knew that it wasn't just me who would like it. Out of season, yes, but out of bounds for holidays? I was now convinced it wasn't. Agni would not enjoy quite so many luxurious ocean-going yachts in January but its isolated beauty remained. It lost nothing by comparison to the summer.

"It has been good to speak with you, my friend," he said as we shook hands. If you need anything else, let me know. You have my number." And with a cheery wave, he was gone. The lights flickered through the trees by the hotels and the houses and the rain still fell heavily. I decided to get my storm clothes and take a late night walk down to the causeway at Kanoni. For some odd reason, I don't mind getting soaking wet and tonight it was just as well. It goes without saying that I was alone as I strolled down the steep and slippery steps. I could hear wind chimes from the middle distance across the causeway to Perama but apart from that, and the howling of the now strong wind, there was nothing. For once, the airport runway lights to my right were fully illuminated so a flight arrival was imminent. I had specifically requested a room that overlooked the lagoon – that is to say the runway – in the hope and expectation that I could spend time on my balcony watching the planes land and take off in slightly fewer numbers than in the summer, but – hey! – there would be a good few, wouldn't there? As it turned out, there wouldn't be a good few; there would normally be three flights a day, all to Athens, one in the morning, one at lunchtime and one at night. Ah well. It was a nice view.

And this time I wasn't disappointed. Through the murk, way in the distance to the south east, were the unmistakable lights of a large aircraft. I made my way to the centre of the causeway where I had watched so many planes before in glorious sunshine. There are huge landing lights before the causeway to guide the planes in. This one, an Aegean Airways A320 Airbus flew over Mouse Island, roared over the causeway and hit the runway with a double thump. A bit of reverse thrust and then back to the noise of the wind and rain. With a final glance down the coast towards Benitses, it was time to dry off.


Anyone who has done a package holiday to a European island will probably have been given the opportunity to go on a boat trip. Certainly in Corfu there are a good few trips from the various resorts. There are trips to the mainland, there are trips to Paxos and its baby sister Anti Paxos, the latter of which can closely resemble the old 'Bounty' advert ('The Bounty hunters – they came in search of paradise,' ran the commercial, not adding, 'But ended up with a two-piece coconut flavoured chocolate bar') and nowadays there are even day trips to Albania.

As the reader may have already gathered, these are not the musings of a sophisticated culture-vulture, as my long-suffering partner will testify, all too willingly, so the guided tour of something of historical value and interest will probably not be on my radar. I can spend all year learning all about history – not that I do – but apart from reading books, my annual Greek sojourn is not there to unduly tax my brain cells. I know which tavernas I like, I know which beaches I like and I also know that for me, there is only one place to go for boat trips: Theo's Boats.

Theo Gasteratos has been running Theo's boat trips for over 30 years and I have had the good fortune of enjoying a good number of them in that time. There is nothing to Theo. He is five foot not a lot, usually clad in little more than a flamboyant pair of shorts and a scruffy hat. The day trippers on his boat can be the 24 hour party people from Kavos (don't worry: that trip is solely for them) which ends up in a 'Cave Rave' or, more commonly, families and couples of all ages, enjoying the trip up the coast of Corfu or across to the mainland. It is, I promise you, the best boat trip anywhere, ever.

A typical trip would leave Corfu Town in the morning, chug out into the channel as people gradually begin to wake up when the music will start and people will lie across all parts of the immaculately maintained boat until it reaches the mainland where everyone disembarks, participates in water sports, grills pleasantly under the hot sun and a little bit later people gather at the barbeques to consume sensational chunks of pork or chicken, salad and Tsatsiki. Oh and have a few glasses of very, very nice wine. Throughout all this, Theo is the perfect host. He has a great sense of humour, his excellent English enables him to be fluent in banter and he spends the entire day ensuring that everyone is happy. His energy is incredible which is just as well since this is not a 9 till 5 Monday to Friday job.

"We usually begin the boat trips from the end of April and finish around the end of October," says Theo. "But this can vary according to the season. We operate seven days a week throughout the summer season."

"Seven days a week?  That must be very tiring?" I said.

"I am passionate about my job, which is actually not a job for me.  After my family, I would consider it to be my second love, my hobby, if you like, which gives meaning in my life.  I love British people.  I have spent half my life working with them and part of me now feels British!"

You press the button with Theo and off he goes, always giving, filling up my notebook.  "We run trips to the north of Corfu or a tour to the mainland.  The one and only Theo's BBQ is always on the list!"

"I've been on that one a few times," I said.  "The food is always terrific and so is the wine!  I'll bet I'm not the only one who keeps coming back?"

"There are a lot of people who keep coming back again and again," he smiles.  "I have seen children who used to come with their parents coming back as teenagers and then coming with their own family.  It's like a tradition that when someone visits Corfu they come with us once again."

"Is there a secret to your success?" I asked.

"I think people know that no matter how much time has passed since they were last with us, they will get the same smiles, the same enjoyable atmosphere and the same quality service," he said.

"It's not just you though, is it? There are other familiar faces on the boat!"

Theo laughed: "It has always been a family business with three boats. But now my brothers have retired, I am the only one running the business with one boat. My son Harris, who is going to take over the business in a few years, my wife Maria and two other sailors work with me."

The impression you might get from Theo's boat trips might be that here was someone who enjoyed a good party all year round. This was, after all, the man who is a born entertainer with a microphone in his hand. I remember being on his boat as he went slowly into the very beautiful Kalami Bay with him wishing good day to the holidaymakers drifting around on lilos and pedalos, one topless lady I remember "with the big boobies". And he got away with it because of what and who he is. It was no more threatening than a seaside postcard although much, much funnier. And here was the man who was not shy with the spray foam, although he always got more back than he gave out and he always ended up in the sea! But it turned out the partying was for the summer season only. The winter was very different.

"I was born in Lefkimmi and I still live there. The winter for me is all about repairing and preparing the boat to get it ready for the next season. As soon as the summer ends, the boat has to get out of the water so all the work can take place and that requires a lot of my time. So a normal winter's day for me begins at 8.00 am and finish at 5.00 pm."

"So winter isn't boring?" I asked.

"I have no time to get bored. After a tiring day I really enjoy an early evening nap. I have no other work in the winter as boat cruises are not very popular during winter because in Corfu winter is cold and rainy.

"I rarely go out in the winter. I am not that type of person. Instead, I enjoy my family life and I prefer inviting friends and relatives and friends at home for dinner. After working so hard in the summer and dealing with thousands of people, I look forward to relaxing at home. Also, I will visit my daughter who lives in Dubai."

And I totally get that. I know just how hard Theo works in the summer. These boat trips are not just for a few hours: they are all day and every day. And that's just when they are at sea. No wonder he is looking to hand the business on to his son. I am not getting paid for saying this but make sure you sail with Theo before he goes back to Lefkimmi for the summer as well as the winter.

I asked whether Corfu would benefit from direct winter flights from the UK. These are Theo's exact words:

"Corfu would be an ideal weekend destination

for couples and families during winter. There is a beautiful, historic centre with shops and restaurants to visit. They can also explore our picturesque villages together with the tropical green countryside and taste our local wine and olive oil. It is an island fully dependent on tourism so any visitors' increase during winter as well would be an enormous enhancement for our economy."

I am not going to pretend that my findings are in any way scientific and for all I know, the overwhelming majority of Corfiots might be appalled at the prospect of small legions of Brits visiting in mid winter as well as during the summer, but I doubt it. Theo, who treasures his 'down time' with his family, even if it isn't really down time at all, what with his work on the boat, believes that direct flights would benefit the Corfu economy. The bigger picture cuts across everyone's thinking. Not, 'How much money can I make?' but how can additional tourism help the island to benefit business in general. They really were all in it together.

With that Theo bade farewell. He was flying to see his daughter in Dubai in two days, something he was really looking forward to. I promised that my family and at least one other family would book a trip with him in the summer of 2015.

## 11. A winter's tale

Having never before written a book, I wasn't expecting my best-laid plans to turn into something else, but that was exactly what happened. My long-held dream to visit Corfu in winter, to see and report back on what it was like, particularly in the resorts, was finally achieved. I had certainly got the 'feel' for this beautiful island 'out of time' and it turned out to be pretty well how I expected it to be. The people I met, some by accident, some by design, drew different kinds of pictures but generally the winter was a season to be enjoyed, not dreaded. The contrast between winter in England and summer in England was not that great in many ways. In fact, it was much the same in terms of sunlight and rainfall. It was just the temperatures that shifted. In Corfu, they did have seasons. To only slightly misquote Rod McKuen and Jacques Brel, "They had joy, they had fun, they had seasons in the sun." Well, not all of them.

There is the presumption that Corfu is a summer island and that's that. People go there for the sun and the sea and there's nothing else to it. But if that was true, and all people really did want was the sun and the sea, people wouldn't bother to travel that far. Instead of a 1000 mile flight, with transfers at both ends, sometimes lengthy, stressful and usually tedious transfers, we'd all go to the Costas, wouldn't we? Or Portugal? After all, summer in Spain is not much different temperature wise to Corfu and in winter it's warmer. Do we really go just for the sun and sea? You could take it even further. Do people go to Jamaica just for the sun, sea and rum punches, or the Maldives to eat seafood and go snorkeling? If they do, it's an awfully expensive way of holidaying when they could fly somewhere much nearer and much cheaper and do much the same thing? No, it isn't as simple as that.

We go to Corfu for all sorts of reasons. We love the sun, of course, and we love the beach, the sea, the pool and the sun bed. We also love the scenery, we love the hospitality, we love the food, we love exploring and we love the variety. We cannot get that in Costa Del Pom, with its miles of unspoilt 'English' pubs. (Other Costas are available.) We are not blind to the attractions of other Greek islands. It's just that we are in love with Corfu. And we visit the island every summer. There is no doubt that some aspects of Corfu are exclusive to the summer experience. The waterparks at Agios Ionannis (Aqualand) and Acharavi (Hydropolis) can only be summer attractions. The enormous holiday complex at Aqualand lies dormant for six months of the year because no one wants to go on the rides in the depths of winter. There is no potential for winter holidays there, not least because in the case of Aqualand it is, relatively speaking, in the middle of nowhere.

And Kavos. Who would want to visit the party capital in the depths of winter? I am of an age where a winter visit to Kavos is infinitely preferable to a summer one but let's be realistic: a vital component of a clubbing/boozing/18-30 type holiday will be the weather. The same would apply to Ayia Napa in Cyprus, San Antonio in Ibiza and Malia in Crete. It just won't happen, forget it.

But beyond the beach, I began to realise, as you have probably gathered, that I began to see a huge potential as Corfu the winter holiday destination. Many people who come to Corfu in summer might not see the attraction of Corfu in winter. It is a time to grill gently and contentedly under the Ionian skies, putting behind you that long year of hard work in the real world. Speaking purely on an anecdotal level, because I have no idea whether statistics actually exist, I get the impression that a large percentage of visitors never leave the resort in which they stay. They have a routine that they like. Why waste time travelling the length and breadth of Corfu when you can instead walk 10 feet to the pool bar for another Mythos? I get that. I've been that man. I've also been the man who has flown to Tenerife in midwinter for a seven day culture-free break where the need to speak the local lingo is not required and the food is, comfortingly, English. More importantly, whilst the sun was not exactly scorching hot, it was warm and dry. It is satisfying in a warmed-up Blackpool kind of way. And there is nothing wrong with that, either. It takes all sorts.

So in terms of package beach holidays, then forget Corfu in winter. It's the perfect summer island for splashing around on a pedalo but you would need wet gear to do the same thing in winter, which rather negates the effect. I do not pretend to have carried out a scientific opinion poll of Corfiots and British ex pats as to whether they would welcome winter tourism, but I am in no doubt that a lot of people would welcome it. We are not talking about mass tourism here because I doubt whether the numbers would be there, but I do see potential, a gap in the market. There is one main obstacle though: direct flights.

EasyJet runs many flights to Corfu from the start of the season right up until November. From Bristol, my local airport, there are already three flights per week. Whilst the big charter companies like Thomas Cook and Thomson fly on the big 'change' days – Monday and Friday – easyJet flies throughout the week, especially from Gatwick. And in more recent years, Ryanair has launched flights to the island, after much negotiation with the business community who have invested significantly with the airline.

The arrival on the market of 'low cost' airlines reflects the change in which we book our holidays. They do not offer package holidays where the accommodation is included (although easyJet does have an 'arm' which books accommodation, flying is their main priority and earner) and those who travel make their own plans. This was almost unheard of when I started going to Greece in the 1980s, but now it's commonplace. The independent traveller would be the more likely to visit Corfu in winter. I think it would be too complex for a charter company to run what would effectively be a niche operation out of the normal holiday season and fill the flights and hotels. I would never say never, but I cannot foresee a situation where the charter companies would look to launch package holidays to Greece out of season.

So I look to the low cost airlines to open the doors to a winter in Corfu. One argument I heard was this: if the airlines thought they could make money from winter flights, they'd have launched flights before. And after all, they do know a little more than I do about the travel business! Perhaps they have already assessed the possibilities and concluded it wasn't worth their while. Profit margins with low cost carriers can be narrow. Put simply, airlines are not a charity and they will not launch new services unless they think they can make money. The purpose, the new, evolved purpose, of this book is to put forward an argument that there is much to see and do in a Corfu winter and that airlines could make money by starting direct flights.

There is nothing wrong with the Aegean Airlines' services to Athens and then on to the islands, in this case Corfu. The scheduled flights I took were excellent. And it seems they have flexibility in their operation. For example, I was told by one of the Aegean officials that if a particular flight to an island was especially popular and there were too many potential customers for a small propeller plane, they'd insert a much larger jet aircraft, an Airbus, into that slot. In fact, I really enjoyed the experience of flying to Athens for a connection to Corfu. It was time-consuming, for sure, especially on the way home, but it didn't bother me that much. Mine was, in any event, a flight of business and pleasure. The flight was part of the deal. But how easier could it have been with a direct flight from Bristol? The way things worked out, a direct flight would have saved me more than a day, more time to explore the island and spend more money.

I was surprised at just how quiet the airport was in winter. Other than the flights from Athens, three a day, there was nothing from anywhere. This is probably more than enough for Corfiots, many of whom utilise the ferries when they go to the mainland and because they will not necessarily want to go to Athens when they go there. Winter, at the moment, would be the worst possible time for a plane-spotter to visit Corfu. Even with winter flights, I doubt that this would change very much! I would imagine that the airport would be the most significant and visible ghost town in Corfu and that many of its employees were hired on a seasonal basis. It was unmistakably Ioannis Kapodistria airport, it's just that most of it had the shutters up. For half the year, it was certainly not an international airport.

On my flight from London, a fellow passenger, also travelling to Corfu, remarked that it drove her mad flying over the island on the way to Athens. Couldn't the airline arrange for a brief stop on the way, a bit like a bus service? Well, that was never going to happen. It's either to the Greek islands via Athens or nothing.

Whilst this book is about the resorts, many of the potential winter attractions would be inland, historical features, a lot of which are closed in winter. But need they always be? They're great places to visit, but not always in the summer months, when temperatures are in the 80s and 90s. If you are interested in the history, wouldn't you consider the possibility of visiting the island out of season? I'm afraid I have no class at all when the sun is shining and I want to be out in it. Corfu's history is not totally lost on me, but once I have been touring a monastery or a museum whilst the sun is blazing, I start looking at my watch.

You do not visit Bath Abbey, the Natural History Museum in London or the Clifton Suspension Bridge in Bristol because you want to get a good suntan, but you would visit Corfu because you did. And you can visit the historical sites too, although not necessarily at the same time as you come for your sun tan! When I went in winter, some, but by no means all, of the attractions were closed. In any event, I had no time to visit them, nor any real inclination given my hectic timetable. But in the last few days of the expedition (a slight exaggeration, perhaps), I made a whistle stop tour of Corfu Town, viewing as many attractions as possible, buying up local guides and pamphlets. It was probably when the day was over and I was settling down for a quiet beer at the Libro d'Oro on the Liston when it really registered that there might be something in this winter in Corfu malarkey. The light was gradually beginning to dim, I was sitting outside, but under cover (if you know what I mean) and next to me was a heater which made sitting outside bearable. My beer arrived almost as soon as I ordered it (everyone else was drinking coffee, as usual); I sat there gazing through the trees, across the grass area (the outfield to the cricket square), and then to the magnificent Old Fort. All I needed, to complete the French image, was an odourous Gauloise cigarette, some swish sunglasses and a leather jacket. But then I remembered that I had given up smoking over 21 years ago and it would probably not be a good idea to start again now. I knew that I would be happy to sit here with this view at any time of year. The crackling atmosphere was little different to the way it was at the height of summer and there seemed to be no fewer people. "Another Ionian Pilsner!" I said to the waiter, in perfect English.

Everywhere I looked, there was something of interest. Agios Spyridon, the Church of St Spiridon, Campiello, Old Corfu Town, the Old Fort, the New Fort and that was just for starters and I barely had to walk any great distance to get to any of them. With a car, or as part of an organised trip, the world was one's lobster, as Arthur Daley used to say. And so was Corfu.

I looked at the benefits of winter tourism and there were plenty of them. I looked at the negatives and there weren't any. It would be a win-win situation for everyone. More tourism would benefit Corfu businesses and those who work for them in ways I had not even considered. These were still difficult times in Greece. Unemployment was still catastrophically high, wages and pensions were down, nobody trusted politicians, although I recognise that the latter is not exclusive to Corfu. The day after I left the island, a general election saw the old guard in politics defeated and humiliated as the charismatic Alex Tsipras took his left wing Syriza party, with its opposition to austerity, into government. At the time of writing, I have no way of knowing how things will turn out in Greece. Will they remain in the Euro? Will the new government choose a path away from austerity? To the untrained and uneducated eye, nothing ever appeared to change in Corfu, but there was no doubt that things were much worse on the mainland.

I do not profess to any level of expertise on the Greek tourism front either and no one is paying me a backhander to promote the island (sadly) and perhaps I could see something that no one else did, or I saw something that wasn't there. I was intrigued by the place, especially the resorts which were where I spent most of my time. Although some were devoid of all forms of human life, some ticked over with the presence of a few locals and others, like Arillas and Kassiopi, carried on looking like, well, Arillas and Kassiopi but with a lot of boarded up shops and tavernas. Some places aren't real places at all, built purely for the tourist drachma as was, the

Euro as is. They were easy enough to spot because there was no village centre and no community to live there even if there was. But that doesn't mean they're not worth a visit: far from it. It might be handy if just one small café was open to catch tourists in winter and you suspect that if direct flights from the UK were to commence, the crafty Corfiots would be smart enough to catch on!

We are not talking additional development here, just utilising what's there already. As Dimitris Kourkoulos from the Brouklis Taverna in Arillas would say, the aim is not to develop Corfu, it is to make it better. There was a time, as we have noted earlier, when Corfu strayed near the point of over-development, threatening to take away the very reason people like me went there in the first place. No more. The over-development almost happened at places like Agios Georgios in the south, where it was feared that the magnificent dunes between the resort and Issos would be ravaged to make way for more hotels and apartments. I do not know whether it was by accident or design, but the development has stopped and the dunes remain wonderfully intact, offering beautiful views to the north and a little solitude and quiet away from the throng of happy holidaymakers. I shall come back to this later, but Agios Georgios in winter was a very pleasant surprise to me. There was no one else there, certainly by the sea front, but the place was well-tended and clean. It obviously matters a great deal to some people.

The winter tourist to Corfu would obviously need to dress differently from the summer tourist. No need for garish shorts and vests and flip flops. I took my storm clothing which I had previously used in England's Lake District and found that I had not wasted suitcase space. I should have taken sturdy walking shoes or even boots, although my trainers got me through. An umbrella would have been a waste of time given the winds I experienced for much of my stay but each to their own when it comes to dealing with the rain! I still needed my sunglasses, a late addition which I had been assured would not be needed! I can report that when the sun shines on a Corfu winter's day, it is still very bright. Yes, the darkness can descend for days on end but Corfu's weather is, as Forrest Gump might say, like a box of chocolates: you never know what you're gonna get! Unless you look at the weather forecast, that is.

My story, such as it is, concerns the resorts, so I decided for my 'Corfu – a winter's tale' section, to carry out an imaginary clockwise tour starting at Kanoni, travelling round the island and ending up back in Corfu Town. And then afterwards to highlight some inland attractions.

I really was surprised by what I found.

## 12. On the town

Corfu Town is certainly worthy of a chapter of its own. If the truth be known, it's entitled to a book of its own. My journey, in my imaginary Hyundai Something took me past the Bay of Garitsa to my left, before veering slightly in-land on the way to Kanoni.

The first port of call is the Menekratis monument in Garitsa itself. It's a circular tomb, built in 6 BC in the ancient cemetery of Corfu. It is believed to show one of the oldest inscriptions in Greece. The monument is a cenotaph in honour of Menekratis, who was, according to my guide book 'consul in Corfu Oianthia'. Do you want me to be honest? I had never previously heard of Menekratis until I saw the tomb many years ago but the tomb itself is incredible. There's only one monument anything like it and that's in Lindos, Rhodes.

Menekratis Monument is located in Garitsa, the limits of the ancient cemetery of Corfu was opposite the gate of the port of Alcinous. The circular tomb was built in the 6th century BC by striking archaic inscription, which is considered one of the oldest inscriptions in Greece. This funerary monument is a cenotaph in honour of Menekratis, consul in Corfu Oianthia, near the present town Galaxeidi. According to the inscription, the municipality recognizing his work, erected the monument. The Corinthian alphabet inscription dating to 600 BC (one of the oldest surviving Greek inscriptions) and the architectural style of the cenotaph is dated in 570/540 BC and there is only one similar monument in Lindos, Rhodes. The Archaeological Museum of Corfu kept a marble lion, adds my guide, the 'Lion of Menekratis', so named because originally there was the impression that was placed on the cenotaph of Menekratis.

My old favourite, the number 2 'Blue Bus', covers all the attractions on the way to Kanoni and the next stop, to the left, by a major archaeological site, is Mon Repos. It's a magnificent neo-classical villa built on the Kanoni peninsula and was built in 1831 for the British High Commissioner Sir Frederick Adam. Britain handed Mon Repos to King George 1 of Greece in 1864 when we withdrew from Corfu, though not before we gave them cricket and ginger beer!

And a famous Brit was born there, none other than Prince Philip himself! As befits a prominent member of the British royal family, our Phillip was born of the House of Schleswig-Holstein-Sonderburg-Glücksburg and into the Greek and Danish royal families. Philip didn't stay in Corfu for very long. At the age of one, the family was forced to evacuate as the military government that came to power after World War 1. His uncle, King Constantine, was arrested, politicians were captured then executed. Philip was smuggled out of Corfu in a fruit box onto a waiting British navy vessel.

The rest is history. In 1939, Philip (18) started corresponding with a 13 year old girl called Elizabeth and after abandoning his Greek and Danish royal titles, converting from Greek Orthodoxy to Anglicanism and finally becoming a naturalized Brit, he sought and obtained permission from King George VI to marry her, obviously not when she was 13, but eight years later when she was 21.

As for Mon Repos, it fell into disrepair as a result of lengthy legal disputes between the municipality of Corfu and the former King Constantine of Greece. Eventually, the municipality fully restored the old building and it's now open to the public and, in my opinion, well worth a visit. It also worth taking a walk to the south end of the grounds to see the ruins of a Doric temple from 500 BC.

Across the road from Mon Repos, are the ruins of the early Christian Basilica of Paleopolis. It's on both sides of the road and impossible to miss. It's an early Christian basilica, built by the Bishop of Corfu, Jovian, on the ruins of a Roman Odeum before 450 AD. It has been destroyed and rebuilt on numerous occasions, by the Goths and Vandals of the 6th century and then the Saracens and the Normans of the 11th. Next came the Turks in 1537 and to put the tin hat on matters, literally, the air raids of World War II wrecked it again. After the Second World War, all the early Christian architectural parts, parapets, capitals etc., were collected and stored in the Old Palace Museum and the mosaics of the church restored.

And so, onto Kanoni. The one-way street towards Kanoni is roughly at the same level of the Halkiopoulos lagoon, before it ascends steeply to the site that everyone associates with Corfu. Straight ahead is the small convent, Vlacherna which opens in summer for the sale of souvenir items, and just beyond it is the small island of Pontikonisi, also known as Mouse Island. The name Kanoni is easy enough to work out: it was the site of a gun battery, a cannon, established by the French during Britain's blockade of Corfu from 1810 to 1815. There's still a cannon today, albeit a Russian one which was installed around 40 years ago. You can find it on the viewing terrace by the café and the gift shop. Although the cannon is not the real deal, it adds to the atmosphere and helps convey the history of the place.

In summer, a fleet of small boats chugs back and forth to Mouse Island. You buy a return ticket on one boat and return whenever you want, although there is not a great deal to do there. There are thick trees covering much of it to give a welcome break from the blazing Ionian sun. There's a small, minute even, church on Mouse Island, the Byzantine Church of Pantokrator on Pontikonisi, built, it is believed in the 11th or 12th century. There's not much in it apart from some marble wall plaques which have recorded royal visits. You used to be able to buy an ice cream there too! I always think it's worth a visit, even though there's nothing much to see.

Many guide books are critical of Kanoni because it overlooks the entire airport runway which itself 'slices through the lagoon.' Well, it's true, it does slice through the lagoon but my non scientific calculation is that the view of the runway and the sight and sound of departing and arriving aircraft is a major attraction. Yes, it is true that without the sound of planes, it would be a far more tranquil place from which to enjoy the views, which on clear day really do seem to go forever, but you only have to stand on the viewing terrace to see what happens when an aircraft comes across Mouse Island to land, or when one trundles down the runway before turning north to take off. In 30 years, I have never seen anyone complain about the noise. People love it. In winter, the views are still there but the planes, by and large, aren't. And the café viewing area where the cannon remains is inaccessible. Obviously, the reason for that is there are no tourists, but if there were...

But the out of season views are still mind blowing, with the blazing sunshine replaced by the winter rains. As I have explained elsewhere, it is a real treat to sit in the excellent Café Kanoni with its uninterrupted views of Vlacherna and Pontikonisi, whilst you clasp a delicious and warming coffee! At the foot of the steps down from Kanoni is a small café, which only opens in summer. The walk around the small causeway to Vlacherna is bracing and the bay itself does not look at its summer best with large amounts of rubbish which have drifted in from the sea. To be blunt, the odours are not the best either, reminiscent of the smells of Corfu Town in the 1980s.

The causeway linking Kanoni and Perama and the road south is a pleasant enough walk, except when you are confronted by a motorcyclist coming from the opposition direction. They don't tend to slow down for you!

Kanoni is a good base too. It's close enough to Corfu Town – it's arguably an extension of the town – and there are a good number of excellent hotels, including the Ariti where I was fortunate enough to stay. Aside from the causeway to Perama, there's not a lot of walking to be done, but there's enough to hold your attention on a winter's day. On a summer's day, I always plan to visit Kanoni when it's at its busiest!

And one more thing about Kanoni. There's a touching scene in For Your Eyes Only where Bond meets Melina as she arrives at the causeway on a boat. It's changed less than you might think.

Heading south on the east coast, the traveller passes through Perama which seems to be a series of hotels and tavernas and not much else. The first major resort is Benitses. I have visited the story of Benitses's chequered past before but it's worth mentioning again. It remains, unquestionably, a summer resort, but it is not the summer resort it was 30 years ago. I was staggered by the Benitses I saw in 1985, going through in the early hours of the morning.

Massive nightclubs absolutely rammed with young revelers, dance music thumping out into the night; no one slept in Benitses. Well, not during the night they didn't. By day, the street cleaners were out in force, removing the beer bottles and cans, wiping up the vomit (I know, it's not nice to read) and by noon small groups of befuddled young men with pure white bar tans stumbled out for their full English brunch, with the inevitable accompaniment of a pint of lager and a fag. This really was Benitses from May to October. Once a pleasant fishing village, then a hell hole (my opinion) of excess. And now Benitses has returned to something like its former self.

There are still reminders of the Benitses that was, before it was shipped off to Kavos, in terms of blocks of hotel accommodation and a surfeit of bars and tavernas, but the whole atmosphere has changed. Obviously, when I visited in January there was no atmosphere at all since nothing was open. I had been tipped off by English friends that the Big Bite was the place to go if I fancied a fry up ("the best in Corfu", I was advised!) but I didn't. You might think that there would be nothing worth seeing if you were there in winter, but you'd be wrong. The Corfu Shell Museum was closed but is, from all accounts well worth a visit if you like shells! Also, the owner apparently claims that Steve Irwin was his best friend. Please do not hold me to that if you visit!

If you are particularly energetic – and I am never particularly energetic in the summer! – you can walk up a well marked path on a steep hill to the water springs. I tried this once in the height of summer wearing flip flops, which was not one of my smarter moves. Far more accessible are the remnants of an old Roman bathhouse, which is situated just off the main strip, down an alleyway and through some lemon groves.

You might not want to do anything in Benitses but that's fine too. The views across the bay to the Greek mainland, up to Kanoni and Corfu Town to the left – I could think of worse places to sip on a warm drink. Since the days of nightclubbing and partying, a new Marina has been built which only adds to the new sense of sophistication about the place. If you are particularly lucky, as I wasn't, you can enjoy the sight and sound of arriving aircraft, so close by that you can make out the heads of the passengers and see the pilot at work.

Further down the coast is Moraitika which is essentially two places. The Moraitika you see as you drive into it is a main road packed with pubs, clubs, bars, cafés, tavernas and shops. It is often referred to as being 'dusty', although it was more muddy as I visited in driving rain. Ano Moraitika is a different kettle of fish with its tiny houses overgrown with bougainvillaea and a very pretty church with a quaint belfry. The beach is situated behind the pubs, cafés etc. It's a nice shingle/sand beach with the usual facilities. If I am being honest, this is not the most interesting place to visit in terms of culture but it fulfills its summer purpose. Ano Moraitika is such a contrast to its bigger, more brash brother, it's hard to believe they are in the same place.

As you pass through Moraitika, the road to the south curves to the right. To the left is Messongi. This is what Messonghi's website says about the resort:

"In Messonghi you will find a smattering of shops which sell all kinds of souvenirs and beach goods. Taverns and Bars vie to attract clients with their menus of delicious dishes and exotic cocktails. Many places have dancing or karaoke for your entertainment.

A wider range of Bars and clubs can be found just across the river in Moraitika for those who seek a livelier evening. Along the beach are a number of leisure activities. Pedalos are available for about 10 euros and for those not afraid of heights, Paragliding is a must (about 25euros). On the Messonghi river there are BOATS offering daily cruises (Boat trips) for exploring Corfu coastline or mainland Greece and Paxos island."

So, plenty to keep you going throughout the summer months, for sure, but absolutely nothing for the winter. The tree-lined beach curves gently to the south, with large hills beyond and what a lovely beach it is. Carry on the coastal road and you reach the small resort of Boukari which is renowned for its excellent fish restaurants. But the 'smattering of shops', as well as the bars, karaoke bars and clubs – not that I particularly wanted to do any singing and clubbing in the middle of January! – were all firmly shuttered up. Put bluntly, winter in Messonghi, for all its charms, had little to offer, unless you could find an apartment to enjoy the solitude and quiet. There was certainly plenty of both.

Some 400 British people work in Kavos during the summer. This goes down to 0 during the winter months. And the reason? Because Kavos is unquestionably and irretrievably a summer-only resort. The reasons people from the 18-30 group go there are quite simple: sun, extreme drunkenness and sweaty, unsatisfying sex. Only one of these was of much interest to me: yes, sun.

My reasons for promoting Corfu as a holiday island out of season are straightforward: it has much to offer tourists of many shades of cultural diversity. As we will discover, Corfu is rich, fabulously rich, with history, it has some of the finest views in Greece, there are countless wonderful walks. I am sure that if there was a will by the airlines, it would be simple to fill a direct flight during the winter months. But it wouldn't happen in Kavos.

There are two kilometers of sandy beach at Kavos and much of it is very attractive. The mainland is only slightly more than a stone's throw away. But the trouble with Kavos is, frankly, that it isn't real. In summer, it is a long drag of the usual bars, clubs and fast food joints, interspersed with motorcycle hire companies, pharmacies and medical facilities (I think there is a connection) and in winter there is a long drag with the same places. And the difference? No one is there. I compared it earlier to Pripyat, the abandoned city next to the Chernobyl nuclear plant which exploded in 1985. If anything, Kavos is worse, albeit without the Geiger counters.

So why did I visit Kavos? I had not been there for almost 30 years and I wanted to go there for novelty value, partly to see if it really was as bad as I remembered. It was. You would certainly not visit the place for the culture, unless the culture you were looking for was British drinking culture. The one thing you don't see in Kavos is anything remotely Greek. I just think to myself, why? Drive to the end of the drag – and it really is a drag – you soon reach Akrotiri Asprokavos, Kavos's baby sister with a few attractive modern apartments and again some great views. On a clear day, you can see Paxos to the south. Asprokavos is worth the drive. It would be worth taking a flask of coffee because you certainly won't be able to buy one in winter but I found Asprokavos was certainly a welcome relief after leaving Kavos.

I know I am extremely biased, but I see nothing attractive about Kavos in summer and whilst winter is mercifully quiet, the overall feeling of the place doesn't change one iota. Kavos certainly didn't disappoint me. It is unremittingly grim and I hope sooner rather than later that Corfu decides to deal with it. I appreciate there may be an aged related issue here. I do not think someone of my vintage is meant to go to Kavos on holiday, but then again, I hated it when I was young as well. I have returned on enough flights to the UK in the company of young people who have spent their holidays there but apart from the odd blistering sunburn on some people, you would never have guessed anyone had left the country, but that is not the point. This is a place devoid of character, there is a complete absence of history and culture and no one cares. But don't take my word: see it for yourself, but preferably when the 18-30 brigade have gone home!

Agios Georgios (or St George South as it is often known) has little in common with Kavos. The resort has basically evolved from nothing, adjoining as it does a fabulous 12 km of sandy beach. To the south, which can be reached by walking through olive groves, but would be more sensibly be reached by car in the height of summer, is the large village of Argirades which carries on as if tourism had never arrived, which for them it hasn't. The village itself would probably benefit from a by pass because even in winter I found myself held up for ages, negotiating my way through parking on both sides of the narrow road and vans, trucks and buses growling their way through. Oddly enough, Agios Georgios had lost little in comparison to its summer self. Drive to the front, passing the legendary Mad Mikes to the left and then turn right before the beach and there is everything for the happy holidaymaker, albeit not in January and why should there be? There is a small supermarket on the way in but that was life as we knew it in the depths of winter.

To be fair, on a sunny day, it doesn't feel much like winter in Corfu and it certainly doesn't in Agios Georgios. As I have mentioned before, the development that threatened to destroy the beautiful dunes appears to have stopped. If it hadn't, a major reason for staying there would have gone forever. The beach itself, with its blue flag status, is narrow and heads out to the west before you reach Issos which in summer has a café/bar but that is dismantled for the winter leaving precisely nothing apart from the wooden frame. That said, the views from Issos are excellent. And of course the aforementioned James Bond saw his girlfriend murdered here, near his beachside house of which there are no remains these days. Slightly further north is Lake Korission, or Limni Korission as it is called in Corfu.

I regard Lake Korission, which covers some 6000 acres, as one of the crown jewels of the island and an essential port of call for nature lovers as well as those who love stunningly attractive lakes. Like so much else in Corfu, the saltwater lagoon was built by the Venetians who built a channel from the sea and flooded the nearby marshlands. Commercialisation has not got anywhere near the lake, although it can be accessed from a narrow road running from the junction at Messonghi. Agios Georgios is hardly the party resort of Corfu but it's Kavos to Corfu's Lake Korission, wonderfully tranquil and scenic, bordered as it is by low hills. To the north you can see Mount Agios Mattheos. On the lakes shores are cedar trees and juniper and reeds. There are flowering plants everywhere – spring arrives early in Corfu, at least in horticultural terms, and there are a variety of orchids to admire. In summer, the colours are ablaze, but even out of season there is enough to enjoy.

The lake has provided something else too. 'Twitchers' will appreciate the fact that over 120 species of bird have been seen at the lake and winter visitors will include teals, shelducks and mallards, as well as waders like greenshank. The lake is full of fish too and there are often fishing nets to catch fish such as grey mullet. At the far north of the lake is a fisherman's hut.

It is a million miles away from the accepted view of Corfu. If you had been blindfolded, flown a thousand miles and dumped there, I reckon you would struggle to work out where you were. No foam parties here. Walkers, nature lovers and people who just like to walk in beautiful places and breathe wonderfully fresh and unpolluted air – this is the place for you. And it's another example, an unusual one granted, of what this amazing island has to offer.

Lake Korission is not going to change in a hurry, either. It has protected status under the Europe Nature Information System and is an important stop for migrating birds on their way from Africa to Europe. At some times of the year, some 2000 birds are in residence. A twitcher during my brief visit would have had a field day, not that I can tell the difference between one bird and another, with an incredible number and variety on display and, more importantly to me, you are at one with nature here. All right, nature didn't actually build the lake, the Venetians did, but you'd never guess as you soak in the beauty and sheer tranquility.

Further up the sandy west coast are the beautiful resorts of Glyfada and Agios Gordis. The former has one of the best beaches on the island and is much favoured by all inclusive holiday companies in recent years. Here, over-development has taken a terrible toll on the coastal hills. Like many hotels on the island, especially in the resorts, they are not open in the winter months and life retreats to the small villages beyond. Myrtiotissa was described by Lawrence Durrell in his book 'Prospero's Cell' as "perhaps the most beautiful beach in the world" which is surely stretching things a bit. I would argue it isn't even the best beach on the west coast of Corfu, but these things are, I know, entirely subjective. There's also a lot less of the beach than there used to be which seems to be a developing theme on the island.

The major resort as we get to the north east of Corfu is Paleokastritsa. Here mountains tumble into the sea, huge tree-clad slopes line the way down. The resort is the end of the road, there is one way in and one way out. I find that in the summer, Paleokastritsa is a disappointment. The beaches at Agios Spyridon are small and packed, the nearby road is noisy from the sound of arriving vehicles, especially the numerous tourist buses that arrive in a continuous flow. There is more noise from the watersports too, as well as from the numerous boat trips that chug round the cliff grottos and caves. The latter are well worth doing by the way.

High above Paleo stands the famous Bella Vista taverna which is high above the bay. Whatever the weather – and I have eaten here during a monster of a thunderstorm – the views are to die for and I really did think that was a possibility when the lightning bolts were lighting up the hillside. Many years ago, during his travels of Greece, Keith Floyd visited the Bella Vista and thoroughly enjoyed the experience. The drive up the hill is an exercise in tedium and concentration, so steep is the road that you are rarely able to get out of first gear, assuming the car makes it in the first place.

If I am being honest, Paleo has been a disappointment to me. This is probably a matter of taste – and I am not renowned for having any – but whilst there is a wonderful sense of arrival at the terminus, there has been a reckless amount of development. That is not to say it isn't a good place to stay because you only need to see the number of tourists in season to see that it certainly has something.

The major tourist attraction, apart from the village itself, is a monastery which is dedicated to the Virgin Mary. Now pardon me when I say that

I come from the school which says that once you have seen one monastery you have seen them all, but there is something about this one, the foundations for which were laid in the 13th century. It is situated up the hill just by the beach and in summer buses operate to take visitors to the top. Whilst the foundations were laid in the 13th century, the building as it is now was built some 500 years later. There is a church at the heart of the monastery where hangs a painting of the Last Judgement. I remember the spectacular bougainvillea when I went there. There is also a garden with a terrace from which there are stunning views of the Bay of Liapades and beyond. Below lies the appropriately named Paradise Beach. There's also a collection of bones (!) and shells in a small museum. I guess if monasteries are your thing and you don't want to visit them in the blistering summer heat, a winter holiday would be an idea.

As for winter, it's like anywhere else: it's closed.

Agios Georgios, the north western version is closed too, with barely a handful of people living there in the winter but it barely detracts from its beauty. There has been development here too, particularly crass by the beach front, but overall it remains otherwise unspoiled and picturesque. To the north is Akrotiro (Cape) Arillas and to the south Akrotirio Falakron. Whilst there is 'nothing to do', as you might say, Agios Georgios lies in a particularly good area for walking. In summer, many of us have been on the well-marked walks, wishing for the only time on our holidays that it would just cool down a tiny bit. And the walks are rewarding for the exquisite views and the occasional discovery of a much-needed kafeneion or taverna. I shall return to this subject later.

You would expect me to recommend Arillas, given that I have been there every year since 2004, and you would be right. One supermarket, at the bottom of the hill, and one taverna, the enduringly excellent Armourada, remain open throughout the winter, the rest of Arillas sleeps, but not too deeply since it is a real 'live' village with a large indigenous population. The Akrotiri bar at the top of the hill between Arillas and San Stefanos, a real high point of any visit to Corfu, opens only at weekends during winter. The seafront is little different during the winter, although the beach is even narrower and covered with rocks and pebbles which are brought ashore by the winter storms. Here, as we have learned earlier, the community acts as one during the winter months to improve, not develop, the resort. Arillas reminded me that the colours do not change that much in Corfu. The green foliage remains to an extent, it just gets greener as it gets warmer. The blue skies and sea seem to be a lighter shade than they do in summer and the light itself is more harsh, so if you feel the need to visit out of season, make sure sunglasses are on your list. Whilst Arillas is slightly off the beaten track, there is a direct road to the north via a variety of lovely country roads and villages and, once you navigate the tight turns on the way out of the town, Corfu Town itself is less than an hour away, a lot less than an hour if you drive like the average Corfiot! (Just kidding, but only just.)

There's also some classic Greek mythology in the shape of Gravia Island. It's yet another rocky islet, of which there are many, off the Corfu coast and it is claimed that it is the ship that Poseidon turned to stone in revenge for the Phaeacians transporting Odysseus home to Ithaca. This may or may not be true – the odds suggest that there is at least some doubt about it – but what's not to love about the story?

San Stefanos to the north is much the same except that unlike Arillas, there's hardly anyone about and everything is closed. In fact, most people who work and own businesses in San Stefanos live in the village of Avliotes which is just north of the resort and, as in Arillas, as many of the businesses are locally owned and maintained there is a great deal of pride among the community in the resorts and it shows. There are the remnants of an old harbour here, as well as a modern fully functional one. San Stefanos, when I visited, and as I mentioned earlier, bore a closer resemblance to Cornwall with its surfer-type waves powering up the beach.

You can approach Sidari from a variety of different directions but you know you have found it virtually straight away. It used to be two villages but they have merged into one sprawling and still expanding resort which is alive in winter, just!

I have noticed in recent years, and particularly since the arrival of low cost airlines from the UK like easyJet and Ryan Air, and similar carriers from other European countries, that independent travel has become the norm rather than the exception. The larger resorts, like Sidari and Kavos, still have a large majority of package tourists, appealing to very different types of British holidaymaker. Kavos, as we have learned, attracts the young Brit who, putting it bluntly, wants to gets wasted for a week or two whereas Sidari attracts the Brit families and couples who like being abroad but also like a bit of home from home. To that end, Sidari boasts countless bars and pubs which advertise the full English breakfast, the Sunday roast and of course John Smiths Smooth. There are go karts, a small waterpark and all the trimmings in terms of shops and facilities. Now this is not a bad thing and I am not making a judgement. I am a total philistine on holiday, my idea of culture is drinking a pint of a Greek beer and lying on a Greek sunbed – I am exaggerating only very slightly – and we are all of us very different. Imagine if every British tourist went to Corfu in search of nothing but monasteries. God knows there are enough of them, but we'd spend all our time queuing to view fascinating preserved works of art and candles. Just like having enough John Smiths Smooth, you can have enough monasteries. Thank goodness for diversity.

None of this is to compare Sidari with somewhere like Blackpool. It's just a bit different from many of the other resorts. But it's very unlikely that, in the event of British winter tourism, there would be much in it for Sidari. Blackpool is in a world of its own, where even at the height of summer it can feel like mid winter with the ice cold wind blowing in from the Irish Sea, but much of it is the same whatever the season. Sidari doesn't have the pubs and clubs, and certainly not the piers, so don't expect Roy Chubby Brown showing up anytime soon! And I cannot imagine the summer karaoke singers and tribute acts will be there much beyond the end of October.

But there are still things to see, places to walk. The stunning site of Canal 'd'Amour, its sandstone eroded by the waves of time doesn't pale even in the depths of winter. According to tradition, couples who swim through the narrow canal will get married soon. I would not recommend doing this other than in the summer, unless you are prepared with suitable winter wear and safety equipment which would, I suspect, spoil the romance a little! And there is still some history between the modern glare of Sidari's bright lights. Walking along its main street, you can see painted trees (to ward off disease, apparently: I never knew that), with little seats and a seahorse fountain by a bandstand which is covered in the usual bougainvillea and geraniums. For culture vultures this is a rare oasis! Also, situated on the north side of the square stands the Church of St

Nicholas with its lamps and a lively icon which has been painted on to its interior.

I can see the attraction of Sidari for a summer, but in its near deserted tranquility I found it strangely charming. The beaches were awash with winter flotsam and jetsam and, like Kavos, not a little rubbish had washed up in the winter storms and whilst the resort is not aesthetically pleasing it was a nice place to walk round. And of course the north coast, right through to Kassiopi, is mostly flat with only the occasional mild ascents and descents on the roads. It would be easy to travel between local villages and towns by bicycle, certainly by the time you reach Roda, something I would only recommend in certain parts of the island and definitely not in others.

But a winter holiday attraction? In all honesty, not really. It is what it is. There is a surfeit of history and winter attractions elsewhere so if it ain't broke, let's not try to fix it.

I suppose I should write a damning critique about Roda, given that my new friends the Connors and the Mansells live there and because I don't want to spoil it for them by attracting legions of extra tourists to puncture the tranquility of the place. I could say what a tawdry, smelly, rundown, downmarket hovel it was but that would not be true, far from it. Another resort that positively sparkles in winter, I would put it down as somewhere that really should be visited. Again, it's alive in winter.

Greek people live there – I know, this really is unusual in some Corfiot resorts – and there are a wide variety of businesses that don't close down for winter. I think Roda is fabulous.

There's a lovely old church up the main road called the Church of Agios Georgios which is in a square full of lemon trees and leaving Roda there are the remains of a Doric temple to Apollo which dates back to the 5$^{th}$ century.

Roda is very well served by roads too, with all points west, east and south well served. Obviously, the north is slightly more problematical what with the sea being in the way. The views to Albania are however stunning.

There's no getting away from the fact that Roda itself has been heavily developed, certainly since I first visited 30 years ago, but critically the developers have not overplayed their hands. Whether it is by accident or design, Roda remains a special place to visit. Yes, there is a place where you can buy the finest fish and chips, but so what? I can buy top quality Indian food just down from my house in Bristol, or have Chinese food and pizzas delivered to my door. There is no law that says you have to eat nothing except food from the place in which you live.

There's not that much history in the resort of Roda but it has a charm of its own. Great for walking and cycling, possibly good for horse riding too and certainly excellent for lovely winter walks and relaxing in the many hostelries that remain open all year round.

I am an unashamed fan of the north coast road. It's in good condition and it's wide which is dead handy when local drivers overtake at high speed, in this instance relatively safely. (They normally wait for a narrow road and a blind bend to overtake, usually more than one car at a time.) Driving east from Roda, you soon come to Acharavi. If the north of the island had its own capital, it would be Acharavi. If Roda is alive, Acharavi is buzzing, even in winter. The beach is set back from the main road by a fair old distance but it's quite beautiful and like Roda, it is in an advantageous position in terms of getting around. The other side of the road from the beach stands the magnificent Mount Pantokrator, which can be accessed from the road inland (it is a very windy road and, as you near the top of the mountain, very scary too – I'll come back to that!), as well as beautiful villages of Episkepsi and Lafki. Olive groves proliferate up here and suddenly you are in another world.

Agios Spiridon is the next port of call as you head into the north east of the island. I came here in 1986 on the advice of many people in Kassiopi who told me it was the great undiscovered beach in all of Corfu. When we got there, it was hard to disagree. At the height of summer, the only visitors were locals with their little beach mats which they carried on the back of their little mopeds. It was a little bit of heaven on earth, disturbed only from time to time by the wash from the huge ferries passing by between Corfu and Albania and the inevitable mosquitoes. That changed forever in the early 2000s following the construction of an 800 bed all inclusive hotel called the Blue Beach Escape. Summer days were transformed from tranquility to 18 hours a day of hectic activity and not a small amount of noise.

In winter, the change is dramatic. The hotel is closed – why would you stay there when its one attraction is the sun – until spring, the food huts and bars shuttered up and removed, it looks like Colditz but without the prisoners. But you know what? Come away from the concrete and put your blinkers on and the rest of Agios Spiridon crackles with life and retains its beauty. To the west is the Antinioti Lagoon, a nature reserve right on the edge of civilization, at least how we know it. In summer, the lagoon is mosquito hell but in winter you can have a stress-free walk around it, observing the wild flowers and fauna. And because of the generally mild Greek winter, things are still growing. The lagoon is not as big as Lake Korission to the south west but equally as welcoming and, compared with the rest of this new resort, totally unspoiled.

I was surprised enough to discover the lagoon in summer, having typically turned up without having made any preparations. I am quite fortunate as regards mosquitoes because they don't usually find my blood attractive – this could be due to the high concentrates of Mythos and Metaxa – and the lagoon was a joy. It was full of fish too, but don't ask me to name the varieties. I am as clued up about fish as I am about cars.

The entire north coast so far was utterly fascinating, unquestionably offering potential for out of season travel. From the limited charms of the slightly ramshackle Sidari to the natural beauty preserved at Agios Spiridon, it is a walker's paradise. But to me, nothing compares to Kalamaki, which is roughly halfway between Agios Spiridon and Kassiopi.

Kalamaki is a beach resort and nothing more. Or is it? Certainly there is a long, flat beach and it is incredibly safe for bathing, the water being very shallow for hundreds of yards. To the left is a long, rickety wooden jetty which, in the quiet months of winter, is home to scores of hooded crows. (The jetty was described to me as a pier by one local, which I think is stretching things a bit!) Nothing is open, but Kalamaki is utterly charming. I could imagine renting an apartment or even a house at the back of the beach purely for the relaxation of the tranquility and isolation. And it is very near Kassiopi which, although it is not exactly a winter hive of activity, does have certain facilities including a supermarket, always assuming you are not moved along, as I was, when you want to use it.

Whilst there is nothing in terms of facilities, I would not write off or disregard Kalamaki. If I was going next week, I would certainly pay a visit.

You can see Kassiopi from Kalamaki. And, to the north west, you are barely a couple of miles from Albania. Kassiopi has a slightly fiddly one-way system so that when you are arriving from the west you pass by virtually the entire village before turning left, passing between shops, tavernas, bars and apartments on the way down to the port. And what a port it is, a proper working port where, in summer, the fishermen mingle with the hired boats out to the open sea. I was surprised to discover just how quiet it was when I was there. Almost everything was closed. I had expected to see happy smiling locals everywhere, the smell of baking bread and cafés serving coffee and extremely fattening cakes. Well, I was hoping to, which is a different story altogether. I would describe the port as picture postcard pretty and whilst life was hard to find, there was plenty of history.

For all the modern development – and there is considerably more of it now than when I first visited in 1985 – you don't have to look hard for history. It was the Romans who colonized the village and before that a prehistoric settlement, then a Corinthian city. Kassiopi gets its name from the remains of a temple to Jupiter Cassius that lies beneath the village church. Many famous Romans passed through Kassiopi, including Nero, no less, as well as Cato, Tiberius and Cicero.

On the headland past the harbour there lies the ruins of a castle which I observed on countless occasions in the 1980s but, to my eternal shame,

I did not bother to research it until now, far more interested was I in buying drinks and pizza from the nearby café. The headland was fortified by the Romans and in the 13th century the castle was built by the Angevin rulers of Corfu. The Venetians, whose paws are all over Corfu, promptly destroyed the fortress and built their own, the remnants in the form of an old wall still encircle the hill. Kassiopi's church has a bit of history too. The church is dedicated to the Blessed Virgin Kassiopitra and it has an icon of the Virgin which claimed that she had miraculous powers. Kassiopi became a village that saw pilgrims arrive long before the current patron saint, Spyridon, came along.

At the far side of the headland are small shingly beaches and flat rocks where visitors take in the rays, although not in winter. Much of the development in the village is behind the harbour and there is a lot of it.

Kassiopi is certainly hugely popular with tourists and I can see why having stayed there on three occasions, but it is anything but a classic resort. Whilst there are some nice beaches to the south, they are not what attracts visitors. It's the quality of the accommodation, the facilities, it's liveliness in summer and that splendid harbour. It has an atmosphere all of its own. And because it is not the classic summer resort encourages my belief that there is much to be said about Kassiopi as a stage to be taken in during a winter tour. Some fascinating history and some great walks.

The north east coast is arguably the most picturesque part of Corfu. Small villages and resorts are reached through tumbling narrow roads, Albania is at its closest point, the ferries are so close you can almost touch them. High in the hills, especially near Agios Stefanos, is Kensington On Sea. It's not really called that but it's the Rothschild estate where the great, the good and the not so good (that is to say the very rich) come to stay in summer or even for summer.

Agios Stefanos is a fishing resort, albeit a very quiet one in winter. But even in summer, it is not exactly a raucous place to be. At the bottom of the narrow road, through the inevitable olive groves (have I mentioned olive groves before?), the visitor is confronted by white-washed buildings and cronky wooden jetties (out of service for the winter). Agios Stefanos has little by way of history but what it does have is some lovely walks to the north, all of which are well-marked and well used.

Everyone who knows anything about Corfu knows about the Durrells. Gerald wrote about his early life there in his richly entertaining book, My Family and Other Animals. His brother Lawrence, however, wrote the brilliant Prospero's Cell when he lived in the famous white house in Kalami from 1935 to 1939. He described it as "set like a dice on a rock already venerable with the scars of wind and water". The white house these days is a taverna with apartments on top, although it retains a plaque acknowledging Durrell's life there. You could almost imagine drawing back the curtains and seeing the gorgeous blue sea before you and find it very difficult not to write meaningful prose. Perhaps less so these days, given that the view from the south of Kalami has been affected to its detriment by the construction of modern apartments gouged into the hillside. For all that, Kalami remains an idyllic place to stay, although it is hard to make a case for winter activities. As with other resorts, Corfu's excellent climate means that the streets of the resort, even in the depths of winter, are flanked by groves of lemon and orange trees, so close that if you felt so inclined you could pick them!

Before the village of Kentroma lies a narrow road down a steep hill. At one time, there was a sheer and utterly terrifying sheer drop to the sea, now there is a crass looking but probably necessary wall. The road winds at the bottom and eventually straightens out, leading to the small pebble beach. On either side of the road there are small houses, allotments and car parks. The car parks are for the three excellent restaurants in the tiny bay of Agni. They are from north to south, Taverna Agni, Toulas and Taverna Nikolas. The length of the beach is barely that of a football pitch, the width not much more than a cricket pitch, but the restaurants are huge attractions for those staying in villages near to Agni and, like us, from halfway round the island.
Only Taverna Nikolas looks anything like a restaurant in the winter with its genial owner Perikles Katsaros and his family living upstairs in

the family home. Toulas looks like a house and Taverna Agni looked like a bomb had hit it, with builders bashing and crashing away. As I have documented at great length, Perikles was incredibly generous with his time and he was probably the main reason I became convinced of Corfu's potential as a winter holiday island. Whilst he is closed for the winter, he imagines that the Taverna could be something like a cookery school, where visitors buy the food, return to the Taverna and cook it, under supervision, of course. He could, perhaps, open at weekends if the demand was there, that demand surely being generated from direct flights from the UK. The man himself was part of the business community that helped to convince Ryan Air to fly direct to Corfu. Airlines are not registered charities and the only reason they would consider winter flights would be if they thought they could make money from them. And airlines like the budget airlines have very tight margins. I doubt that they make £1000 from each flight from the UK, so would they go the trouble of flying to Corfu once a week throughout the winter? Remember also, that with the low cost airlines there are only so many 'cheap' seats and once they have gone and the number of seats is less, the ones that remain go up in price to the extent that they rival regular scheduled companies. I was told by many people, especially Brits, that price mattered. Those who travelled to the UK maybe once a year could put up with the hassle of going via Athens. I do not pretend to be an expert but I am just trying to start a debate.

I digress.   Agni in winter bore a close resemblance to summer in every sense except the state of the three tavernas that encourage people to visit this special place. The jetties were inoperable for the winter and there were – obviously – no sunbeds but the tranquility was exactly the same, there were just less bodies. Strangely, despite the relatively minute size of Agni, it is more suited to winter visitors than anywhere else in Corfu.   And let's be honest: Perikles could charm the birds out of the trees and could probably persuade me to visit the local sewage works. Persuading me to visit Agni was a given.

South of Agni lie a number of small and attractive villages like Kaminaki and Nissaki, with its stunning waters for the divers to enjoy and then Barbati, before dipping down into Ipsos, the long straight resort under the rugged slopes of Mount Pantokrator.   Ipsos, and its neighbor Pyrgi, are known as the 'Golden Mile' which is not as bad as it seems and certainly not a Corfu version of Blackpool!

After Ipsos comes Dassia, with its big hotels, shingly beach and its range of shops.   Shortly after there's Gouvia which boasts an impressive yacht marina.   Like Dassia, it's a summer resort but there remain the arches that belonged to the Venetian shipyard and they're well worth a visit. And how can you not admire a place that boasts an eaterie called the Vergina Taverna?   It's reputed to be very good, too!

And those are the resorts. You pays your money, you takes your choice. I do have favourites – that is blindingly obvious – but even someone who is not overly fond of some resorts has to admit that for one reason or another, anywhere in Corfu is worth a gander. Even Kavos!

# 13. In the town

For anyone who has been to Corfu on a package holiday, you will be familiar with the 'Welcome Meeting'. Your holiday representative will arrange meetings at the accommodations for which s/he is responsible at particular times at which the holidaymaker will get information about the resort in which they are staying, advice on what to do in emergencies and, most importantly, details of trips that the package holiday is offering. I say 'most importantly' because it's most important to the holiday rep who makes their commission from trips in order to top up their normal wages.

I haven't been to a 'welcome meeting' for over a decade now but I well remember them. And in Corfu they were always pretty well the same, although there would be variations depending on where in the island you were staying. There was always the 'Grand Island Tour' which was basically a bus trip visiting the visual highlights such as Kanoni, Paleokastritsa and the Achillion Palace. The quite magnificent 'Theo's Boat Trip' (see Chapter 10) was always an essential too, trips that were always tailored to the needs of the holidaymaker. And that old favourite, 'Corfu Shopping By Night'. You would leave your resort at tea time, endure pick ups all along the route and then park near the Old Fort whereupon you would have until 11.00 pm mingling with other holidaymakers down the lovely little lanes and roads in the town.

In the middle of summer, Corfu is always hot and Corfu Town is even hotter. Travelling in July and August, I have not so much as taken a pair of full length trousers or even a warm top to Corfu. It just isn't worth it, day or night.

In my early days of visiting this most special of towns, I waddled penguin like through the busy streets, stopping as frequently as if I was on Oxford Street and, it has to be said, sweating profusely. I did not notice, never mind pause to view, the history and beauty on every corner, the incredible Church of St Spiridon or the Liston itself, except as somewhere to get a beer and watch the cricket. Even then I was old enough to know better, but – hey – I was on my holidays and I'll do what I want! "Bottle of Metaxa, Sir?" Why not? "A tacky T shirt?" Has to be done. "Would you like to see my pottery? Good price!" Where do I pay? Not exactly the height of culture, was it, but then, I travel with baggage: British baggage.

In many ways, the 'Corfu Shopping By Night' trip was both tiring and boring. It was tiring because spending many hours trudging up and down the lanes, reprising some several times over and repeatedly crisscrossing others, in 80 degrees of sapping heat, can take it out of you. And the novelty of shopping in Corfu Town can wear out pretty quickly if you are not a naturally enthusiastic shopper. My partner will vouch for the fact that after a while, sometimes a very short while, I have a tendency to become crotchety and impatient. Once you have seen

323

one jewelers, you have seen them all and you only need to know my regular dress sense and general taste in clothing to know that haute couture does not feature very high on my radar!

The point about the 'Corfu Shopping By Night' trip is that you have to do it, with the package company or independently, because it's such a nice place to visit. The atmosphere on a balmy summer's night, with voices echoing down the streets and the Liston, is something to behold. It took me a few years to look beyond the souvenir tat and take in the history, but it was rewarding, oddly rewarding to me who has a pitiful lack of interest in history at the best of times. It was not just the facts that gripped me, it was the myths too, the myths that many believe are facts. But no matter. They're stories worth listening to and, later, telling. I could never go to Corfu the island without at least once visiting Corfu the town. It's against the law, apparently.

There is a wonderful sense of arrival in Corfu, particularly when you arrive from the north and turn left by the port. The town buzzes, everything and everyone is on the move. Huge cruise ships, modern tenements on water, sit alongside the ferries going to and from the mainland and Italy. Travel agent shops mingle with the cafés and bars and, turning right you feel the hubbub of the town. I always knew much of the architecture was Venetian without really knowing why or what it meant, but a little knowledge, whilst sometimes being dangerous can often be more than useful. From the south and west, arrival in Corfu Town is a little dull, passing supermarket after hardware store after car showroom. You know you are nearly there when you see the end of the runway that ends at the main road, a set of traffic lights that's used every time a plane takes off from the town end of the runway. This is because the wings of the larger planes virtually cross the road at this point. I once stood there whilst a Dan Air Boeing 727 took off a few feet away from me, reducing my hearing ability to the same level as if I had just seen The Who at full volume.

It makes more sense to take a left before the town, but when did sense come into it? Drive straight ahead down the ever narrowing road to reach the Bay of Garitsa, turn left to see the Old Fort, up the hill you are at the Esplanade. There are few better routes in Corfu.

Of all the places in Corfu, this is the one place that, unsurprisingly, doesn't change much from one season to another. How could it? It's a fully functioning real town where most Corfiots live. It's not like many of the resorts where everyone leaves at the end of the season. More likely, it's even busier in winter because the people from the resorts are here. The little back streets behind the Liston were much quieter when I was there in the winter of 2015, but the more modern shopping area beyond was anything but quiet. In fact, if anything it was even busier than it is in summer. People, mainly young people, sat outside the cafés, dressed in smart modern clothing, albeit wrapped up against the elements, shops were busy, Corfu Town was certainly open for business.

I simply loved walking up and down the lanes in winter. They were quiet, very quiet, and at times I was the only person there. Perhaps this was because it was raining and I was showing my Great British Spirit, or maybe the locals were showing more sense and staying indoors? Although the lanes were dark, I felt perfectly safe. Some of the shops were closed for winter but these were the tourist shops. Everything else remained open, including all the eateries. I think it was on one of these little streets, midway through a drizzly, slightly chilly evening, when it really registered with me. Why was I the only tourist in town? I walked and when I stopped walking, I started walking some more. I was walking through all this history and before I went home I would have to learn a bit more about it. The next day, I started by surfing the web to find out more about the town and then went into town, yet again, to collect as much information by way of leaflets and booklets that I could. Corfu Town would be a great winter getaway place. I'm very serious about that.

If I was to tell you that the Liston, on the western edge of the esplanade was a French tribute to the Parisian rue de Rivoli and at the northern edge was the Palace of St Michael and St George, symbol of British neo-classicism, you'd probably say that I'd either made it up or I'd nicked it from a guidebook. You'd be dead right about the latter, if I am being honest. I am to British neo-classicism what Alan Carr is to cage-fighting so I am not going to pretend that I am incredibly knowledgeable on some historical aspects. But there is so much to see and learn about Corfu Town. It's not exactly London in terms of size but you would be surprised what actually is there. There's a shedload of history, interesting enough even for a philistine like me, and there are plenty of watering holes and places to eat all around the town.

I start with Campiello, Old Corfu Town, situated between the Old Fort and the New one. The buildings are mainly Venetian and they stand alongside and either side of the mazy little lanes and streets. In between many of them are stone stairwells, some bigger than others, and there are small passage ways dotted around the lanes. These buildings are up to four storeys high. I was told, I can't remember by whom, that the reason the houses got so tall is because everyone wanted to live within the town walls, so they simply built extra floors on top! A lot of these buildings are in various states of disrepair but lose nothing aesthetically as a result. There are occasional Venetian motifs on some houses, others hang out their washing high above the streets, a relatively short exercise in the summer months, essentially pointless in the wet season (winter). The ground seems like it is paved with the smooth flagstones you would find in an Olde Worlde English pub. Every night I was there, I heard a brass band – Corfu has four such bands – practicing upstairs in one of the houses. Honestly, they sounded absolutely terrific but I dread to think how loud they must have been inside the houses. As you walk along, a courtyard will appear, or perhaps a religious symbol or a terraced garden and everywhere there are places to eat and drink and then eat and drink some more.

Many people who are asked about what their favourite spot is in Corfu will often answer, The Esplanade (The Spianada) and the Liston. It was those busy Venetians who cleared the medieval town that lay in front of the Fortress. This had nothing to do with their dislike of the original architecture and everything to do with having open ground in front of the Old Fort to defend the town against an attack from the landward side. I read this all as a matter of fact, which it was, but I could not understand what the point of this would be because if someone had control of the old town, barring the odd cannon shell being fired from the Old Fort, the invader could effectively ignore them until they got fed up or ran out of supplies. You can see why I am not an historian, can't you?

The surviving buildings remain on Kapodistriou Street (as well as having an airport named after him, old Ioannis has a street, too!) but on the Platela there is the terrace of arcaded buildings called the Liston. If I had ever been to Paris I could give the reader an accurate description as to whether the Liston really was built in the style of the Rue de Rivoli, but I shall leave it to them to decide! It does say so on the internet too, so it must be true.

At the southern end of the Esplanade, separated from the Liston and the cricket pitch that's in front of it by a small but busy road – watch out for those little mopeds hurtling round! – is a park which features landscaped flowerbeds and a bandstand where the aforementioned brass bands belt out their tunes every Sunday afternoon, but only in summer. If you really want something to make you feel at home, I should point out that there is a McDonalds here too, quietly decorated, but still garish. I should point out that fast food is not just a British disease: every time I went by there was a regular flow in and out of young Corfiots. This probably was an example of where the exception proved a rule, that being if a place was frequented by the locals, it would be worth visiting! And the thing about McDonalds is that it's always the same. No one would return home after a fortnight's holiday in Corfu and say, "Do you know what? There's a brilliant McDonalds in Corfu! It's SO much better than the one down the road!"

And another surprising downer? Not all the cafés on the Liston were open in the winter but where they were, a group of enterprising 'Looky Looky Men' tried to unload their wares on locals and me. In recent years, they appear to have spread their wings and flown from the Canary Islands and brought with them the usual bootleg tat, especially by way of DVDs and CDs. Having seen them at work in the charmless concrete of Tenerife, I wondered what would be next? Cockney Timeshare touts, acting like Chuggers on acid? Karaoke in all the bars on the Liston?

Lap Dancing Clubs?  Nah – not in Corfu Town, but don't give Kavos any more ideas!

You can walk Corfu Town by day in winter, you can walk it by day in summer.  One is more bearable than the other.  Similarly, you can do your shopping in winter, apart from the tat that appeals to people like...well...me!

I am not a religious man but the Church of St Spyridon is really something else.  You simply cannot miss the bell tower with its enormous red dome.  It's one of the standout views of this standout island.  Although the church looks quite unexceptional from the outside, it's pretty exceptional inside with various candelabras, paintings and icons.  And most importantly, in a white casket are the mummified remains of the saint himself.   What a saint he was too, expelling the plague from the island, as well as saving the island in 1716 by seeing off the second great siege.  Not bad for a man who died in 348.  The remains are exposed every year, the most significant being on 12 December (St Spiridon's Day) and also at Easter and 11 August.

I saw the church on numerous occasions when I was there in the winter of 2015 and it is a stunning site.  The bell tower is brightly lit at night and the very size and beauty of the building has an aura of its own.  Even if you have no faith of your own, it is a moving sight and hugely symbolic to the devout.

It shows my complete lack of culture that my main memory of the Old Fortress (Palaio Frourio) is the massive punch up in the movie 'For Your Eyes Only' but its history is somewhat richer than that. The first fortifications were established in the 6th century. They were Byzantine and were built after the old Corinthian city of Palaiopolis was destroyed by Goth raiders. The seemingly ever-present Venetians got in on the act yet again some 900 years later, building and extending the wall and excavating the moat, called the Contrafossa, which remains to this day.

You just can't miss the Old Fortress. It's situated at the far side of the Esplanade. Pass the right hand guardhouse, the gatehouse of which contains the Byzantine Collection of Corfu, across the bridge to the Church of the Madonna of the Carmelites then up a steep climb past the Venetian Clock tower to the inner peak, the Landward Castle. And then, 72 metres high, there are great views of the town itself and, to the north, the imposing sight of Mount Pantokrator. I have now done this climb in both winter and summer and I can assure you that in winter it is much easier. It was more than a little breezy when I reached the summit, clasping my guidebook and holding onto my hat. The wind had really got up, or perhaps it was just windier at the top, and the rain was starting to pour down. Way in the distance to the south, past the Bay of Garitsa, one could see the dark clouds advancing to the town. Over Lefkimmi, it must have been as black as night, some achievement since it was early afternoon when I was there.

Apart from the noise from the elements, you could obviously hear nothing else. If anything, the winter view was even more impressive and so was the Old Fortress herself. She had been there for a very long time and been battered continuously by storms not unlike the one which was about to hit Corfu. There were a few people with me at the top, taking photographs, speaking Greek (I think!) and breathing in this amazing atmosphere, where only a few years ago Eric Burdon and the Animals played an outdoor gig!

In fact, the Old Fortress really sums up what winter tourism could be about. Not many people will visit Corfu in July or August with the sole intention of clambering up its mountainous steps. It would probably be an optional day out, a day away from the sun bed. But away from the blazing Ionian sun, you can do and see so much more. You will probably not see Melina Havelock flying over the Fortress in her helicopter (I cannot remember if this was before or after her parents were killed in their boat at peaceful old Kalami), or see that big punch up featuring Topol who by now wouldn't have had to worry if he was a rich man. Essential visiting, probably half a day's work and then you've got the Esplanade and the Liston for lunch. Not a bad day out, eh?

## 14. Walking

An island of such beauty deserves to be walked extensively. I have walked a great deal during my many visits to Corfu and there is consistently one outcome: I get hot, sweaty and crotchety. And the walks are almost always – no, correction due there – the walks are always taken in order to get to a bar or taverna. Getting hot and bothered is all the more bearable if there is a cold glass of beer waiting for you. But walking in Corfu as a holiday?

I have some friends who do just that. They fly from the UK to Corfu on the first flight of the season, usually at the beginning of May, and embark on a walking holiday. They absolutely love Corfu but they can't abide the summer sun. This is all a bit bewildering to me since the Ionian sun is one of the main attractions for me. But I suppose it is a problem. You love the place but you can't abide the weather. That's my relationship with the UK summed up in one snappy sentence. That's why I go to Corfu.

It is quite easy to see where this is going. Corfu is an amazing island and it's an amazing island of contrasts. Stunning beaches, lovely scenery, spectacular views, a wide variety of resorts – oh I could go on all night – and it's got so much more. In summer, you can only really go short distances on foot because of the heat and I suspect that many people don't particularly want to walk more than a short distance because that's why they're on holiday in the first place. It's all too much effort. Why bother to leave the pool or the beach when it's far easier to stagger a few feet to the bar? Anyway, that's enough about me.

I started walking short distances in Corfu way back in the 1980s and 1990s. This had nothing to with the nearby presence of unofficial naturist beaches, you understand, and everything to do with me enjoying being on my own without only my loud music induced tinnitus for company. For instance, in St George South, I would set off at the end of the beach where now stands the grandly named Aquis Sandy Beach Resort, turn right and walk up the beach, over the dunes for what seemed like miles, passing Issos and then carrying on to Lake Korission. The only problem now would be that I would be slightly weary and the walk back would be troublesome, requiring urgent medicinal attention by way of Mythos, which I understand can cure anything.

For easy walking, you can't beat the south of the island for the simple reason that it is relatively flat. There's arguably less to see as well, which you certainly would not say about the west and the north. But there are a lot of brilliant walks in the north of the island too.

I have been greatly helped in my research by the excellent Castaway Travel (www.corfucastaway.com). On their website they detail both easy and serious walks, all of which look absolutely sensational and were compiled by Corfu resident Fried Aumann. I had thought about, and indeed was given permission to, copy the entire walks onto these pages but in all honesty it would be a waste of paper and Kindle (other reading tablets are available) and you, my loyal reader, could make up your own mind. But having said all that, the near six hour marathon (how appropriate for Greece!) from Kakoskala to Old Perithia, The Nun's Path and the Dandolo Ruin does not look like one for the summer season.

There are other excellent reference points too, none better than the Corfu walks of Hilary Paipeti which are accessible through her excellent website http://realcorfu.com/the-corfu-blog-by-hilary-paipeti/ as well as in a number of excellent books.

And whilst I am on the recommendation front, by all means check out the books of John Waller, in particular Walking the Corfu Trail: With Friends, Flowers and Food which is what it says on the tin and is richly entertaining.

To be honest, I mention walks because Corfu is rich with them. It's something that I had not really considered due to the heat when I visit, but out of time, provided it's not chucking it down, which it often is in winter, the world is, in the words of Arthur Daley, your lobster.

As well as the above tips I would offer you a more basic one: Google Corfu walks, or some derivative thereof. A lot of people came up with the idea a lot quicker than I did but that doesn't mean it's a bad one.

That, in many ways, is what books like Steve Ford's Corfu villages, which you can buy from his excellent website http://www.corfuvillages.eu, gives you. There is a man who cares passionately about the island of Corfu and shares his extensive knowledge of the place. Even after all my visits to Corfu, there are many places I have never even heard of, never mind visited. If you enjoyed this bumpy ride around Corfu with a typical British tourist who has done little to learn the lingo, you will surely enjoy Steve's somewhat more educated efforts!

So, walking in Corfu is a decent idea for winter and, if you are mad enough, as another friend of mine is, so is mountain biking. There is at least one mountain on Corfu to make you think twice, though!

## 15. A winter paradise?

People are always coming up to me in the street and asking why I so love Corfu! Well, they're not really, but now and again, I get asked why we keep going back. There are scores of other Greek islands of varying levels of beauty. Shouldn't I really try somewhere else?

It's a mixture of things really. As I wrote earlier, I first went there with 'the lads' on what wasn't really a 'lads' holiday at all. I have never been someone who was very keen on 'clubbing', always preferring a pub with a decent atmosphere and, more importantly, good beer. The lads – and lasses – holidays have barely changed over the years. They were, and remain, all about what is referred to as 'partying', which covers a multitude of sins, including getting extremely drunk (a given), meeting members of the opposite sex for brief, sweaty carnal relations and that's about it. There are optional extras, like water sports, dancing and fighting, but drinking and "sexual relations", as Bill Clinton put it, are at the top of the list.

Now I can understand the drinking bit. I like a drink as much, if not more, than the next man, although I am not one for getting blind drunk, especially in Corfu. That is not to say I have not been blind drunk in Corfu – on an early visit to Kassiopi (hardly the party capital of the island), my friends and I sat on our balcony and recklessly consumed insane amounts of some kind of Jamaica Rum products and we felt sick

337

for days – but it was never my main priority. Neither was meeting girls because I felt I spent far too much time, usually unsuccessfully, chasing girls at home, so why spend too much time doing so on holiday, given the money it was costing me.

So my early lads holidays rarely involved anything more daring than staying up drinking into the early hours in the deserted harbour at Kassiopi outside the Wave Bar, long after the owner Kostas had gone to bed.

In the 1980s, as we have observed, Corfu was at a crossroads. It was developing rapidly, it was over-developing rapidly. It seemed that everywhere you looked there were half-built houses and huge swathes of land were being dug up for all types of properties. Wherever you stayed, no matter how small the town and village, it seemed to get bigger every year. You could see why it was happening: local business people felt they could make a lot of money from developing resorts but by the same token they were running the risk of destroying the very reasons you went there in the first place. A beautiful green island with stunning views and scenery, surrounded by beautiful blue seas was threatening with something very different. Something had to give.

In winter, I could evaluate what had happened after the development days of the 1980s and 1990s and conclude that they had got away with it. In my opinion, they got lucky or they made a brilliant decision with the mass expansion of Kavos. You may be surprised to read this, but the growth of 18-30 tourism in the village has hugely benefited the rest of the island. I am no fan of the place, as you may have gathered, but in terms of preserving and improving the rest of Corfu, it has, possibly unwittingly played a pivotal role.

The transition of Benitses from an attractive fishing village to 24/7 party town was both a tragedy and a travesty. I never saw it in its initial fishing village state but I certainly saw it when it was at its brash peak. Honestly, I thought it was utterly hideous, a terrible advert for Corfu. If you were staying in the south, beyond Benitses, you could not avoid the drunken Brits because you had to drive through the place. At night, you could almost feel the ground swaying underfoot, there were so many people heading for the bars and clubs, not to mention the endless 'English' style eateries. And that was another thing I noticed then and I noticed now: it was almost entirely Brits who went to Kavos. Many a Greek shook their heads at the behaviour of some of our young people, many a travelling Brit cringed with embarrassment.

But Benitses is saved. Whether it was a strategic decision to cleanse the town, I have no idea, but the night clubs have all long gone. It is somewhere you would choose to visit again, with its impressive marina, small beach and wide variety of facilities, including the legendary shell museum. Moving the blot of Benitses to Kavos was a masterstroke. It's a good distance from the rest of civilization, except Lefkimmi, and the party-goers rarely leave the place apart from – yes, you guessed it – booze cruises. In other words, you never need see them, apart from at the departure airport where crowds of young men in their long shorts, vests and silly hats commence the drinking orgy in the departure lounge, and at Corfu airport when they are sitting around, lobster red, huge bags under their eyes and strained croaky voices, having done nothing other than drink themselves into near oblivion. I never mind seeing them – I was young once, believe it or not – but Kavos is still a blight on the island and does it no favours.

But it's not just Benitses that has been saved. Ipsos was not dissimilar, a long sliver of shingly beach separating the sea from the bars and clubs. I always had a soft spot for Ipsos and stopped there a few times whilst travelling to other places. Somehow, it always had a friendlier style and attitude to Benitses. There might have been excess, but never quite as much as its bigger brother to the south of Corfu Town.

So if the far south east of Corfu took in the 18-30s, Sidari in the far north west developed in a very different way. It is not my cup of tea, assuming you can get a decent cup of tea in Corfu, which I haven't managed yet, but it ticks all the boxes for many people. If I am being honest, there are a lot of things I miss when I am in Corfu. I miss Asda, I miss Thatcher's Gold cider (although I do know a supermarket in

Arillas that sells Stowford Press, so all is not completely lost), I miss my bed – oh, there loads of things I miss too much to live there but having said all that I do love being there for a couple of weeks, maybe longer, every year. But I don't want it to be too much like home and for the most part it isn't like home.

Sidari is for the British traveller who likes home comforts, who wants to be in Greece but also wants a fry up, football on the telly and a pint of John Smiths. I am not saying there is nothing wrong with this. I love watching football as much as anyone, I like a decent fry up too, although I'll draw the line at John Smiths in Greece as much as I would at home. I have met countless people over the years whose idea of heaven is going to Sidari every year and that's why Sidari matters. I also know people who spent their first Corfu holiday in Sidari and then found places on the island that they loved more. Let's not get snobby about it.

I love the smells of Corfu, starting with the hot, heady mix of jet fuel and flora you get when the aircraft doors are opened upon landing at the airport. I like the screaming of the engines as we disembark the plane, the ridiculously short bus ride from the plane to the terminal building and the sight of your luggage coming through on the rattly old baggage reclaim area. And there is, unquestionably, a sense of real arrival in Corfu as you exit the building, between the reps with their smart uniforms and the locals with their handwritten cardboard signs reading things like,

'Mr and Mrs Scuttle, Tranquility Apartments, Kavos'.

The smells are certainly unlike 30 years ago, when a small walk towards Garitsa Bay provided an odour that was anything but floral, rather more the type of stuff you grew things in. It was as if it was muck-spreading season, except that they did it over there in August, which was my first wildly inaccurate reaction. When I hear the expression that "I left a bit of me in Corfu", this was certainly true around Corfu Town in the 1980s. This was hardly unique to Corfu because not far from where I live in Bristol lies the pretty seaside town of Clevedon. It was not that long ago that Clevedon was the not particularly proud owner of five large sewage pipes that deposited the entire town's waste, untreated, into the Bristol Channel and didn't you know it when the tide came in!

There was also the suspicion, belief among some, that Greece in general and Corfu in particular, was somehow dirtier than back home, that the Greek lifestyle wasn't as clean as ours, that you might not be able to trust some of the tavernas for their cleanliness. For all I know, this used to be true. I remember using toilets that stank to high heaven in the back of bars and tavernas, all the while thinking that if this was what the toilet stank like, would the kitchen be any better? There was a bar in the south-east of Corfu (I will not name it) where I once, some 20-odd years ago, had a full English breakfast and very good it was too. But then I paid a brief visit out the back and was horrified with what I smelled and, frankly, what I saw. It was blindingly obvious that the WC had not been cleaned in weeks, or else the clientele was particularly disgusting. I did not go back for years, but when I did finally pluck up the courage, they had brought in the builders and plumbers.

And you still cannot put paper down the toilet. This was a bit of an unwanted novelty at first that I thought would soon be remedied but no such luck. The man who invented Greek drainage is not someone I would be calling in order to correct my own bathroom facilities. Even in the hotels I have stayed in over the years, the pipes still cannot accept paper. I do not envy the maid her daily duties, especially in somewhere like Kavos where, I was assured, most of the British contingent are virtually incontinent for the durations of their stay.

The noisy, chaotic summer airport could not be more different in winter. The car park is closed, there are a handful of taxis hanging around but nothing else is open, not a single shop or café.

It would probably be easier to list the things I don't like about Corfu rather than the things I do, there are so few of them. But let's stay positive.

Despite the presence of a McDonalds just off the Liston – which I have used, more than once, in recent years: sorry about that – Corfu Town is an unqualified pleasure, any time of the year. Given the time at my disposal last winter, I got to know the streets very well. All the local ones remained open, the tat shops – my favourites, it goes without saying – were firmly closed. The old town is pedestrianised, which you can't say about the rest of the town, and on a still, hot day in summer it is advisable for asthmatics to bring their inhalers and for more vulnerable people to stay away altogether. You can feel the heavily polluted air getting into your throat and lungs, you can taste the sulphur, literally. I can only imagine what somewhere like Athens is like on a still summer's day. Corfu Town is choking enough.

I love driving in Corfu, although I do wish they would adopt driving on the left as a norm, if only to annoy the Germans. I'm used to driving on the 'wrong' side of the road by now, but now and again I still fumble with the window when I am trying to change gear. And it frightens my partner half to death when my concentration rambles when we're driving along some painfully thin road with a sheer drop to the right and she is virtually looking down to a premature ending. I have to pretend that I knew what I was doing all along. The cars must be very sturdy in Corfu, particularly in the suspension department, because there are pot holes and there are pot holes. The small ones cause a small bump, but the big ones cause an almighty 'CRASH'. "I didn't see it love!" 'CRASH' again. Damn. Half a bottle of mineral water spilled into her lap. "Look, I didn't do it on purpose!"

The drivers used to be completely mad in Corfu. Everyone wanted to get to their destination before they'd really started. Overtaking was more of a dare than a motoring manoeuvre; just wait for that blind bend before doing it. Actually, that's still the same. I still drive too slowly, at least in the minds of some Corfiot motorists who I often lead in an accidental convoy when I am negotiating the road between Dassia and Kassiopi and I am far more overtaken than I am overtaker, although I have managed to outpace the odd slow moving vehicle in recent times. I adopt the old Greek classic – "no problem" – whilst holding up the traffic.

I like finding somewhere new when I am in Corfu. Even after 21 visits, I still see names on the map that I have never heard of, never mind visited. It is quite unforgiveable really that until 2014 I had never before been to Kaiser's Throne. I had been to the little town of Pelekas many times but for some inexplicable reason I had never come across it. Worse still, I had never heard of it. The view from Kaiser's Throne is so utterly stunning that it really should be compulsory viewing for every single tourist, though not at the same time because there is only a small car park. Tucked away to the west of the island, as Kaiser's Throne is, you can see all the way up to the inevitable Mount Pantokrator, Corfu Town, Kanoni on the north east and on a clear day the Greek mainland is clearly visible. And it's so high up that I felt as if I might accidentally fall off at any given point.

I love the small villages of Corfu, although I have visited very few of them. For village lovers, I can only but recommend once more Steve Ford's excellent book 'Corfu Villages'. Most of them remain totally unaffected and unchanged by the onset of mass tourism, as if it didn't exist at all. Groups of men sit outside small kafeneions and drink coffee and smoke endless cigarettes (I believe this is compulsory in Greek villages). And many villages seem untouched by modern dentistry, hence the gap-filled smiles of so many people.

I love the contrasts of Corfu. The west coast beaches bear no resemblance to those on the east. The west boasts beautiful sandy beaches all the way down, many reached by steep roads and others by no roads at all. The east coast, from Kassiopi southwards is more shingle and pebbles, at least as far as Barbati, but it is far more accessible by road because the coast road snakes its contours all the way south. By contrast, the west coast does not have a major coast road at all.

The north east coast road is a marvel of Greek construction (I am guessing it was the Greeks, but who knows, what with those busy Venetians?). It's one mad hairpin bend after another, then another, through tiny villages that are all but on the road itself. It is not the place to pass a large bus, although they always seem to turn up when I am around. Not only are the bends tight on the switchback roads, hundreds of feet above the sea, they are often unprotected, that is to say there is nothing to stop the careless traveller from meeting a premature end in the Ionian Sea. The views are stunning, for sure, but when I was alone, I quickly made the decision to keep my eyes on the road. As there was no one else around for much of the time, it might have taken until the summer season to have found me in my Hyundai Something had I taken a wrong turning.

I did not make a point of exploring the heart of Corfu this time, meaning the substantial majority of it. And there is plenty of it to see. In all my years of visiting, there are still substantial chunks of the place I have never been near, let alone visited and there lies a difficulty for the summer traveller. If you are being honest, the main reason you went to Corfu – or anywhere else in the Med for that matter – was because it's usually hot and sunny. If I am being honest, and that's always a good idea when I am writing about it, it's still the main reason I go there, but with added love of the place. Corfu has become a home-from-home to both tourists and ex-pats. I certainly have all the feeling of going on holiday when I arrive on the island, but there is the secure feeling of security and familiarity too. I do not have to spend the first week wondering where the hell I am. As I get older, familiarity has become a loyal friend.

So is Corfu a viable winter destination for a short break or a holiday? Well, it was for me. It looked much the same in January 2015 as it had done during all my previous summer visits. There were only a few differences:

- There were no direct flights
- The weather wasn't very nice
- There were no other tourists on the island
- Most of the resorts were shuttered up

The first issue was flights. I always wanted to go to Corfu in mid winter but I knew the lack of direct flights was going to be a problem. I booked scheduled flights with Aegean Airlines via Athens and it was not much of a problem. The flights were not that expensive, either, much less expensive than I had expected and of course the bonus of scheduled flights is you get more leg room and a meal thrown in. The disadvantage was that I had to travel from Bristol to London Heathrow, which was time-consuming and dull. But I always find it a great experience when I fly from Heathrow, used as I am to flying from smaller municipal airports on budget or package holidays.

So flying to Corfu from London did not require extensive planning. Athens is a major airport and easy to navigate for even the most simple of passengers and they don't come any more simple than me. I had, for some reason, expected to remain airside in the capital and it came as a surprise that I didn't and had to pass through security all over again. I naively assumed that once you had done all the security stuff in

London, that would be it, unless you actually chose to leave airside.

Finding my connecting flight to Corfu was a relative formality and, at least outbound, the connection was little more than an hour. However, the return flight from Athens to London did require a four hour plus stop over. The powers that be scheduled a direct flight to London to leave at the moment the Corfu flight arrived. And we thought British Rail was bad.

The aircraft from Athens to Corfu will vary depending on the load. The airline will schedule a small propeller plane if few seats have been sold, but will use an Airbus A320 for a busy day. It's only a short hop to Corfu from Athens, less than an hour usually, so it's not a massive inconvenience.

In winter, Corfu airport is as closed as most of Corfu. The usual departures lounge at the top end is all locked up and you depart from the same end as the arrivals hall. It is a very strange feeling when you arrive because normally you will expect to see an apron full of planes and a terminal full of sweaty passengers. There are always taxis waiting and I got one immediately even though I was one of the last passengers to emerge from the baggage reclaim. They don't get a lot of winter business, so the drivers hang around until the very last customer has left the building.

I felt flying via Athens made the whole thing more of an experience, but then I had time to burn. Not everyone would be so lucky. The ex pats were pretty unanimous in telling me that direct flights would be a considerable boon, as did a large number of business people but not everyone believed it might happen. One of those who didn't was Sue Tsirigoti from the excellent Castaway travel.in Acharavi, who said: "Both Ryanair and EasyJet have shortened their original seasons due to lack of bookings. There has been talk of a direct UK winter flight for years but I don't want to be the bearer of bad news but it is very unlikely to ever happen. It is just not viable. It does not to have to be expensive to get here but is likely to remain via Athens for the foreseeable future."

That certainly dampened my evangelical call for winter flights. I soon got swift confirmation of Sue's comments after a few simple enquiries with other parties but I suppose you can never say never. Ultimately, the decision of an airline to launch direct winter flights from the UK to Corfu will be driven by demand and given they know their markets far better than I do, one would imagine direct flights are not likely to commence anytime soon, if ever.

Any decision whether to attract winter visitors will be one made initially by the tourist authorities themselves. They will be the ones to generate the business and encourage us to travel out of season. And doubtless it would cost money.  It always does when you are trying to attract airline interest.

I am not an expert, far from it, but as soon as I got in my hire car on the first day of my visit, I knew that winter is Corfu was a winner.  I still had the solitude I wanted, it had bucket loads of history I would not usually bother with in the summer because of the need to lie in the sun all day and there was still plenty to do and see, as well as places to eat and drink.  It could be that winter breaks would be solely aimed at Corfu addicts who already visited in summer, but who knows?  Cruises arrive in Corfu in the early and late season, disembarking tourists from all over the world including the USA and Canada.  People I know who have arrived by cruise liner have never complained for want of things to do and see.  In fact, they say they didn't have enough time.

I certainly wouldn't allow the absence of direct flights to put anyone off going.  There are plenty of nice hotels although I would advise anyone who is going to ensure the hotel is heated.  Night time temperatures can plunge alarmingly.

The weather itself is the problem, or maybe the attraction.  The winter storms can be severe and can restrict activities, so bear that in mind and it can rain seemingly for days on end.  Don't go in winter for a sun tan.  Sue from Castaway travel runs guided walks and said that due to the winter storms, she had had to cancel a number of tours.  That said, she did agree that winter was undoubtedly the time to walk on Corfu. And so say all of us.

The winter weather isn't always very nice and I was very lucky. I got drenched a couple of times and on one trip I had to abandon ship (almost literally) due to the ferocity of the rain and the excessive standing water. Frankly, it didn't feel safe. And it can snow. If you Google 'Corfu' and 'snow' you will see some photos which will amaze. But don't let it put you off. Don't stay in: hire a 4X4! I would draw the line at driving a snowy north east coast but most places would be fine to visit. I have set out some Corfu weather history later in the book.

It would have be nice to see some tourists in Corfu but I felt strongly I was the only one and I suspect that not a few people thought I was a few cents short of a Euro. It could have been the type of places I went to, though! I did not expect hordes of drunken teenagers rampaging the streets of Kavos, for example, but there were no obvious signs of visitors anywhere else, which was actually quite liberating.

I am not normally one for organised cultural tours of anywhere, not just Corfu, but even I could have been persuaded to visit the Achillion Palace, Kaiser's Throne, Paleokastritsa and of course Corfu Town with a guide who could add to my picture. But I do like unorganised visits to Corfiot resorts. I took rather less photographs than I should have done because, in retrospect, there was so much to photograph. As well as the classic Corfu landmarks, the views are not as different from summer as you might think. In winter, Corfu remains lush and green. Some days it was just me and the elements.

Was the fact that the resorts were mainly shuttered up a bit of a downer? Not really, but I was surprised that some places were. Kassiopi, which I like very much, was as closed as anywhere in Corfu. It wasn't the weather and it wasn't the time of day. There was just nobody there. The harbour was as breathtakingly beautiful as ever, even devoid of small craft. Sidari, which I don't really like very much, was more open with people doing their day to day jobs. The north coast in general was more alive, places like Roda and Acharavi were well and truly open for business. Step back from the main drag and main road and Corfu, the real Corfu, carries on as if the tourists never came. And in the small villages off the beaten track, tourists never go. More fool them.

I was warned not always to listen to, or take seriously, the thoughts and concerns of the ex pats but this turned out to be an enormous generalisation because, like in anything else, there were different types of ex pats and I liked both kinds.

The first type of ex pats was like those in Roda, who were not just emigrating for an English life under someone else's sun but were actively, willingly integrating with village life and indeed contributing to the community. It took me around five seconds to realise this! And when you live in another country, they told me, have a hobby, an interest. The happier, more fulfilled ex pats all had hobbies and interests, some they had never considered before they arrived in Corfu on a permanent basis. And this matters. How many people have you heard complaining about immigrants to the UK, who never learn the language and live in their own ghettos? Certainly not as many as those you hear complaining about emigrating to, say, Greece or the Spanish Costas (in particular) in concrete communities of their own, living the English dream. I saw them too. They were nice people too, but there was an element of sadness, of emptiness in their lives. The endless dinner parties and boozy evenings were the staple of their lives and everyone who visited from the UK came armed with suitcases full of their favourite British things.

I remain unconvinced that everyone is pleased that they upped sticks and moved lock, stock and barrel to Corfu. No one says they regret a thing, but apart from the weather, they tell you in a roundabout way that many things "over here" are much worse than it is "back home". It's warmer in winter, for sure, but it's not the Canary Islands (thank god). I repeat: the weather is not an incentive to visit in winter but the island itself has plenty to offer.

There are plenty of places to stay, almost all of which are in and around Corfu Town and Kanoni. Why would you want to stay anywhere else during wintertime in an island so small? My hotel, the Ariti Grand Hotel, was excellent. Very reasonably priced, served by a bus you could set your watch by. But in town there were countless other lovely looking hotels that have all achieved more than favourable reviews on Trip Advisor.

I rather liked the island in closed down mode, even if you can't visit some of the more famous attractions, but if there were enough visitors, who is to say they might not open for them, even just once a week? And the lack of tavernas in the resorts was a pain, but then again, take a trip away from the main road and there are villages, many of whom have their own kafeneions, packed with characters, serving excellent coffee and cheap beer. It was certainly a mistake I made. I visited so many resorts and found myself moaning about the fact I could not get a coffee, but it was only when I returned to England that I remembered that actually Corfu doesn't grind to a halt at the season's end. People don't live in the resorts, they live in the little villages. More fool me.

And there's that old truism: eat and drink where the locals go. Perikles Katsaros, the man from Taverna Nikolas, took me to one of these, The Three Pigs in Corfu Town, and it was stunning, absolutely excellent. Simple, fresh food cooked right in front of you, lots of it, reasonably priced and absolutely delicious. Corfu Town is packed to the brim with everything from highbrow restaurants to lovely little grill rooms. You cannot fail to find the right one or indeed put on weight.

Perhaps, after all, Corfu doesn't need the winter flights to flourish out of season but it will get them if there is the demand and the demand will only come when people show an interest in going there when it's not so hot and dry. But even without the flights, Corfu is well worth a visit. I only wish I had stayed longer.

I'll go again in winter for sure and next time maybe I won't go alone. But then again, I just might. Like in summer, you can still find the solitude if you want it, but even more so. If you want to mingle with people, Corfu Town still buzzes and of course the villages never shut just because there are no tourists. In fact, the seasons barely affect them at all.

Perhaps for many people, there's just not enough to do in winter. Certainly the traditional British idea of a foreign holiday – the full English, John Smith's Smooth, Bingo and the Sunday Roast – is nowhere to be seen (thank God, I hear you say). So you'll still have to go to Blackpool which is far colder and, without trying to be too disrespectful, rather less easy on the eye.

But there's more than enough history to go round, there are numerous walks to be had all over Corfu and there is plenty of company, although you'd do well to learn better and more Greek than I managed, despite the fact that most people speak passable English (a bit like me, really).

Above everything else, it was the resorts that did it for me. I came to Corfu to stay in a resort and I've been coming back to them for 30 years now. There is no doubt that the island has so much to offer but even when the resorts are closed, I still love them best. The contrast is incredible, walking down a road where in a few months the bars, tavernas and shops will be absolutely heaving, but in winter the noise is just from nature. Even Kavos, which is a blot on anyone's landscape, was a must-see for me. As mentioned elsewhere, it lived right down to my expectations, maybe even lower, but I loved the experience nonetheless.

It's a winter destination all right, but not as we know it. And I couldn't recommend it enough.

## 16. Scratching the surface

'Corfu...not a scorcher!' was not the end of my writing journey. It was certainly a dream realised, an ambition fulfilled and an itch scratched – choose whichever cliché you like. There was more, much more, about Corfu than I ever realised and I knew I had barely scratched the surface.

Even when planning my trip, it had not really occurred to me how life might carry on in the holiday island when hardly anyone was over there on holiday. I had rightly assumed that the Corfiots did not spend all winter sitting around watching the Greek equivalent of 'Bargain Hunt'. Although they never described it as such, summer was a seemingly never-ending slog from the start of May to the end of October, a seven-day week for six months solid. Not 9.00 to 5.00 days either. Horrendous early starts, late night/early morning finishes, 18 hour days were not the exception. If I was one of them, I'd have probably needed to have slept for the rest of the year, but then if I was one of them, doing nothing all winter, Corfu would not look so utterly splendid when the first passenger plane arrived.

Corfu Town was as bustling as in summer. Not all the shops were open – those not being open were almost invariably the tourist shops – and the little lanes away from the main part of town were often eerily deserted. But the cafés and bars were very busy, seemingly all day. As I found out, people drove a long way from around the island in order to have some kind of social life. If this had been a British town, the bars would have been rammed with people drinking cider and lager and I would have been one of them. But this was Corfu and the young people seemed to consume nothing but coffee. Perhaps this was why they all looked so young and attractive and why no one wanted to fight at kicking out time?

There was far more I didn't see than did. I didn't even set foot in the town of Lefkimmi, even though it is right next to Kavos, and I saw few of the real little villages of Corfu. That would certainly have made for an interesting insight and maybe there's the next book. To my deep shame, after 30 years of visiting the island, I know hardly any of the villages, let alone the people who live in them. It hadn't occurred to me that even in winter, people commute on the buses from small villages, especially into Corfu Town. For most people, life on the island goes on as it does for the rest of the year; it's not just for the benefit of you and I.

I really did feel as though I had the island to myself as I travelled round. Ambling down into Kalami, I did seem to have the place to myself, the only signs of life being some washing hanging out on the line of Lawrence Durrell's famous white house. In fact, there were many more people in the tiny village of Agni when I went there (four, I think I saw). Sidari was certainly alive and just about open for business, the exquisite harbour of Kassiopi was spotlessly clean, quite possibly on account of the fact there was no one around who could make it dirty. But even at its most quiet and uninhabited, Kassiopi has a character of its own. Look around the boarded up bars and tavernas and imagine in a short while the place being alive with holidaymakers.

Going to different places, seeing them as they were in winter but knowing what they were like in summer, was a fabulous experience. I even enjoyed visiting Kavos for all its many negatives. I am not sure I would enjoy it quite so much in the foam party at the 'Sex Club' but I suspect I do not come into the category the 18-30 clubbers are looking for. There was nothing of any real interest to look at and nothing to do and that was in the summer. In winter, there's no one there either. My earlier comparison with Pripyat, the town next door to Chernobyl following the nuclear explosion of 1986, was frivolous, of course, but only just. Granted there was not quite so much radiation in the air but it sure felt like a nuclear winter. I am approaching old codger territory so you would not expect me to be full of praise for the place, but then I never was. But someone, actually quite a lot of someones, regard it as the place to go as soon as the sun is shining. Well, someone has to!

My reaction to Kavos when I was walking down the main drag was of the tut tut, shaking my head variety. I was probably behaving like my granddad when he first saw the Rolling Stones. I suppose if I'd had ten pints of lager, washed down with shots, ate a sumptuous "stake" (sic) dinner from one of the top notch restaurants and then danced the night away in the 'Sex Club' – oh, and I was 20 again – it might just be for me, but I doubt it. I was far too boring. Even then, I'd have enjoyed just about anywhere else on the island. But if you are there in winter, you must not miss Kavos. It's terrible, but unmissable.

So, what of the future? Corfu will be as much part of my future as it has been the past. There are an awful lot of Greek islands I have yet to visit so I shall fit in some of them to my vacation schedule before the grim reaper shows up. I haven't finished with Corfu in winter, either.

The great Perikles Katsaros, the King of Agni, placed in my mind a possible project for the future: a kind of road trip from Athens to Corfu. Now that would be interesting, to say the least since the only time I have ever set foot in mainland Greece, apart from on one of Theo's Boat Trips, was Athens Airport. I have a lot to learn. Perhaps, he could be James Taylor and I'd be Dennis Wilson in an Anglo-Greco "Two Lane Blacktop". God, that would be something to write about it. I'm pretty sure he meant it too. What a story that might be. He'd certainly know where to stop to eat and he owns a hotel on the mainland too. That would either be after Perikles has retired from running Taverna Nikolas and handed the reins to his son, Nikos, or during the spring, autumn or even the winter.

'Corfu...not a scorcher!' taught me a lot I didn't know, probably because I hadn't thought much about it. The people work incredibly hard in the summer and don't just sit idly by in the winter, either. The British ex-pats are an eclectic mix of those who integrate and those who like being Brits abroad, living as Brits do but under the Ionian sun. I get that and if I lived there, I'd undoubtedly be somewhere in the middle. I mean, I'd be rubbish at traditional Corfiot dancing but I would visit the local kafeneon as regularly as possible. You have to blend in, don't you, even if it means going through the hardship of consuming Mythos and Metaxa in order to show my best efforts at living the Corfu life!

I've already addressed the question of whether I could ever live there, but I'll try to elaborate. I could live there, but I wouldn't want to. There are many, many positives that the fully integrated Brits can enjoy. I saw that. They often have two sets of social lives, one with their fellow ex-pat friends (which I totally get) and another with the locals with whom they have made great efforts to integrate, by learning the language and getting into the Greek customs and traditions. My impression, especially with the Connors and the Mansells of Roda was that they were more than just Brits abroad, more much-loved fixtures in the community.

You could certainly live a good life there all year round. If you preferred, you could get a cable TV package to include all the things you would watch at home and again, regardless of living within the Greek community, why not? Just because you choose to live in another country, it doesn't mean that you stop enjoying the BBC in favour of the Greek equivalent. Nor would you give up your love for Earl Grey tea or mature Cheddar cheese. Or real ale, pork scratchings, the Sainsbury's deli counter, the Harbourside area in Bristol, granary bread and cricket. I could cope with the Corfu climate in a heartbeat, even with all that ghastly winter rain, but the things I'd miss, ridiculous though they might seem absurd (all right: some of them *are* absurd), Corfu as a place is for my holidays or, if my numbers came up, the base for a second home.

There are a few times of the year I would love to experience in Corfu. The start of the summer season, when all the resorts are fresh and re-opening and the first planes arrive from the UK. That first day, when the airport goes from three daily flights to and from Athens to a constant roar of landings and take offs and the last day of the season when the final charter aircraft to the UK taxis along the runway. The day after the last day must be the moment when you realise you are there for the winter, there for keeps. And Easter, of course, which is regarded by many to be of greater significance than Christmas. All that pot-smashing – feels like my kitchen!

My experience of winter in Corfu was a positive one. It made me want to go back, it made me want to encourage others to go. The way things are, with the journey via Athens, it is actually quite exciting, if a bit longer and further. It's more of an adventure too. I'd love to see and do more, but of course it would be nice if more attractions were open (and I don't mean Aqualand). But travelling around the island, loafing around Corfu Town, sitting on the dock of the bay (in Kassiopi) and walking through a Ghost Town (Kavos) is an unusual, almost unique but incredibly enjoyable experience.

## 17. Saturday Morning 4.00 am

Just like being on holiday, the last thing I wanted to do was to go home. I had seen but a small part of Corfu in winter and if I had stayed for a month or more, I still would have found things to write about. For the first time, I was on my own in Corfu, doing what I wanted to do (as I normally end up doing anyway, I'm ashamed to say), going where I wanted to go, planning where I should go. The latter part didn't work quite so well as I had hoped.

Proper travel writers like Paul Theroux and, my favourite, Bill Bryson would doubtless have planned everything to the Nth degree. My nature is to plan stuff and then try to adapt in changing circumstances. In my case, I half-heartedly planned things and then made almost everything up as I went along. It was certainly more fun that way. If I planned to go somewhere, but another place attracted my attention, I would go with it. Sometimes I would find nothing of interest, at other times I would find something of interest. I certainly had a plan for my last day in Corfu. This would entail getting up at stupid O'clock to take a drive round the town for no other reason than I could.

"Should I book a taxi for tomorrow?" I asked, the night before I flew home.

"There's no need," said Helen, reassuringly, behind the reception desk where she seemed to be 24/7. "The taxi company is just down the road. They'll be here in a couple of minutes." I believed every word she said. You just do with some people. It is a Greek thing, a bit of the "no problem" attitude of the people. I am used to some English taxi firms who promise you a taxi and you spend an age trying to find out where it is when you most need it, only for the damn thing to turn up just when you start to panic. I just wondered why the local taxi firm would be operating at 7.00 am on a Saturday morning. Was there much call for taxis at that hour?

On the balcony of my room, wearing three layers of clothing, I sat with a glass of, frankly, terrible Greek red wine. Perhaps it was a very poor buying policy on my part, but it seemed, to my uneducated palate, that most Greek wines were terrible. This one was so bitter you wouldn't have put it on your chips, but I suppose if I was going to look the part and gaze wistfully across the bay, thinking poetic thoughts, then I would have to make a small sacrifice. I opened a small packet of salted peanuts to take the taste of the wine off my palate. You would think with a climate like Greece that it wouldn't be that difficult to produce decent quaffing wines, something to have of an evening or with a meal. But to be honest, the stuff I was used to drinking was more like the sort of stuff you might put on your chips. Chateauneuf du Sarsons, if you will. I am told that actually the Greeks do make a decent selection of fine wines, it's just that rather like the Germans with their high quality estate Rieslings, they keep the best stuff for themselves!

It was a little after 10.00pm. There was a brisk breeze and everything was slightly damp following an earlier shower. The visibility was good and the lights of Corfu Town shimmered in the middle distance. The airport runway lights were on so, at last, I would finally see a plane land during my stay. I had expected a regular flow of aircraft during my stay. At long last there was some excitement of a sort. But disappointingly, and entirely predictably, the plane that finally did arrive was not a roaring jet, but a small and slightly wobbling Dash 8 propeller plane. This I feared would be my transport to Athens tomorrow. It would be a first for me because I had never before been on a propeller plane and had no real inclination to do so. It suddenly appeared from the south and roared into sight with all the power of a small moped. It probably had a lot more power than a small moped, but the sound was very weedy. It soon left the runway and came to a standstill outside the terminal building. Silence descended once more, just the whistling down the wires, a clanking sign from somewhere down below and a car horn.

There was no real point in sitting on the balcony because it was cold and it was dark and my room was warm and light, but I stayed there for a while anyway. I had been to this wonderful island so many times but never in winter. I had done so much in so little time, I had covered pretty well the entire island several times over. All right, it wasn't exactly Australia, but it was a big thing for me. I was ready to go home but I didn't really want to. This makes no sense, I know, and I can't explain the feeling beyond saying that once I know it is time to leave somewhere, I'd like to just get it out of the way.

To make sure I didn't oversleep, I arranged for an alarm call, I set my alarm clock and I set my telephone, all for 4.00am. All this for a light sleeper. My flight was not until 8.30am, but you can't be too careful, can you?

I wondered what the resorts were like at night. I had done none of them during the evenings but perhaps I should. I know that places like Arillas had large local populations but other places, like for example Agios Georgios South seemed to have very few. There would be no noise there, other than the noises of nature. And it would be very dark. Agios Georgios South was quite dark away from the front at the height of summer. In mid winter, it would be nearly black. Next time, I reckoned. Next time.

At 4.00am, my small orchestra of alarms went off within a few minutes of each other. I had already packed the night before to ensure I would be in no rush to leave for the airport. By 4.30am, I was in the hotel lobby, nodding to the night staff who must have thought I was completely mad, with good reason, I would say. It was cold this time, very cold, with horizontal rain blowing up from the south. Avoiding the huge puddles outside the hotel, I reached my Hyundai Something (I'm afraid I had still not worked out the actual model) and started the engine. Soon I was driving down the one way street towards Corfu Town.

Barring the street lights, there was no other light. I was the only person mad enough to be taking a leisurely drive long before the dawn on a Corfu Saturday. I made my familiar way to Garitsa Bay and once again followed the bay up to the Old Fort. The trees swayed in the strengthening wind, the rain splattered the windscreen. I found a parking space near the Liston and braved the elements to see this most beautiful of island capitals as I had never seen it before. It was a good half hour until I saw anyone – even the McDonalds was closed – and the streets, with everything closed, were much darker than usual. I felt completely safe though, even when taking the narrow lanes. I did jump a little as a large rat passed by six feet away – it was the size of a cat, I tell you – but that was the nearest I got to being mugged.

Then, right at the far end in the main part of town, was a 24 hour takeaway, the lightest place in the town by miles. And there were people eating, two young couples who looked as fresh as I felt knackered. Perhaps they had been out clubbing, although there was nothing else nearby that looked remotely open, or recently closed, or maybe on their way to work. In any event, I was not alone.

The Liston is such a special place, even when nothing is open and no one is around, except two men sitting outside of one of the bars, long before dawn, slowly puffing on cigarettes, who looked for all the world like the looky-looky men you see in the Canary Islands. Occasionally, a motorbike would buzz past, its rider helmetless as usual, and maybe a car heading who knows where. But mostly, just the elements. As I said elsewhere, you rarely heard the elements at work in summer because generally the air was still. You could hear people and all the sounds that people make but this could have been the Cornish seaside to listen to.

Driving down to the harbour, there was life down there. There were no boats on the move, but some offices were open, small groups of men stood around waiting for what I don't know. It was much lighter down here too, passing Spianada Square, the new fort high to the left. I don't know why I had decided to get up so early. I had learned nothing and had seen next to nothing. I think it was a bit like the Sunday night feeling when you are in a job you really don't like and you hang on to the night before the Monday raises its ugly head. I didn't want this silly little expedition of non-discovery to come to an end. I would soon be embarking on the long trip home. I was looking forward to the travelling – I enjoy that side of it – but not leaving this place behind. And these lovely, lovely people who had made me so welcome.

At this ungodly hour, there were people who appeared to be on their way to work, armed with rucksacks, dressed for a cold winter's day, which this wasn't really, at least by northern European standards.

What on earth had possessed me to set out this early, I don't know. I suppose I just wanted to feel what it was like in Corfu Town when most of it was asleep. I looked over the bay of Garitsa one final time, lights flickering in the early morning breeze, gazing into the middle distance, posing, basically. God, I thought to myself, how much do I love this island which I first visited 30 years when I was still a slip of a lad? Just for one moment in time, Corfu was mine.

I could not fault the Ariti Hotel. It was spotless, the facilities were excellent and at night you could hear a pin drop. At 7.00 am, I quietly left my hotel room and made my way to reception. The person on reception kindly presented me with a bag full of edible goodies to keep me going! Some lovely fresh cake, a drink of orange juice, a lovely croissant and yes, some more cake. "Can you arrange for a taxi for me, please?" I said in my usual exaggerated tones. I feared I might be sounding as I would when speaking to someone who was profoundly deaf. Believe me, I am not proud of my failure to learn even basic Greek.

I was just about to sink my teeth into a piece of cake and a taxi rolled up, barely 30 seconds after it had been ordered. Very impressive. A farewell wave to the receptionist and off I went. I was very sorry I had missed Helen. Maybe I'd pop in during the summer. (As it happened, I did exactly that, the following August, when the weather was typical hot, Helen was typically cool and the hotel full.)

"Of course," replied the young man, reaching for his phone. And it the vehicle pulled up within 60 seconds.

The taxi had an odour of stale cigarette smoke, or maybe it was driver who did. We drove through the sleepy streets with which I was now so familiar and in no time we had pulled up at Kerkyra Airport, known as and named after one Ioannis Kapodistrias, a former Greek foreign minister of the Russian Empire (it says here). Sadly, he was assassinated in 1831 and never got to see the airport in its splendour. In fact, he never got to know that the airport would eventually be named after him, not least because aircraft would not be invented for many years following his passing.

"12 Euros!" announced the driver, depositing my small suitcase by the airport entrance.

I didn't know the Greek for, "Do you have change of €15?" or indeed, "You what?", so I gave him a 25% tip. I was just relieved to be there absurdly early. I arrive everywhere absurdly early. It is part of my condition and I start to get anxious if there is any remote possibility I might be late or even on time, which is much the same thing in my book.

You can still alight directly outside Corfu airport. It's very different over there. None of this parking light years away malarkey. At Corfu, it's how airports used to be. Pull up outside, walk the short walk to the terminal building.

If you have ever been to Corfu airport at the height of summer, you will know what it's like. The far end is for departures. There is a relatively small hall with countless check-in desks and the traveller watches the screens above to find when theirs is about to open. Then people crawl to the desk, check in their suitcases, have them handed back to them, and finally give them to security staff who put them on the conveyor belt through the x-ray machine. Miraculously, despite the apparent chaos of people shouting at each other (to be fair, many a Greek conversation resembles an argument when it is nothing of the kind), suitcases have a good habit of ending up where they're supposed to. Then, it's through security and into the lounge itself, which of course is completely rammed and houses the most average facilities imaginable. Thankfully, package flights rarely allow a great deal of time in departures and at Corfu that's just as well. In the depths of winter, the main departures hall is closed.

It was around 7.20 am when I joined a very small queue. Security wasn't up and running just yet. A couple of smartly dressed women stood by the desks and checked in the luggage of the handful of passengers who were flying. Eventually, uniformed security staff who were clearly employed by a private security company conducted their searches.

"What is that large bottle in your suitcase?" asked one of them, gazing at the X Ray machine.

"It's Metaxa," I replied, adding unnecessarily, "Seven star Metaxa."

"Okay," he said. "Go through."

We were searched as thoroughly as if we were about to board a packed 747 headed for Jerusalem, never mind the short hop to Athens. It was still dark as we entered the tiny area that had been allocated as the winter departure lounge. Silly me for complaining about the lack of summer facilities at the airport because there were none whatsoever on this cold winter's day. I chomped through my croissant. By 8.00 am, there were maybe 40 or 50 passengers in the lounge.

With so few passengers going to Athens, I had resigned myself to flying on a small rattling propeller plane, when from the south appeared an Aegean Airways Airbus A320. This seemed a little excessive, but it soon became apparent as to why a larger aircraft had been used, albeit only really for the inbound flight. The steps were attached to the plane and a flood of people disembarked and they kept disembarking. And it was only a Saturday morning. Kerkyra's football team did not have a home game that weekend. Very odd.

Except it was obvious. The next day was when a General Election was to be held and in Greece people return to their home towns and villages to vote. It must have been an expensive bit of democracy for some voters but plainly it was still a thing of great importance. I suppose when you had been through what the Greeks had been through in recent years, you damn well wanted to vote.

No sooner had the plane emptied than we were told to board with immediate effect in best Ryanair fashion. I had booked my seat on-line but the truth was that I'd wasted my time fretting about it. The plane was certainly more than three-quarters empty for the short hop. I had empty rows in front and behind, never mind empty seats next to me. Once we had all boarded, the captain wasted no time in starting the engines. The cabin staff played a video (I don't expect it was actually a video, but you get the idea) of the safety instructions and before you could say Spiros, the plane was taxiing to what I refer to as the 'town end' of the runway. We had already been cleared to take off as the plane hurtled off down the runway. I was seated on the right hand side, looking to the west, as the plane rotated, steeply at first, over the causeway and Perama and Benitses to the right. Soon, in the dawn's early light, Lake Korission appeared and below, on this side of the island, were the resorts of Messongi and Kavos and the town of Lefkimmi. On a flight from Corfu to England, taking off in this direction would normally necessitate a tight left hand turn and then flying to the north of the island and onto the Adriatic. But this flight was to Athens, so the views of the south of the island were breathtaking to behold. Then there was darkness until we reached the outskirts of Athens. There was just enough time for the stewardesses to serve coffee, but not enough time to drink it before we started to descend into Athens. The plane bumped through the heavy clouds, allowing me to spill much of my coffee onto the seat next to me.

Everywhere below, as far as the eye could see, were wind turbines. We were briefly in a holding pattern above Athens. This gave us the opportunity to admire who knows what since the captain had gone mute since before we took off. This is one my pet hates about flying; the captain and first officer rarely come on the PA system to tell us where we are and where we're going to be. It can't be that hard because, for much of the flight the aircraft flies itself. But this pilot confined his commentary to "Cabin crew – prepare for landing". Being a keen aviation enthusiast, I had managed to work out for myself that the swift descent may indeed had been because we were preparing to land. And with a gentle thump, we were on the runway and being advised by the cabin crew to stay seated until the aircraft came to a standstill.

As we taxied alongside the runway being used for departures, I noted a long line of Aegean A320s waiting for the call. One of them, I was almost certain, was on its way to London Heathrow. A slight alteration to the scheduling could easily have made this a connecting flight, but no, the London flight was sent on its way while I was still bumbling along to the arrivals gate. Luckily, I only had a mere four hours to kill before my flight left. This resembles the policy of my local railway company which has no interest in what used to be known as connections. No matter that it would be dead handy for many of us to connect to a flight leaving for our ultimate destination in a short space of time, given the state of the Greek economy, it would be better if we could spend some money in the airport.

Eleftherios Venizelos, or Athens Airport as we know it, is a modern, airy airport, opened as it was in 2001. And according to the souvenir blurb I came back with, the airport is 'well-appointed'. That's a term with which I normally associate estate agents in their house descriptions. It certainly sounds better than 'badly-appointed', even though I am not sure what 'well-appointed' really means. There are countless shops, cafés and shops, as well as the other essential features you would expect to find in a new fangled airport, like a prayer room, a museum and a McDonalds.

I passed up the opportunity to visit the prayer room – well, you never know who you might meet – and instead decided to buy a quality English newspaper. Unfortunately, there wasn't one, so I went for the best of a particularly bad bunch and bought a Daily Mirror, where I learned about all manner of "celebrities" of whom I had never heard. It must have taken all of five minutes to read it from cover to cover. I bought the paper from what appeared to be an open plan Greek version of a WH Smiths and noted some excellent calendars, a good few of which featured the wonderful photographs of the Greek photographer George Meis. Now this was excellent news. I went through the various calendars and to my dismay – actually, amazement – found they were old calendars, some as much as three years out of date. In fact, there wasn't one for this year never mind next year. Now I have been known for my gullibility, but this was taking things just too far. Somehow, I couldn't imagine this happening back home, except perhaps on Oxford Street where some less than scrupulous street traders might try and persuade innocent foreigners to part with their tourist cash for something equally useless.

The good news was that Athens airport had a goodly selection of tat for people like me to look at and, in a moment of brainlessness, purchase. Luckily, for once brainlessness eluded me and next I saw a sign that intrigued me. There was a museum in the airport. I am not usually that interested in museums and, if I am being honest, this one was no exception, but with three hours to kill, and because entrance was free, I decided to have a browse.

I picked up a leaflet that explained the history of and reasons for the museum and learned that the airport, in cooperation with the Ministry of Culture, had set it up with a number of archaeological findings "dating from the

Neolithic and early Helladic periods, right through the Post Byzantine period". It turned out they'd dug up the findings when the airport was being built and I guess probably thought it would be a good idea to preserve them and put them on display. There are 172 separate items and "(the museum) aims to highlight the rich cultural heritage of the area." I am not trying to over-emphasise my ignorance on the cultural side of things – you have probably worked it out yourself – but it was very interesting. I'd love to have stayed longer to enrich my understanding of Greek history, but having casually left my packed lunch on the flight from Corfu to Athens I was famished.

There was plenty of choice, that was for sure, and the food on offer was general airport fare, nothing Greek about it, apart from the odd Feta baguette. And then I saw it. Up several sets of escalators, there was a McDonalds. And not any old McDonalds but one with a blinding view, the view to end all views, of the assigned take off runway. I would stay here for hours. Sheer bliss. Yes, yes, I know I should have had something vaguely Greek, but vaguely Greek, I promise you, was all it was. If I had been eating relatively healthily during my stay in Corfu, here was a golden opportunity to put it right, or rather wrong. The magic words simply drooled off my tongue, "A double sausage and egg McMuffin with a hash brown and a coffee, please." I could not deny that this highly calorific meal would probably not be life-enhancing and certainly not life-lengthening, but my god it was lovely, in a greedy, bloating kind of way. The runway was like an international airport runway should be like: busy, busy, busy.

A few seats away, an old man slept across some seats, occasionally snoring himself awake. The 'restaurant' wasn't that busy so I guess the staff concluded he wasn't doing them any harm and they left him there. In the meantime, I watched the planes. In fact, lots of people had chosen their seats so they had a pristine view of the planes taking off. I wasn't the only anorak in town!

I wasn't really tempted to get a bus into Athens during my four hour stay at the airport. The airport was a fair way outside of the city and given my notorious lack of sense of direction, my almost total inability to speak Greek and my basic lack of knowledge about anything in Athens, here was a golden opportunity for me to miss my flight to London.

Stavros Flatley came round the 'restaurant' collecting rubbish. I decided to buy some more coffee, more to pass the time than to satisfy my further need of caffeine. The planes just kept on leaving, the sun kept on shining.

After a while, I noted that the gate was announced for my flight. I had already worked out which gates were where – you never know, do you? – and sat down and waited to board. It was all pretty eventless, really. I accidentally joined the wrong queue – for business class – but was waved through anyway. The airport staff probably recognised an idiot when they saw one. This Airbus A320 was probably half full too and once again I had an entire row to myself. Soon we were on our way back to London, my Corfu adventure behind me.

15849207R00211

Printed in Great Britain
by Amazon